# In Search of Coherence

# In Search of Coherence

*Introducing Marcel Jousse's Anthropology of Mimism*

EDITING, TRANSLATIONS, AND INTRODUCTION BY

# EDGARD SIENAERT

FOREWORD BY

# WERNER KELBER

PICKWICK *Publications* · Eugene, Oregon

IN SEARCH OF COHERENCE
Introducing Marcel Jousse's Anthropology of Mimism

Pickwick Publications
An Imprint of Wipf and Stock Publishers
199 W. 8th Ave., Suite 3
Eugene, OR 97401

www.wipfandstock.com

PAPERBACK ISBN: 978-1-4982-9796-7
HARDCOVER ISBN: 978-1-4982-9798-1
EBOOK ISBN: 978-1-4982-9797-4

*Cataloguing-in-Publication data:*

Names: Jousse, Marcel. | Sienaert, E. R. | Kelber, Werner, foreword.

Title: In search of coherence : introducing Marcel Jousse's anthropology of mimism / Marcel Jousse ; editing, translations, and introduction by Edgard Sienaert ; foreword by Werner Kelber.

Description: Eugene, OR : Pickwick Publications, 2016 | Includes bibliographical references and index.

Identifiers: ISBN 978-1-4982-9796-7 (paperback) | ISBN 978-1-4982-9798-1 (hardcover) | ISBN 978-1-4982-9797-4 (ebook)

LSCH: Jousse, Marcel. | Gesture. | Oral tradition. | Rhythm.

Classification: BF591 .J66 2016 (print) | BF591 .J66 (ebook)

Manufactured in the U.S.A.                                        11/07/16

Cover picture: Beaumont–sur–Sarthe, Old Roman Bridge

There is, in Beaumont-sur-Sarthe, a little bridge that goes very far back, to Roman times it is said. Now what did they bring us, those risible Romans who called themselves pontifices—bridge builders indeed, who did not even bring us bridges. For this old bridge is the sturdy Gallic bridge straddling, in paysan fashion, the pre-Gallic, enduringly paysan Sarthe river. Whenever I return to visit it again, as we all return to see again our childhood laboratories, I wonder if I am equal to this dense, slow, frighteningly rich Sarthe. Truly, there is in water, in this liquid, a whole universe, and this universe I need to understand in myself so that you in turn might understand it in yourselves. As did my masters, the Druids of Gaul, I will ease myself in the flow of what a few lectures hence I will decisively call: human mimism.

École d'Anthropologie, 6 November 1950

\*

A poplar stretches to the sky above the Sarthe river. This poplar I feel like an insistent call for me to reach out at my mother's heaven. This is clearly a geste once made in me, mounted in me, now set off in me by the thing itself. This is true hominization grown out of both a child's spontaneity and an adult's consciousness. All global gesticulation possesses such hominizing power.

Sorbonne, 17 December 1936

\*

What I call consciousness-raising is specific to the anthropos: it means that I know that something came into me that remains in me as a mimeme.

École d'Anthropologie, 13 November 1944

\*

We have then in us mimemes. What are these mechanisms? They are interactional in the sense that they are not incoherent. We do not have an object here and an object there. The norm is to always have coherence and that is what is meant by interaction.

École d'Anthropologie, 20 December 1943

*

We are formed by our deep-rooted mimemes.

Sorbonne, 23 December 1939

*

Style is the flow of mimemes that pour in us. We may not always be conscious of these mimemes but we have a duty to bring them into our consciousness. That is what being human is about. Consciousness may become so acute that the conscientizing process no longer impedes the spontaneous flux of gestes. That should be our aim, this wonderful and powerful mastery summed up as The style is the Man.

École d'Anthropologie, 1 March 1937

*

The style is the Man. It is Man wholly offering himself to the real, wholly receiving the real and wholly replaying the real: that is style.

Hautes Études, 12 February 1941

*

I am the style of the Sarthe.

Sorbonne, 25 March 1943

*

Coherent Man carries his coherence with him everywhere.

Hautes Études, 9 June 1936

# Contents

## Part 3

## Marcel Jousse: Five Essays on Mimism

# Foreword

Marcel Jousse is a name little known in the humanities and social sciences, and his scholarly contributions have remained largely unreported in academia. This is not a situation that has always existed quite in this way. For approximately a quarter of a century, from 1931 to 1957, the French anthropologist commanded the attention of a significant following among the academic community in Paris. At that time, his reputation heavily rested on a major book and most significantly on some one thousand lectures he delivered, mostly without the assistance of a script, at the Sorbonne, École des Hautes Études, École d'Anthropologie, and the Laboratoire de Rythmo-Pédagogie. During those years, Jousse's ideas were the subject of considerable debate and proved influential in shaping the thinking of a number of intellectuals. Among his hearers was the classicist Milman Parry, pioneer of the Oral-Formulaic Hypothesis, which revolutionized our understanding of the oral-compositional structure of the Homeric epics. Jousse's impact on what came to be called the Parry-Lord Theory has been profound. As Milman's son, Adam, has reported, it was Jousse's major publication of *Le Style oral* in conjunction with his Paris lectures that made his father realize that the Homer he had viewed as a traditional poet had to be understood more accurately as an oral poet. Similarly, we have a report from a friend of James Joyce who accompanied the writer to one of Jousse lecture-performances during which a group of girls enacted a parable of Jesus in Aramaic. Joyce, we are told, was inspired by the performative style of the lecture, and deeply impressed with the demonstration of spoken words being shaped by gestures. Jousse's oral delivery and unconventional performance style fired Joyce's imagination in writing the polysemic and encyclopedic *Finnegans Wake*, the book that had as its aim the reorganization of speech, writing, and print into a new communicative model. In our time, finally, the thought of Marcel Jousse has left its mark on Walter Ong's frequently cited *Orality and*

*Literacy* and contributed to its core thesis concerning distinct profiles and contrasts between the two modes of communication. Still, despite Jousse's considerable popularity in France in the first half of the twentieth century, his manifest impact on individual scholars and writers, his theoretical contribution to the Parry-Lord Theory, and his occupancy of a number of prestigious academic positions in Paris, his reputation fell into rapid decline almost immediately following his death.

To be sure, Jousse's work is being collected, developed, and even commemorated in certain academic circles in France. Moreover, owing to the persistent efforts of Edgard Sienaert, author of the present volume, the bulk of Jousse's lectures has for some time been in the process of being made accessible in English translation, although it remains to date the only language in which Jousse's French work is available. Still, within the larger context of international scholarship Jousse's work has remained unacknowledged, and his ideas have played next to no role in the major intellectual debates of the second half of the twentieth and the early twenty-first century.

There is, however, one aspect of Jousse's work that has in recent years received a measure of acclaim, at least among a number of mostly North American academics. It pertains to his book mentioned above, *Le Style oral rhythmique et mnémotechnique chez les Verbo-moteurs* (1925), translated and published in 1990 by Edgard Sienaert and Richard Whitaker. In terms of format and content, *The Oral Style* is an exceedingly unorthodox book. Far from being an authorially composed oeuvre, it is made up almost entirely of quotations excerpted from hundreds of secondary sources. The stylistic idiosyncrasy is best explained as an expression of one of Jousse's basic convictions. Throughout his professional life he aspired to attain a global synthesis of all he had gathered up and lectured on. Such a synthesis, he thought, was not to be obtained by way of an authorially constructed philosophical system abstracted from reality but rather by giving evidence of how multiple and diverse parts quite naturally cohered in a desired whole. In different words, the concept of a true synthesis would not obliterate the many parts, but would let them stand and interact with one another. The parts are the whole.

*The Oral Style* was a work of groundbreaking innovation, more so even in terms of content than of compositional format. In it Jousse takes the position that oral style, composition, and structures of thought distinct from writing culture were a subject worthy of exploration. He was the first, or at least among the very first, to conceptualize orality. Indeed, the designation of "oral style" hardly even existed prior to Jousse's lifetime. What the evidence collected in *The Oral Style* was designed to prove was the existence of a verbomotoric culture which managed life intensely verbally, interactively, and communally. There existed, Jousse's endeavored to prove, definable similarities between oral means of communication, techniques of memorization and recitation, and faculties of imitation among peoples in continents as different as Asia, Africa, and the Americas to warrant the premise of universal anthropological laws.

To be sure, the fact that he was able to amass a vast mosaic of scholarly citations pertaining to the oral phenomenon made up of gestures, rhythmic schemas, parallelisms, formulas, recitational style, repetitions, antitheses and many more proves that aspects of orality had been widely recognized and commented on long before him. It was in fact the basic rationale of Jousse's book to demonstrate that the many parts had been in place without his doing. Nonetheless, it was Jousse who raised the issue of media and communication in a novel and unprecedented way by discerning and assembling the many parts, thematizing orality, and elevating it to a principle of fundamental, and indeed global, significance in human culture. It is, therefore, entirely justified when in recent media and orality-scribality studies he has come to be regarded as the trail-blazing intellectual who conceptualized oral style, composition and structure of thought as a cultural phenomenon sui generis.

There is a tendency, even among those who acknowledge Jousse's pioneering significance, to depreciate him as architect of the Great Divide, the thesis that has fallen into disrepute for driving too crude a distinction between the oral and the written. And yet, within the context of humanistic scholarship, Jousse's exposition of the oral phenomenon assumes a noteworthy, a unique position. What may be called Jousse's ethnography of speech and speaking cultures reawakened sensibilities long eclipsed by a dominantly textual intellectualism. Whatever the specifics of his work, the apprehension of a universally valid Oral Theory marked a groundbreaking innovation in Western intellectual history.

Jousse's *Le Style oral* was in tension with, and in fact a deliberate challenge to, a humanistic scholarship that is almost entirely grounded on written texts. Indeed, the concept of Greco-Roman antiquity that had been constructed for centuries by the two ancient academic disciplines of biblical studies and classical philology was that of a tightly textual, documentary culture. Never having himself experienced the full impact of the digital medium, Jousse could reasonably claim that a textual ideology, reinforced by typography, had become the near-exclusive way and predominant perspective of thinking about history, knowledge and religion, and most other aspects of human culture. When in a surprisingly forceful statement he asserted that "[i]n the past, the accepted norm for human mental and intellectual aptitude was that of white, adult, bookish intellectuals, civilized according to our Greco-Latin culture," he was rebelling against a centuries-old literary, educational, cultural apparatus of Western values. Both *Le Style oral* and, we shall see, *In Search of Coherence* are the products of a man who viewed himself as "a resistance fighter," working "in defiance" against "the dogma of the Academy" which in its "bookish ethnicity" and Eurocentrism had chosen to silence the speaking majority and to make null and void a very large portion of human history and experience.

There is, finally, a feature that should be noted for being conspicuous in both *Le Style oral* and also in *In Search of Coherence*, namely, a preoccupation with "Jeshua of Nazareth." As the author readily confessed: "Jeshua of Nazareth has always been my true scientific obsession." Jousse was a priest and a member of the Societas Jesu, and deep interest in the language and person of Jesus permeates many of his lecture performances. An expert in, among other things, Semitic languages, he insisted on the historical signifi-cance of the Targums, Aramaic renderings, and expositions of the Hebraic Scriptures. He was of the view that Jesus' scriptural citations were not from the Hebrew texts but from their Targumic explications which, he claimed, had been in existence as early as the first century CE. And so Jousse became a lifelong student of the Targums, "attempting to have on my lips the very language of Jesus." In his more detailed philological studies, moreover, he was able to demonstrate how many of the Jesus sayings, when retranslated into Aramaic, displayed manifestly oral features—word plays, assonances, alliterations, repetitions and various other sound patterns—many of which had been obliterated in the Greek, not to mention in their modern translations.

In point of fact, Jousse's preoccupation was driven not merely by lin-guistic concerns. For him, Jesus, the Galilean rabbi and Teacher of the To-rah, was the true representative of the Palestinian verbomotoric culture of an oral, rhythmic, catechetical disposition and frame of mind that preceded Christianity's migration into Hellenism: "True Christianity is Ieshuanism before Christo-Graecism." Jesus the Jew was the personification of pure hu-manity and the epitome of the global synthesis. Grounded in his Galilean Judaism, he was the universal Man. It is not unimportant to understand that at a time when anti-Semitism in Europe was on the rise, anti-Judaism penetrated biblical scholarship, and the de-Judaizing of Jesus was increas-ingly in vogue, Jousse was a steadfast voice holding on to the Jewish, and specifically Galilean, identity of Jesus.

Much in the foregoing account of *The Oral Style* applies to *In Search of Coherence* as well, setting the stage for and helping to fully appreciate this book. But, as the subtitle suggests, the anthropology of mimism adumbrates a subject matter broader than anything pertaining to orality. Put differently,

*In Search of Coherence* approximates more closely than *The Oral Style* the global synthesis Jousse had aspired to achieve. But not unlike his first book, *In Search of Coherence* makes significant demands on its readers. In part this is due to the fact that "as far as possible" Sienaert's Introduction "left the stage to Jousse" by adopting his citational style, excerpting relevant passages from his lectures, which are introduced by and interspersed with a miminum of editorial comments. These seven lectures and five essays, which, in addition to Sienaert's Introduction, constitute the bulk of the book, also pose a challenge because they typify a performative style that flowed directly from a disposition that was largely oral in origin and organization. I suspect that ideally Jousse ought to be heard and listened to, and preferably in his native French. First and foremost, however, *In Search of Coherence* introduces readers into a new (or rather very old) mode of thinking unlike any of the traditional schools of criticism practiced in the humanities and social sciences have ever prepared them for. Jousse's conceptual apparatus and investigative vocabulary appears to be entirely outside the scope of customary humanistic categories. Throughout the book, philosophical-theological terms such as will, intelligence, or consciousness—key concepts in Western intellectual history—are being substantially reformulated and metamorphosed. Moreover, Jousse experiments with largely self-made terms, creating, as it were, a language of his own. Words such as intussusception, mimism-mimemes-mimage, conscientiousness-conscienciation, algebra-algebraization, verbigeration, rhythmicity-rhythmism, and numerous others are intended to wrench readers away from conventional manners of speaking and conceptualization, and to ease them into novel and as yet unsuspected thought processes.

For all these reasons, readers may be well advised not to peruse *In Search of Coherence* at a leisurely, meditative pace as if reading a conventional book, but rather to proceed fluently and to consume large parts rapidly as if listening to lectures. The point is to seek to grasp the world of Jousse by immersing oneself in his language, or rather to let his thought infiltrate us, the world of the readers.

The two issues that are central to the book are anthropology and mimism. If at the outset Marcel Jousse was introduced as an anthropologist, we now need to elaborate this designation. Anthropology for him was not confined to the traditional categories of paleontology and pre-history, but the discipline comprised the synthesis of all that makes up the anthropos, as Jousse was inclined to call the human species by its Greek word. Because anthropos was a single but complex whole, a compound, to use one of his favored terms, anthropological study required the confluence of a plurality of disciplines, preeminently of psychology, physiology, psycho-physiology, linguistics, pedagogy, philosophy, and last but by no means least theology. Given this understanding, anthropology, as conceived by Jousse, demanded detailed research of "the greatest possible number of ethnic milieux", including among many others the ancient Egyptians, Sumerians, Greeks and Romans, as well as present-day, living peoples of the Arabic and Chinese cultures, African tribes, the Malagasy and the Bulgarians, and also the Amerindians, of whom his visit to the United States had provided him with a first-hand experience. Importantly, however, the objective was not by any means to sanction specialization, let alone ethnocentricity, but rather the very opposite: to identify and link together the concrete cultural complexities into a coherent anthropological synthesis.

The other key issue of the book is mimism, a term coined by Jousse and derived from the Greek, which connotes the deeply ingrained human habit of imitation. Mimism for Jousse is what is fundamentally constitutive of the anthropos: "Man is by nature a mimer." Prompted by this conviction, he entertained a lifelong, professional interest in the study of children's behavior and development. For children, he reasoned, make unceasing inquiries and learn by imitation, and thus ideally demonstrate that mimism was a congenital condition of the anthropos. As he put it memorably: "In the beginning was mimism." And it is to this concept that Jousse returns over and again, approaching it from different angles, reiterating and developing it in manifold fashion. Knowledge itself is defined by mimesis, for it is through imitation that anthropos seizes upon the world, and internalizes it as mimemes, or units of memory. And insofar as anthropos is the carrier of mimemes, s(he) operates as the custodian of memory, and is nothing if not the embodiment of memory: "Memory is the whole of Man, and the whole of Man is memory." Once again, this extraordinary elevation of mimesis and memory has to be appreciated against the backdrop preeminently of classical philology and biblical studies. The former represents a prime example of text-bound thinking which has little use for the role of memory (except for some of the most recent pioneers of orality-scribality studies), while the latter has only recently begun, but only just begun, to exploit the interpretive possibilities of memory. Jousse himself was fully aware of the dilemma when he expressed his discontent over a humanistic culture that was customarily inclined "to bypass memory, secure in the knowledge that, if need be, everything would be found in an appropriate book or encyclopedic dictionary."

Among the many additional issues that are being covered in this book, four are of particular relevance in enlarging our under-standing of the central themes of anthropos and mimesis-memory.

One concerns the holistic nature of anthropos. Jousse is unrelenting in his repudiation of all anthropological dualisms, thus undercutting modes of thinking that have been deeply rooted in Western philosophy and theology. As he put it plainly: "There is no division in the anthropos". By way of example, anthropos is not body and is not soul, nor body versus soul, but rather a body-soul compound. As long as anthropos is alive, (s)he is bound to remain an indivisible whole. Only "death is the separation of the soul from the body".

Secondly, it will not escape the attention of readers that Jousse asserts himself as the advocate of a thoroughly corporeal anthropology. Even though anthropos is essentially a compound, the mimemes that motivate and energize anthropos engage the whole body. Hence, anthropos can appropriately be described as "a miming body". It would be difficult to locate another case of a somatically based anthropology quite like Jousse's, although, as will be noted below, it does have a prominent precursor in Western philosophy/ theology which had emphasized the role of our bodily based senses in the processes of cognition.

Thirdly, closely linked with the concept of corporeality is Jousse's rather harsh judgment vis-à-vis a meta-physics which, in his words, were constituted by "ethereal and intangible constructs that can be neither observed nor recorded". Anthropos is composed not of ideas but of mimemes. These are manifestations of the concrete, and they operate in relation to the realities around us. If it came down to a choice between the two philosophical giants of Aristotle versus Plato, Jousse would unhesitatingly prefer the company of the former whom he quotes repeatedly and with approval. "The anthropos does not live in the Platonic world of ideas", but in situations of utter concreteness, to use yet another one of Jousse's favorite terms.

There is, fourthly, the issue of interactionality. Anthropos finds himself/herself situated in a world that is fluid and incessantly in motion. This state of mobility comes about through a process of unending reciprocal communicative interactions: the world acts upon anthropos, and anthropos in turn reacts upon it. Given this condition of anthropos and the world it stands to reason that anthropos and the mechanism of mimism operate in a network of boundless connectivities. It is this very condition of interactionality and interconnectivity that makes a universal anthropology a feasible proposition. In sum, anthropos represents and lives in a world that is light years removed from the artificial and immutable world of print.

At the end we need to return to our earlier observation concerning Jousse's highly unconventional mode of thinking. He would be the first to acknowledge that in a world of interconnectivity, a linguistic and mental style out of the bounds of traditional norms cannot mean totally underived originality. Those among the readers who are familiar with ancient and medieval philosophy/ theology will readily recognize that numerous themes conveyed

across the book are indebted to, and on occasion virtually unthinkable without, Aristotelianism and its medieval counterpart of Thomism. As Jousse observes more than once, the "law of mimism" is a fundamentally Aristotelian
maxim: "Of all animals, Man is the greatest mimer." As far as memory itself
is concerned, it was a deeply held conviction of most ancient and medieval
thinkers that cognition and memory coexisted in close partnership. For
Thomas, memory, not unlike Jousse's mimemes, operated in activist fashion
(actus memoriae), although for the medieval theologian memory was dependent on phantasmata or interior visualization, an emphasis that appears to be
absent from Jousse. Moreover, Jousse shared the Aristotelian premise, reiterated by Thomas, that all cognition rises from sense perception: omni nostra
cognitio a sensu initium habet. The correspondence theory, finally, succinctly
phrased in the dictum adaequatio mentis et rei, suggesting a communicative
compatibility between mind and things, represents a widely used medieval
saying which in Thomas' thinking became a definition of truth. Needless to
say, Aristotelianism and Thomism were an essential ingredient firmly located
in Jousse's educational background.

This Foreword would be incomplete without grateful acknowledge-
ment of the contribution of Edgard Sienaert. For many years he has carried
on as translator, editor, and interpreter of the work of Marcel Jousse. It will
be obvious from much that has been stated in this Foreword that making
Jousse's thought accessible, and accessible in a language other than his native French, requires a superb mastery of both the French and the English
language, as well as superb philosophical sensibilities. I cannot think of any
other academician who could have performed this exceedingly difficult
task with equal talent, intelligence, and empathy. It is rightly being said that
translators are the unsung heroes in our intellectual universe. In keeping
the borders of the humanities (and all other sciences) open and in imped-
ing their descent into provincialism, ethnocentricity, and nationalism,
translators, editors, and interpreters perform a mission that is, ironically, of
particular relevance in our digital age. For all too often, out of a mistaken
technological euphoria, and not without a slight directed against the typographic culture, we are being assured that all print materials are now, or
will shortly be, accessible online. This corrosion of the typographic medium
goes hand in glove with the steady decline of the study of foreign languages
all around us. It is, therefore, a time which is in dire need of the work of
translators as perhaps never before in history.

For all his magnificent efforts and selfless labors Edgard Sienaert has
my sincere thanks.

Werner H. Kelber

# Preface

THIS INTRODUCTION TO MARCEL Jousse's anthropology is in the main by Jousse himself. Of its three parts, parts two and three consist respectively of seven of his lectures as recorded at the time he spoke and of five essays he had published in his life-time; in part one, a synthesis of his anthropology, he has an active voice through extensive quotations. Jousse's own synthesis of his research was still in an early stage when ill-health struck him. Publications during his life-time were few and the posthumous publications do not allow one to gauge the true scope of his anthropology. It is from the twenty-thousand-odd pages, a record of a twenty-five-year lecturing program from December 1931 to March 1957, that emerges a comprehensive and coherent system of thought—a worldview.

In Francis Bacon's well-known metaphoric classification of researchers, Jousse is neither an experimenter-ant, relentless gatherer of data, nor is he a reasoner-spider, spinning heady theories; his methodology is very much that of Bacon's bee: observation and information gathering, first, and subsequent transformation of this old into new. Having opted for anthropology rather than astronomy—to plumb the depths of the human being rather than those of the skies—he would apply the methods of the natural sciences to the social sciences, in order to arrive at what is the aim of all science: a unifying law. His law of mimism was this unifying law, informed by all disciplines and applying to all; a law that is to the human sciences what the law of gravitation is to the natural sciences; a law that, if applied, means a change of civilization.

In 2011, a conference marked the fiftieth anniversary of Jousse's death. Having heard, once too often, no doubt, that his work was an avalanche of technical terms, I prepared to lay that shibboleth to rest in a paper that went under the decidedly unglamorous title: "Marcel Jousse, terminologist." Yet, a dozen unusual terms and easily deciphered neologisms neither an avalanche nor a paper do make. The true challenge lies in Jousse demanding one to rethink and to think otherwise, to ask and seek answers to Socratic questions: What is, in anthropology, this anthropos-human and this logos-science? What is progress, soul, memory? Why do children play? Why do we have flags, salutes, medals? Why indeed does the apple fall? And so tumble, one by one, the tenets of our present-day civilization about our relationship as humans with ourselves, with the other, and with our universe. Our Emperor appears trebly disjointed: a human divided against himself as a "soul, mind, or spirit" and "body"; our writing as the gauge of societal development, dividing humanity in a before and after; our subsequent faith in all-conquering technology. Jousse posits a treble re-conciliation: of Man with himself as an indivisible human compound of musculature and intelligence; of oral and written style cultures with equally respected and effective skills of expression and communication; and of Man realizing that we are what our ambient real is.

My science, Jousse said, can be no more than a science in a dotted line, one that would in the future be joined up into an increasingly complete line. My hope is for this study to have at least put some of those dots into relief.

## Edgard Sienaert

Honorary Research Fellow
Centre for Africa Studies
University of the Free State
Bloemfontein
South Africa

# Acknowledgment

My thanks go to the Marcel Jousse Association for the support afforded me for many years in my research and for the permission to make full use of Jousse's work in this publication. I thank especially the Association's former chairman, M. Jean-Ghislain d'Eudeville.

The abbreviations following the quotations refer to the venues where the lectures were taught: Sorbonne, S; École des Hautes Études, HE; École d'Anthropologie, EA; École d'Anthropo–biologie, EAB; Laboratoire de Rythmo–pédagogie, Labo. S (Labo) refers to the six lectures of the Laboratoire digitized as S 51. The lectures are on two CD's, available from the Marcel Jousse Association in Paris www.marceljousse.com. AA refers to an unpublished article "Anthropos et Anthropoïde" (Marcel Jousse Archive); AGR to *The Anthropology of Geste and Rhythm* (Durban: Mantis, 2000); GB to Gabrielle Baron, Mémoire vivante: Vie et œuvre de Marcel Jousse, 2nd edition (Paris: Le Centurion, 1981); OS to *The Oral Style* (Marcel Jousse, *Le Style oral rythmique et mnémotechnique chez les Verbo-moteurs*, 1925, translated by Edgard Sienaert and Richard Whitaker, Routledge, RLE Folklore, 2015).

# PART 1

# Marcel Jousse's Anthropology of Mimism

# Introduction

## *The Anthropology, Methodology, and Terminology of Mimism*

"Thus, anthropology led me to a methodology that brought with it a terminology." *HE 30/05/45*

MARCEL JOUSSE TAUGHT IN Paris, from 1931 until 1957, at three institutions of higher learning: the Sorbonne, the School of Anthropology and the École Pratique des Hautes Études, as well as in his own Rhythmo-pedagogic laboratory. His teaching varies according to the venue and audience; he thus teaches, respectively, on the psychology of geste and rhythm, on linguistic anthropology, on the origins of Christianity—in particular on the nature, function, and operation of the Palestinian oral style—and on the anthropology of education.

A profession of interdisciplinarity follows all announcements of these one thousand-odd lectures, which constitute his major legacy: "Marcel Jousse's studies in anthropology aim at establishing a link between the disciplines of psychology, ethnology and pedagogy." Indeed, "If we were truly scientific, we would not cut up everything, we would not allow ourselves to say: there is this unit here, another unit there and yet another one there. You should not, when dealing with that immense thing called the universe, which means totality, cut off any of its parts and separate it from the *whole*." *Labo 19/01/38* "All is in all." *EAB 14/01/48* "All is so very much imbricated that it is absolutely impossible to treat even the smallest element of our human, of our anthropological mechanism, without calling up the links that tie it in with all and every one of these matters." *HE 24/01/45*

In a lecture at the Sorbonne on January 12, 1956, Jousse drew on the blackboard a compass rose representing this interdisciplinarity in detail. In

3

this compass, sub-titled "The anthropology of mimism and its scientific orientations," multiple scientific orientations converge in the capital M of the Mimism from which they stem, illustrating Jousse's earlier contention that "From the moment I put mimism in its rightful place, which is at the center, the whole problem of human expression turned around." *EA 26/02/40* "In the beginning was mimism." *EAB 07/01/48* Mimism is at the center and everything converges towards it in a synthesis, in a whole that holds: "The great synthesizers have always reacted against their social milieu's undue drive to carve things up. The true savant on the contrary brings together through new laws, things that were thought to be disparate." *EA 17/02/36*

Jousse's own new law is the law of mimism and mimism is his great synthesis. This law of mimism is not in fact a new law: "Of all animals, Man is the greatest mimer and it is through mimism that he acquires his earliest knowledge. This law was proffered two thousand five hundred years ago by Aristotle and had been ignored; it is the anthropologist who is here speaking to you who established this law as the basis of human formation." By making Aristotle's law the foundation of his anthropology of mimism and so infusing an age-old proposition with new life, Jousse illustrates one of his methodological principles: "The aim of research is to quest for and discover fresh insights and understanding. However, as all seems to have been discovered already, how can we possibly arrive at something fresh and new? We can, by the incessant, meticulous and detailed scrutiny of the old." *AGR 481*

What is new, is Jousse's science of mimism establishing Aristotle's law as the basis for an explanation of the function and meaning of the anthropos in the cosmos and for a definition of the cosmos-anthropos relationship. Thus scrutinized, reformulated, and redirected, the old becomes: "The human is an animal played by the universe. This discovery created the anthropology of mimism." *S 22/01/53* Jousse wanted this *anthropo—logy* of mimism to be a *science* of the *human*, and "Science begins with precise language." *HE 22/03/44*. He wanted a human science with a thought-through methodology, because "Wrong method begets wrong science." *HE 10/11/43* and "I started my training in scientific methodology in that splendid science called celestial mechanics. There, in astronomy, precise vocabulary handles precise things. In anthropology however, anything goes. We use words like soul, mind, intelligence, ideas, all of which are meaningless, really. There are, in fact, neither souls, nor images, nor minds, nor ideas. Where does all this come from? It is nothing but an empty bookish vocabulary handed down to us, and that we failed to question." *EA 12/01/41*

## Marcel Jousse on anthropology, methodology, and terminology

### On anthropology

"Anthropology is relevant for apprehending the anthropos in his prehistory, but even more so for understanding his fundamental, primary nature of two thousand, four thousand and many, many years earlier, and, above all, for appreciating what he is today. Such science, however speculative, will, when done in-depth, have profoundly practical implications. This is why we witness today a reawakening of life. When I take the subject up again next year in connection with the oral style, it will become clear that, in anthropology, we are dealing with an enduring pedagogy that answers the primordial question I posed at the beginning of this lecture: how does the human being, placed at the heart of action of the universe, manage to conserve the memory of these actions within him, and to transmit this memory faithfully to his descendants, from generation to generation?" *EA 03/04/33*

"The main task of anthropology is not to answer exhaustively and successively a string of questions, but rather to identify a number of quick apperceptions by specialists in a variety of disciplines, and to combine their intuitions in a coherent synthesis. This is where Laplace's phrase applies, that I have often quoted you: *Discoveries consist in bringing together gestes that may be joined but that were not joined before.*" *HE 03/03/1943*

### *The anthropos*

"It is a strange creature, this anthropos. I named it after its Greek, as yet unsullied name, anthropos, to cleanse it from all that went under the label *Man.*" *EAB 07/01/48*

"This complex called anthropos, this is to say a human compound," *EA 18/01/41* ". . . is not a body, it is not a soul. It is a human compound. You cannot bring me some water and call it H2O, no, once you decomposed it, it is no longer water. To you, human compound means body + soul. Fine, but only after death. After death, you will have a *corpse* here (a corpse, no longer a body) and a *soul* there. Is that not what you yourselves teach your children—blissfully unaware, as usual, of what you are truly teaching them—when you tell them that death is the separation of the soul from the body? They were not separated before, then?" *EA 12/01/41*

"The normal human mechanism, this is to say this human compound that is, in its present state, indivisible, is a compound (I stick to this term as there is no alternative), a compound of musculature and of intellection of this musculature. It is this intellection of the musculature that we call soul or intelligence. No matter what name your metaphysics fancy, whenever I play whatever movement—miming a dog with his pending ears or a bison with its upturned horns—I am clearly conscious of the fact that I bring my muscles into play. I cannot do otherwise." *Labo 26/02/36*

### The science of the anthropos

"What I bring here is a new science: the anthropology of geste." *EA 05/01/41*

"The anthropology of life, an awareness of the anthropology of thought elaborated by the whole body . . ." *EA 12/03/51*

"In the past, at the School of Anthropology, we were shown rows of skeletons. You saw those too. You first had an anthropoid; this ape then straightened up slowly, as if rising through the ranks; and at some point he came to stand to attention: that was the anthropos. To me however, these bones seemed singularly immobile and the pieces of wire that kept them together seemed all too visible. Faced with this skeletology, I created anthropology, that is to say the science of mimism." S 14/01/54 "Anthropology is in essence the science of the real *living* being." *EAB 07/01/48*

"Next year, we will study the play of the child and we will create an anthropology aimed at the rediscovery of Man. This Man is not a skeleton! This Man is not a creature of the printed book! This Man is not some fanciful creation of our meddlesome art! The human who will stand up before us will do so in the full richness of his muscular might and power. Pay attention now: that musculature is a musculature carrying the universe, and carrying a universe that is understood. That is what anthropology is about: anthropology is the discovery of living and thinking Man." *EA 15/03/37*

### The anthropology of geste

"What I bring here is a new science: the anthropology of geste." *EA 05/01/41*

"Thought, intelligence, mind, what is all this? Nothing but words stuck on phenomena, when these phenomena are immediately and readily observable. The geste is observable, and once we study geste, we have *science* instead of *metaphysics*. The term metaphysics came into being only because some topics had been copied from the manuscripts of Aristotle *after* the part dealing with *physics*. At this point, *meta*physics became the norm for the study of science, and the true study and science of things physical was left in the care of us, anthropologists. It may seem odd and disconcerting that our anthropology broaches such a wide range of subjects, and one might wonder at the kind of science that meddles in just about anything. The fact is that our anthropological science is *the* great fundamental science. Although fleetingly glimpsed at times, it had mostly remained out of sight. Facts, however, cannot forever be ignored and there comes a time when one is compelled to recognize even what one is unwilling to see. What I presently bring into view is the great corporeal mechanism as it manifests itself in geste." *HE 09/06/36*

"One can nowadays, with twin cameras, record simultaneously the gestes of the known object and the gestes of the knowing subject. I can record at once a pine tree on the seaside shaken by the wind, and a child watching the tree being shaken and acting out the scene in his whole miming body its customary precision and finesse. I am able nowadays to observe the small child as a plastic, fictile mirror, and observe at the same time the large real image that has just been mimed. This is where our strength lies as humans: we are able to simultaneously seize the gestes of the things and the gestes of the things as mimed by us.

"My task as anthropologist then is to carry Rousselot's experimental scientific methods into our experimental anthropological mimology. I need to ask questions to the fibers of my body and demand that they answer. The more refined, powerful and accurate our anthropological instruments will become, the more incisive our knowledge of the anthropos will be. I have no doubt that our experimental anthropological laboratory tests will confirm the law of universal mimology, namely, that *we are*, through all the fibres of our body, through all the fibres of our organs, *congenital mimers*. The task I set anthropology is very simple and frighteningly complex: it is to unreel all those reels of corporeal mimismic gestes—manual, ocular, auricular, laryngo-buccal, olfactive, gustative—that will have been recorded by our instruments once they will have been fine-tuned enough to register all these gesticulations. Imagine just how much we still need to learn if we are serious about the science of Man!

"When we enter Professor de Broglie's physics laboratory and realize the technical prowess that managed to tame even the atom, we take fright; yet, today, other atoms still are being bombarded with terrifying projectiles in order to find out how atomic mechanics work. On entering such laboratories where the physical infinitesimally small is being studied, we, anthropologists, cannot but wonder, curious and envious, when we will be able to study the biological and anthropological infinitesimally small. For therein indeed lies a true anthropologist's bewilderment and anguish: in the fact that we think *with all the fibres of our body*." *EA 05/11/34*

# On methodology

## *The methodologist*

"There lie open before us immense fields of research in all these matters, most of them wholly virgin territory. A teacher's role is to sketch an outline, to elaborate a method, and to demonstrate this method's workings and outcomes in a number of connected disciplines. A practising methodologist is a pioneer. His scientific ruggedness stems from the newness of his discoveries and of the trails he clears to reach the eternal Truths." *HE 10/11/43*

## *The method*

"The original and capital sin of our written-style civilization is that it considers itself singularly superior and unique, and believes, moreover, that everything not recorded in writing, does not exist. Because of this, anthropological facts are neglected, and, for the most part, misunderstood. Rather than studying in any depth and identifying which aspects of ethnography are anthropological, human sciences are satisfied with skimming the surface of bookish ethnicity. To counter this mind-set, I decided to change the method. Instead of restricting my field of observation to the dead letters of texts, I opt for a methodology that operates first and above all via the awareness of a living tool: the human geste. Anthropos being in essence nothing more than a complexus of gestes, the most apt and best performing tool available to analyse man is his own performance of his own gestes. This is no doubt the tool to trump all other tools, and, moreover, this tool develops instinctively within each one of us, and becomes increasingly polished as our awareness grows." *AGR 27.*

## *Methodological principles*

### Observation

"Scientific is that what is observable, recordable, and analyzable." *Labo 19/12/34* "As you know, I look here at the objective side only. I have before me the real, a real that I need to observe, to understand, to express. You do realize how complex the subject of my research is, how new it is, sensitive and fluid. What I do here before you is this one, single thing only: to try to observe, to try to understand, to try to explain as clearly as possible. And that, I believe, is science." *EA 03/04/33*

"I am an anthropologist who points out a methodology: the observation of the real." *S 11/03/42* "It is so much easier to invent rather than to observe." *EA 28/11/32* "Discovery I like to define as the act of seeing that what exists. Invention I define as the art of constructing that what does not exist. I press this point because we need to smash relentlessly the old metaphysics of ethereal and intangible constructs that can be neither observed nor recorded." *S 14/12/33*

"Humanity may prove to be formidably old, yet, amazingly, it also proves to be extraordinarily well equipped from the moment it came into being. When we observe the drawings preserved in the prehistoric caves— they are in fact mimodramas—we discover that those people were able to express the real with a refinement, delicacy and precision not yet recovered by our present-day painters. Science needs to ban as entirely gratuitous the notion of an anthropos expressing himself by grunting like an anthropoid. From his very first appearance, the anthropos reveals himself with a body wholly and splendidly equipped, and so very much less desiccated, less worn and torn than we are. Ah, yes, indeed, if this seems disconcerting, it is precisely because we had not observed but constructed Man." *EA 06/01/36*

"We never observed the child, we constructed it. I make the same point at the School of Anthropology in connection with the so-called primitive or savage. We never observed because to observe is hard, while to construct in the air is easy because of language: language allows one to string up words without having to verify their content." *Labo 19/12/34*

## Experimentation

"To know that one only knows well what one has handled is the beginning of science." *EA 14/03/38*

"The anthropos is not something one cuts up into small pieces." *S 17/12/34* "Under the pretext of specialisation, the social milieu offers us no more than a thinly sliced-up real: philosophy here, pedagogy there and psychology here or there. Experience only can convince us of the existence of a single, whole real, one that is cut up because of our inability to study it otherwise." *EA 02/17/36*

"You ought to be the disciples of fact." *EA 14/11/32* "As an anthropologist, I have no bookish dogmas to defend. I have only to observe facts. I apply precise laws to the entire world, and I watch them playing out. I brood over swaying mothers in order to analyse their gestes. They rock to and fro, from side to side, according to the great laws of humanity. I see people living, I see people dying, but always I see balancing from right to left, and lifting up and bending down, and swaying from front to back. I will continue to study all this balancing, lifting and swaying, which I find in all human expression, and in the traditional mechanisms of the Galilean paysan memory." *AGR 301*

"Study the living in its living form, and ban the study of dead books entirely: what is needed is an in-depth study of the living, expressive and rhythmic geste." *AGR 25* "You noticed that I have not defined rhythm. I think that it is very bad method to define a biological phenomenon before having seen it in operation. Some purely metaphysical definitions of rhythm do not square up at all with the facts." *S 23/04/34*

## COLLABORATION

"Science has become so complex nowadays, that in order to advance into some new sector, we must resort to the method of modern warfare: the joining of forces." Foreword to *The Oral Style.*

"I was compelled to create a new discipline. One cannot overhaul a science overnight. I believe that for many years to come there will be no single person able to command all the techniques that I have commanded. There is a need to focalize an appreciable number of disciplines that until now have been widely differentiated. This is why a synthesis of my work will not be possible for a long time because there is not a single appropriate research tool available. One needs equipment that is as living and as supple as life itself." *EA 02/26/40*

"In the investigation of reality, one needs to protect oneself with jealous care, yet, it is equally indispensable for one to know how to get help from other researchers who are as jealously individual in their research. It is through such multiple individualisations that one arrives at a unified and objective discovery. Only through the research of observers following each an independent method of observation can objective conclusions be reached. Such unanimous objective convergence in research is wholly different in nature from the verbal agreement of so many human parrots, who all repeat the same platitudes because they all ingested them from the same books." *EH 08/04/40*

## CONFRATERNISATION

"My greatest strength lies in my contact with the various American milieus, with the Chinese, with the Arabs, Malagasy, Africans. This is how I enabled myself to find my exact and proper place and so, through confraternisation, to arrive at an understanding of each other's specific characteristics." *EA 12/04/43* "In the past, the accepted norm for human mental and intellectual aptitude was that of white, adult, bookish intellectuals, civilized according to our Greco-Latin culture. This kind of ignorant judgement relegated the rest of humanity to 'primitive and prelogical mentality.' Such artificial categories are singularly dangerous to any healthy psychology and are fortunately disappearing. The future promises, wherever possible, to study man holistically as a being of fluid and malleable spontaneity: the anthropos." *AGR 29*

"We have before us, be it in Africa, be it in Asia, be it in the primordial Americas, enough to further enrich all our anthropological gestes, this is to say, enough to convey to us and to etch into our consciousness, the true meaning of what a human being truly is. You realize now that we might see the day when a chief hailing from an ethnic milieu different from our own will appear before us and, on leaving, will tell us: 'You taught us your civilization. Our civilization might be able to teach you a lot more.' That is the point at which we will at last be able to bring into play what I have been conveying to you for the last twenty years: the anthropology of globalism and of planetarism." *EA 19/05/47*

"I am very happy to see the emergence, universally, of civilizations that cannot be called savage, or primitive, or any other such term. They are, these civilizations. Rather than attempting to understand them, which is an impossibility, let us understand that we do not understand them. That in itself will be a step towards mutual appreciation that could develop into agreement." *S 22/01/53* "The younger people must realise the new Man within themselves, the anthropos who, having become conscious of himself in his deepest ethnic being, reaches out towards others in fraternal anthropological interchange." *EA 01/03/48*

## On terminology

### Algebrosis

"How could we possibly have arrived at this alteration of human thought? What is it that led us to impoverish human thought to the point of saying: 'Let x be.' But x what? That in a nutshell is the problem I struggled with when I was twenty and with which I will deal in a moment." *S 01/02/34* "The mechanism of abstraction, which has its origin in a concrete object, may well become algebrozed through overuse. When this happens, one can no longer access the meaning of gestes or words, but one is left with empty automatic gestes, and even religious gestes that are devoid of all meaning." *EA 14/02/38*

"I created the word algebrosis from existing terminology. We can perform no scientific function at present without *algebra*, in which a voluntary process of simplification takes place and signs are assigned meaning by consensus. In *algebrosis* the signs or words, which are gestes, can mean *anything* because we no longer see their connection with the real they originally referred to. We live by a system in which all gestes are diminished and degraded, be they corporeal, manual, laryngo-buccal or graphic, because they are emptied of their original concretism." *EA 14/02/48*

"I realize again and again the critical importance of terminology, and how we are caught in the vice of meaning that is already socialized. No one should be surprised when we, anthropologists, create and use new terms. The fact is that all the current words are socially contaminated. It is therefore necessary for us to recapture each of these words and to carry out a preliminary disinfection, in some way like that of Pasteur. Before we begin, we have to disinfect the vocabulary." *GB 172*


## A new scientific terminology for a new science

"I am accused of logomania, when all I do is to label each of the facts I observe with a name that allows us to discriminate meaning." *S 18/03/54* "The main difficulty for a discoverer is often to find a proper and understandable terminology. Society is hell-bent on keeping its old vocabulary. This old vocabulary needs to inflect towards a new terminology accommodating the discovery of new things." *S 14/12/33* "New facts require new terms. I had to create a sufficiently precise terminology for these facts to be labelled without any risk of confusion. Creating a scientific vocabulary is a delicate operation, with the following possible solutions: one can use common words with a new meaning; one can immediately create a profusion of neologisms; one can create neologisms in reduced numbers, and develop them gradually over a number of years, as and when necessary. The third solution seems to be by far the best because it is the most user-friendly in an unavoidably technical context." *AGR 50.*

"The word *soul*, the word *spirit* came to us from the Palestinian milieu on which our civilization is based: the *nâfshâ* is the breath from the throat; the *roûhâ* is the breath from the nostrils. Put that in Latin and then algebroze it further in French as *anima* = âme (soul), *spiritus* = *esprit* (spirit), and all you did was to play with sounds. Confronted with this contaminated terminology, I bring a purified terminology. This is why rather than to use the word *soul*, rather than to use the word *spirit*, I use the experimental word *mimism*." *EAB 07/01/48*

CHAPTER 1

# Mimism, a Comprehensive Worldview

"We have within us the entire universe."
EAB 03/03/48

"Miming Man holds within him the whole universe."
HE 20/11/34

"What is mimism? It is the universe in front of a living mirror,
and this living mirror intussuscepts this universe and replays it.
That is Man and that is the abyss I try to fill." EA 14/03/49

## The cosmos-anthropos connection and connectedness

### The cosmos: the fog outside the anthropos

"This outside fog is what we call the universe, a word that serves as a cover-up for our ignorance, a word that does not commit us in any way, for we have no idea what it means: 'universe' is 'all,' and to be 'all' is indefinite. It implies that whenever we place ourselves at wherever spot, there will invariably be something else for us to find further on. I once put it to a professor of cosmology: 'Let us suppose we find ourselves in this wishful Universe ◯ and that, with highly perfected flying machines we manage to touch the very outerreach of this sphere. ◯ What will happen? We are most likely to utter the curious remark that, well, Man could place himself at the roof of the world and, extending his hand, he would be adding on to the universe.' Which makes no sense at all, since we do not know what it means not to be inside this mechanism, we are quite simply talking words. Simple examples show up at once both our limitation and the limitations of our experimentation." *EA 09/03/39*

*A tiered order . . .*

Our universe is energy, energy in movement, a continuous movement of energy in interaction, formulated as the triphase law of universal interaction: an acting one—acting on—an acted upon. Human beings thus find themselves in an all-encompassing universal energy that manifests itself in three spheres, each regulated by their own law: a physical sphere of ordered matter, indefinitely in physical action-reaction and governed by the law of universal atraction; a biological sphere of life, made of actions and reflex reactions, governed by the law of instinct; and an anthropological sphere of intelligent life, or consciousness, governed by the law of mimism.

*. . . made of energy*

"There is in the universe one thing only, something physicists study more and more: energy. Paraphrasing Saint John one could say: 'In the beginning was energy—nothing but energy.' Or: 'In the beginning God created energy.' If I had to broach the topic from a purely physical angle, I would show you how energy curls up in small, odd atoms that men of genius, physicists like de Broglie, study relentlessly. What we have there are small solar systems, so to speak, made of clusters of energy." *Labo 04/12/35*

*. . . that manifests in three clusters*

"The following is a quick summary of what preoccupies the modern scientists, classified according to three mechanisms: a physical mechanism, a biological mechanism and an anthropological mechanism . . . all of which try to understand the laws of a force that remains unknown to us, but that we assume, and call energy. All research converges to study this energy. I admit that whenever I talk to you about energy, it is without knowing what it is, but there is nothing unusual about this; we do, after all, for example, talk glibly about electricity without knowing what it is, which does not prevent us from making use it. This energy we say is everywhere, we do not know what it is." *Labo 08/12/37*

*. . . that are triphase interactional*

"In the universe, nothing is cut up, everything interacts." *EA 14/03/38* "The essential element of the universe, constituted as it is, be it in the physical world, in the botanical wold or in the zoological world, is simply an action that acts on another action. That is what I call triphasism. Triphasism is simply a cluster of energy that we call an acting-one that acts in a certain way on another cluster of energy called an acted-upon. What is this agent? What is this acted? It is, so to speak, what will perpetually propel a certain action." *EAB 07/01/48* "The universe is an imbrication of interactions. That is the real to me: a complexus of interactions." *S 11/02/54*

## The anthropos: a human compound

"It is a rather odd creature, this anthropos. I called him by his as yet unsullied Greek name, the anthropos, so as to thoroughly cleanse him from all that we put under that name: Man." *EAB 07/01/48*

In the anthropological sphere, the actions of the cosmos are seized in a system unique to the human being: he captures the cosmic play on him and stores it *within* for possible replay *without*. Miming is replaying out what was first played in. Mimism is the human's unique capacity to turn the cosmological unconscious action, or play, into anthropological conscious reaction, or replay. Where in the biological sphere there is reflex-action—instinct, in the anthropological sphere there is reflective-reaction—intelligence. Man's mimismic system allows him not only to apprehend, but also to comprehend. Man is the intelligizing agent of the cosmos, obeying the law of mimism, formulated two thousand five hundred years ago by Aristotle (*Poetics* IV.2): "Of all animals, Man is the greatest mimer, and it is through mimism that he acquires all his knowledge." *EA 19/12/32*

It is this law Marcel Jousse established as the basis for his explanation of the function and meaning of the anthropos in cosmos.

## The cosmos-anthropos connectedness:
## from action to geste

The function of the human in the universe is transformative: the human has the unique capacity to turn the unconscious interactional universe into consciousness. Movement is action when it is cosmic, geste when it is anthropological. The mimismic process is unconscious physical, chemical, or biological action becoming possible conscious anthropological geste. Geste is what the human makes from the outside world that came in him: how he received it, through one or more of his senses; how he let it permeate his whole being; how he organized it, stored it, and kept it at the ready for possible future expression and communication.

"Do you understand what mimism means? Mimism is the compelling tendency that only the human possesses to replay all the actions of the universe. Geste or action, for we can indeed not ever enter in the actions of the universe, we are obliged to reduce them to gestes in us. Of what is outside us, we only know that what replays in us, and that we can express." *Labo 08/12/37* "In the physical world we have movements that we conveniently call: actions. In the world of life, we have gestes. A geste is that infinitely simple, rich, expressive, scientific thing that espouses the real. If I choose that word geste, it is because to me, the word geste means and calls up something that comes alive in a human compound, and something that can be conscious. That is geste in the strict, human specific sense as I define it." *EA 18/11/35*

"[O]utside us, there are only actions. But these actions will become gestes in the human who receives them and replays them." *EA 01/02/39* "So we have the triphase movement of the real that is a movement. But note: it is not yet geste, because it is happening outside us." *S 06/03/52* "What do I call geste? Specifically, all movement in the human compound. Small or large, microscopic or macroscopic, whole or in part, inchoative or complete, I call all human movement geste." *EA 06/12/43* "[L]ife is never disorganized, it is always organized and that is what I have called geste." *S 08/02/44*

## The mimeme: the nodal point

Etymologically, a mimeme is *something imitated*; in the context of mimism, it is something imitated *anthropologically*—imitated by a human being and, therefore, mimismically imitated or mimed. The mimeme is the unit of the cosmos-anthropos play-replay interaction, or mimismic action, or geste. The mimeme is the concrete expression of the cosmos-anthropos connectedness: cosmic *im*-pression becomes anthropological *ex*-pression. Just as a cosmic action is always a cosmic *interaction*—an-acting-one acting-on an-acted-upon—so is an anthropological geste always an anthropological interaction or *proposition*. In a mimeme, the cosmic mechanical process of interaction becomes the human conscious propositional geste. This process is most easily understood in the laryngo-buccal, oral, or linguistic mimeme that is formulated as a subject–verb–complement relation.

The mimeme is not a metaphysical construct, it is a scientific fact. Mimemes are observable building blocks of a human being: "[T]he geste can be viewed as evolving through various stages of development, advanced, still inchoative or even infinitesimal. This however does in no way change its nature; size does not change the nature of a phenomenon." *S 14/12/33* "[S]cientifically speaking, it does make no sense at all to look at geste according to a scale of visibility." *Labo 19/02/36* Gestes are gestes, be they microscopic or interior, or macroscopically exteriorized. Their sum constitutes a particular unique human being. What is called memory is the sum of our mimemes. In gestual language, a mimeme is a unit of cosmos-anthropos interaction become anthropological proposition. A mimeme is a play-replay unit.

## The mimeme, a unit of cosmos-anthropos interaction

"The mimeme is in mimism what the phoneme is in phonetics." *Labo 09/01/33* "The great fundamental mechanism of human anthropology [is] the mimismic geste, the mimeme." *Labo 20/12/33* "[M]imemes being the very basis of the complex called an anthropos." *EA 20/03/50* "The mimeme is the replay of an external action operating in us, without us, at times in spite of us." *HE 22/03/44* "We have in us mimemes. What are these mechanisms like? They are interactional, meaning: not incoherent. There will not be an object on the one side and another oject on the other side. There will normally be coherence, and that is the interaction." *EA 20/12/43* "In the mechanism of mimism, interaction is the all-important element. A child is not a broken up mirror. When he plays at being a kangaroo eating an aloe, he is not being 1- the static kangaroo that eats, followed by 2- the eating or manducation, followed by 3- the manducation of that particular aloe with its particular shape, if it is an aloe the kangaroo he mimes happens to have before it. That is not how it works at all: he will be the kangaroo-that-eats-the-aloe; he will be the interaction; he will play out the kangaroo-that-eats-the-aloe, and nothing else; he will play at an-acting-one—acting-on—an-acted-upon, and this without any decoupage. That indeed is what the study of formulism will teach us." *Labo 18/01/39*

## . . . gestual and thus observable

"Those mimemes are essentially gestual, gesturally expressed by the whole body, thus global gestes, or expressed in one or other part of the body, and thus manually, ocularly or in any other way. You cannot get away from your human compound." *EA 20/12/43* "[T]hose famous so-called abstract ideas are not ideas. They are mimemes, this is to say things done with the body." *EA 01/03/37* "I mount in me mimemes, I go out, observe and record in me,

8

raw, the moon rising and the sun setting." *Labo 07/03/34* "To think the real means to let the real play out in us as it came to adjust and mould itself in all our fibres. That is what I called mimemes. Corporeal-manual mimemes that invade us, playing in our ocular mechanisms, playing in our auricular mechanisms, playing in our laryngo-buccal mechanisms. That is all we are, and that should be our starting point." *EA 03/03/41* "We have then in us an extraordinary mimismic potential. All the mimemes are there, in us, we need only to let them play out. They are corporeal, our entire body being ready to mime the characteristic geste of the object." *Labo 13/12/33*

## . . . called propositional geste

"The propositional geste is the anthropological transposition of the inter-actional cosmic action." *HE 05/11/41* "[T]he triphase mimeme constitutes what I have termed the propositional geste." *EA 30/11/50* "[I]n celestial mechanics the sun circles the earth. bserved by a human being, this unconscious interaction of celestial mechanics becomes a propositional mechanism that becomes conscious—it is a propositional geste." *HE 05/11/41*. "There is always an acting one—acting on—an acted upon: I eat bread. I drink water. Whatever our written form and whatever our spoken form, human expressions will always take form as propositional geste, in mirror and echo of the interactional cosmic action. We should see the outside world as morphing into the triphase geste of the human, and this is the basic structure of human science, human memory and human logic." *EA 06/03/33* "That is where the great human creation lies: I will be able to take hold of the whole world to reuse it later in the form of propositional fragments." *EA 03/12/33*

"The interaction is the unit of mimismological replay. Once intelligized, it becomes the generally triphase propositional geste: the actor—acting on—an acted upon. It is because propositional geste is ordinarily so little known that people have failed to understand that it underlies language, that it is the basis of language. That is why people studying human expression remained stuck in its superficial phase, ethnic language, and failed to study the propositional geste, which is its anthropological base." *HE 16/04/40*

## Memory: we are the sum of our mimemes

"Thus, the more gestes, the more mimemes of things we receive, the richer we will be." *S 07/12/33* "What do you have in you? That is the question!" *S 08/03/56* "We have in us every replay of our whole life." *EAB 07/01/48* "Omnia mecum porto: I carry all in me." *S 14/01/54* "Memory is the whole of Man and the whole of Man is memory." *S 28/02/57* "Memory, the tireless replay of our mimemes . . ." *HE 10/11/43* "Our primary task is to work in the zone of memory, for Man is above all a memory. Man's worth lies in what he memorized." *S 14/02/57*

"It is most interesting to observe Man in his build-up. How is it possible that until now no-one thought of Man's body, of his geste, of his mimeme as his first and primary tool? Man is first and foremost the creator of his own self, by himself. There was no need for him to look elsewhere. He mounted himself by himself. What we are now going to study is how Man came out of himself." *EA 06/12/34* " . . . motor-camera recordings show us how children are like amoebae, their whole infinitely flexible being reflecting the actions the outside world on them in the form of mimemes. One could also compare the child to one of those small balls of clay children play with: the child is indeed a receptive mass—seemingly nothing, yet, potentially everything." *Labo 19/12/34* " . . . a child is a complexus of mimemes, this is to say of gestes reproducing the various actions of the exterior." *Labo 20/12/33*

## The unifying law of mimism

### All the world's a geste—pangestualism

"Vita in motu. Life and movement coincide." *EA 04/01/37* "Vita in gestu." *S 30/01/36* "All is geste." *S 12/02/53* "In a human being, large or small, it is always a geste." *EA 22/11/37*

"Children are said to be animists. But there is no separate *anima*, no separate soul; there is, however, mimism. To a child, everything is alive, whence the child's normal practice of playing both the acting one's characteristic geste as well as playing the acted upon. The geste is made up of interactional gestes." *S 28/02/52* The so-called animism is pangestualism. Pangestualism is seeing that all is in movement and explaining all movement as a partaking in the triphase interactional universe consisting of a ceaseless interconnecting of an acting one—acting on—an acted upon. Pangestualism gives cosmic action meaning by finding its cause. It is a conscienciation, a hominization of the unconscious actions of the universe. As "geste is any live movement executed in a human compound, and this live movement can be conscious." *EA 18/11/35,* all who remained spontaneous, natural, mimismic, are, not *animistic*, but *gestual*. They see gestes everywhere, their whole universe is an immense geste, their worldview is pangestual.

"Savages, we are told, believed that all things have souls [*animae*]. Not so, rather: they know that there are gestes. Children too play things out and play at things. They sense that all things make gestes and it is these gestes that they replay." *Labo 12/12/34* "Everything is at play, and at play all the time, because all and everything is alive. That is why in children what is called anthropomorphism, or animism, is the norm. It is but normal hominization, which is to say that the things are molded in the child, played inside and outside him. If children take it for granted that all things are alive, it is because *all is alive in them through mimism.* This is the crux of the matter, the supreme mystery that I try to fathom: by its gestes, by hominizing the real, a child emerges from the fog that is the outside world. Not surprisingly, the people you call savage, but who are those humans who remained concrete, who preserved their spontaneity, sense the universe in the same way. Without being prelogical, these peoples will obviously deem it wholly natural that all these live forces intercommunicate, interact, and enter in what can be called a perpetual gestual dialogue of everything with everything." *EA 09/03/39*

"Let me quickly return to the analyses I made over a number of years of anthropological pangestualism in spontaneous people, in people very inexactly called 'primitive.' It is said: 'They see souls everywhere.' No, they see gestes at play everywhere. A Greek poet said, and his dictum was applied to these 'savages': 'All is full of gods.' No, all is full of the gesticulations of Man. I urge the professors and teachers of philosophy I have before me here to make a turnaround and understand that paganism, is, fundamentally, based on anthropological pangestualism." *EA 01/12/47*

"Look at how children play at anything and see this as the great mechanism of interactional play. All the dynamic sources of human expression prove to be the interactions of the universe. This is why I insist that the formula of an-acting-one—acting-on—an-acted-upon be squarely put into the real. In the propositional geste, it is the subject doing the action on the complement. Multiplied by the innumerable gestes there are in the world and conclude how far removed we are here from the simplistic presumptions of progressive evolution." *EA 27/03/44*

## Transience and the fight against oblivion: the death of the mimeme

"As a norm, the human being expresses himself through global mimism. Man does not speak as spontaneously as he spontaneously mimes with his whole miming body, all the objects, all the actions of the objects. Similarly, Man does not write spontaneously. He projects his mimemes, his mimismic propositional gestes, in shadow play that I call mimograms. We project these mimemes on rock faces because of our innate need to render stable and immobile, to conserve and to make last the things that pass." *Labo 20/02/35*

"Nothing horrifies the anthropos more than death. Having analyzed the permanent invasion of death in the life of the anthropos, we now understand better why this is so and why life could be defined as the sum of the forces that combat death. I define the anthropos as the sum of the gestes that fight against oblivion, and I define oblivion as the death of the mimemes." *EA 10/12/34* Indeed, "Man could be defined as 'a complexus of mimemes supported by a skeleton.' When the fibers that hold up the mimemes disappear, only the skeleton is left, the real Man has disappeared. It would be wrong then to direct anthropology exclusively towards the study of the human skeleton. One cannot but wonder at the failure of anthropology to pay attention to what constitutes the true anthropos, this is to say, to the various attitudes adopted by this complexus of flesh in his endeavor to count, to grasp, to intussuscept the outside world, and to mimism, which is Man's intellection of this world that sets him apart from the other animals of the creation. I see as my contribution to this School of Anthropology my focus on the essence of Man.

"Mimemes disappear even before the skeleton is stripped of its flesh. They disappear with that strange phenomenon that we named death, a word that only serves to cover our ignorance. As always easily satisfied, our language defines a dead person as a person who no longer makes gestures. I, however, am not so sure that we dead only when the flesh that clads our skeleton no longer quivers. I believe we die much earlier, we die in what constitutes our essence as anthropoi: in our mimismic gestes, in our mimemes. If we could film a human's mimemes as and when they build up in his human compound, we would be amazed at the difference between the mimemes *recorded on film* and the mimemes *remaining as recorded* in this strange complex of living flesh. We have no idea how this phenomenon works and it should indeed be, along with mimism, a priority for an anthropologist to investigate. This phenomenon we have called *oblivion*: Man is a being who records mimemes and Man is a being who sheds mimemes. Of someone who has lost a number of his mimemes, it is said that 'he is as good as *dead.*' It is fact that, basically, one's loss of mimemes is a kind of death.

"Our concern then, today, is with Man's consciousness of this oblivion, of this flow of things. You know this sentence that I often quoted and will continue to quote because it is the leitmotiv of the anthropology of geste: 'panta rei,' these words so artfully engraved on the medals representing Mr. Bergson's philosophy." *EA 06/12/34*

## Fluidism, formulism and the unifying law of mimism

*Fluidism and formulism: the flow of things*
*and the desire for stability*

"Have you ever, some late autumn evening, lingered for an hour in the middle of a forest? A strange and very instructive sensation invades one. From second to second one senses an ebbing of all things: leaves fall one by one like the tic-tac of a clock, dead branches hit the dead leaves with a snapping sound, pieces of bark come loose and drop with a dull thud. One gets the sensation of the pulsation of the passing of things. Among the Greek philosophers, one in particular remained famous for his perhaps unique sense of this flowing of things—Heraclites: 'All flows.'" *S 06/02/36*

"Here we have, I might say, the foundation and the great anguish of the science of the possible or the impossible. What does the human compound do, instinctively, in this perpetual flowing, in this impossibility to find again in the morrow what he had done or been that eve? He formulated, or rather, formulism happened in him. It is formulism that has us move against the flow of the Heraclitian stream. 'All flows,' says the mechanism of fluidity. 'All needs to come to a halt when rest is needed.' says formulism. This is why, from his very first minutes, the small child is 'formulated' in each of his gestes. He will very soon know how to drink at his mother's breast, how to open his tiny hands to grasp things, how to shift his legs. That is but the beginning, I would say, of the turn, around and upstream, against the flow. On leaving his mother's womb he is, so to speak, fluid, he is wholly the Heraclitian stream, capable of anything. Moving on in life, after a single hour, even, he has lost the fluidity of his first second, and from hour to hour, from day to day, week to week, month to month, you witness his 'tics' as you might call them, or his habits, what I call his formulas. This is the only way to withstand—not to overcome, but to withstand—the powerful law of the fluidity of human gestes. In us, without us will happen and set off that immense and marvellous thing called: mimage. We have in us a hitherto ignored receiving mechanism: mimism. We are fluid, yet static mirrors and whenever we are faced with an object, in us comes into play, rebounds and reverberates an interaction that will repeat once, ten times, a hundred times. This is the interactional propositional formulism that I schematize as: an-acting-one—acting-on—an-acted-upon. It is formulism coming face to face with what could be called *fluidism*. The real offers itself to us in a fluid state, but there is in us that extraordinary power called mimism, a power that bilateralizes and that formulates. These are the formidable great laws of human mechanics." *HE 16/04/40*

"When Man endeavoured to create the physical tool, we saw him inventing metals that allowed him to fuse bronze, and thus to have at his disposal a fluid matter able to harden, once a mold had given it its shape. When the need arose to create an intellectual tool, it is his geste in all its fluidity that allowed him to grasp the multiple actions of the things. This very fluidity, however, rendered it extremely fragile and transitory. Man then became aware very soon that the fluid bronze of his geste could crystalize, could in a way solidify through the insertion of an element he found in himself: rhythm. Thus we arrived at this anthropologically very curious spectacle of a geste that was at once fluid and solid." *EA 19/03/34* "Formulism is a tool of portage. There is however, in the human mechanism, a tendency to distort by which concordant portage or transmission becomes discordant. Man tends to dissipate and the struggle is forever for Man to remain whole. As the Latin poet said: 'Plenus sum rimarum,' I am full of leaks, I leak on either side. If we were essentially Heraclitian and so everything as in continuous flow, we would be leaking from all sides and memory would not be possible. We would never be able to repeat a geste once made. However, dear Heraclitus, it is not so that all flows, for we have this wonderful attribute to redo not only analogically, but identically, in characteristic geste, the global geste that we can transmit to others and it is that 'memory' and 'tradition.'" *HE 17/01/39*

### *The unifying law of mimism: geste, the liquid bronze*

"In his search of a physical tool, Man invented metals fusing into bronze, and so he developed a fluid matter capable of solidifying in the mould that shaped it. When it came to create an intellectual tool, it was Man's fluid geste that allowed him to grasp the manifold manifestations of the real. Yet, the geste's very fluidity rendered it fragile and transitory. Man soon realized that the fluid bronze of his geste could crystalize and as it were solidify by the insertion of an element taken from within himself: rhythm. And so we arrived at this most curious anthropological spectacle of the human geste's suppleness fixed in unalterable form." *EA 19/03/34*

"Anthropology is relevant not so much for understanding the anthropos in his prehistory as for understanding his fundamental, primary nature of two thousand, four thousand and many, many years earlier. Above all, however, anthropology is relevant as it allows us to fathom what the anthropos is today. However speculative such science may be, if done in-depth, it will have profoundly practical implications. It is for this reason that we witness today a reawakening of life. We will take the subject up again next year in connection with the oral style, and it will become clear then that we are dealing with an enduring pedagogy that answers the primordial question I posed at the beginning of this lecture: 'How does the human being, placed at the heart of action of the universe, manage to conserve the memory of these actions within him, and to transmit this memory faithfully to his descendants, from generation to generation?' The problem, I think, is solved. We saw how the anthropos, with only his mute, but intelligent musculature, with muscles capable of fitting in with the things and of fluidly espousing the real, was able to carry and transmit the great human tradition. So it is that, having set out from my assertion that 'In the beginning was the rhythmo-mimic geste,' we arrive at human thought bursting out of all his muscular fibers." *EA 03/04/33*

"We humans have managed to solidify whilst remaining fluid. It is a biological law unique to the human. Animals do not have this capacity because they lack consciousness. They mechanize, they are incapable of mounting multiple mechanisms and to transmit them to others. That is what is correctly called animal instinct. Man however has this dual ability of flow and of exact replay. He shows true strength who is both: Heraclitian and Solomonian, because he will grasp the multiple and fluid and moving new to insert it in new law that will allow him to study it in depth. Men of genius astonish us precisely because of their capacity to be at once multiple and one. Any problem with which they play, they replay in function of their own unique unifying personality. That is our aim and ideal: to be multiple, to try to understand all problems, to adjust to all things and to gather all problems and facts and to integrate them all and to reduce them to a single law." *HE 17/01/39*

Mimism is the human-specific capacity of bringing consciousness in an unconscious cosmos. The continuous cosmic interactional action—the cosmic explosion of energy—becomes a human explosion of energy—the continuous human propositional geste. Having re-made the universe in himself and so hominized the universe, Man can, at will, ex-press and replay a real that now belongs to him. Where interactional unconscious instinct is governed from without, Man's propositional conscious intelligence emanates from within and puts him in charge of his destiny. Conscious of the unconscious flow, he is able to apprehend, comprehend and so to conduct the real that flows in him. Man's geste integrates the fluid real in his human compound's and thus stabilizes this real in time and in space: he formulates the real rhythmically and bilaterally. That is the unifying law of mimism.

# CHAPTER 2

# Mimage or the Process of Mimism

" . . . mimism replays in mimage."

HE 12/02/41

"Man is a natural mimer, a natural propositional mimer: the language of gestes with the whole body is the norm of human expression. Just as the young anthropos walks on his two legs, so, once he has his muscular structures sufficiently developed, does he express himself with the language of gestes, [in mimage], and it is a wholly body-soul play, a global play." *HE 23/11/37*

## Introduction: the three-staged mimismic process

THE EXTERIOR WORLD ACTS on the human and the human receives these outside actions on him through one or more of his senses. He first interiorizes and processes the information within himself and later exteriorizes the processed information for communication. The three-stage process of conscienciation—information, formation and communication—defines the specific function of the human in the universe, defines the cosmos-anthropos relationship. Mimage, the mimismic application of the law of mimism, progresses from the unconscious intussusception, irradiation and globalisation of the exterior actions, to the conscious intellection and conduction of these actions as gestes. This process allows the human to master *his* universe and ultimately *the* universe. Passive instinct yields to active intelligence, a development that is observable and recordable, but remains yet unexplained. "We know very well what mimism is like, insofar as it is recordable." *S 22/01/53*

"Man is an explosive being that explodes in the form of gestes. His gestes however, have a curious specific characteristic that the actions of other animals lack: they are mimismic. Man is an animal (i.e., a small bundle of explosives), a miming animal, and as such able to become conscious of his mimemes, of his mimismic gestes. This consciousness is unique: Man *intelligizes*, understands, his mimismic gestes. If we could define this capacity, we would truly understand the entire human mechanics, but we cannot, and we do not know what to *intelligize* a mimismic geste means. It needs to be experienced." *Labo 13/02/35*

"Mimism is purely instinctive. We have yet been unable to ascertain its cause. Mimism is a fact imposed on us. As our study of the anthropos progresses, we record how the anthropos receives in him, through all the gestes of his instinctively miming body, the stable or transitory actions of the surrounding world, replays them and remimes them." *Labo 09/01/33*

"In principle, the geste remains within us, but it will exteriorise. We will try to cast it out of our self." *Labo 07/12/38*

"Mimism, this force that urges us on, irresistibly, to express ourselves." *S 07/12/33*

"This compellingly propelling energy of mimism in its three manifestations: in intussusception, in immanent replay and in extra-rejection." *EA 16/11/36*

"People who are alive couldn't care less about grammars and dictionaries. They live, they express themselves, and they will do so for quite some time against the dogma of the Academy and against the rules of the dictionary, but their expression is alive! I the end, and invariably, it is usage, it is life that creates the rule. That your splendid psychology handbooks ignore mimism is irrelevant. It is the usage of mimism that creates the law." *EA 01/03/37*

## Information or the reception of the real

### Cosmic play and anthropological replay

In the first stage, the universe acts on Man and cosmic energy explodes in him, as part of the ceaseless universal interaction formulated as an-acting-one—acting-on—an-acted-upon. A seal pressed on wax leaves an imprint: an image comes up in relief. Through this metaphor, Jousse conveys the cosmos-anthropos relation and solves the problem of the origin of language, a problem that, properly put, appears to be a pseudo-problem. The original human expression is mimage: things pressed on us *im*-press themselves in us and are *ex*-pressed by us in relief. The play (im-pression) and replay (ex-pression) is mimism; its process in the anthropos is called mimage. Mimage is first expressed through the whole of the human compound: it is corporage or whole body-soul expression, and especially expression through the hands: manualage. Later mimage expresses through the more ergonomic mechanism of the laryngo-buccal system: as language. Lang(ue)age—expression by the langue (tongue)—is a late manifestation of mimage.

This playing in and playing out is anthropological, it is human specific. *Im*pressed psycho-physiologically, they are carried into the human's consciousness from the moment they enter his mimismic system; and it is psycho-physiologically too that they will be *ex*pressed. "The true way to educate a child (*ex-ducere*) is to let him play, in and out, and holistically, the real he has received in all his fibers. Presenting itself to us as a series of interactions, what is real can be re-played only through mimodramas. Once young people have been introduced to the mechanism of mimodramatic expression, there is no need to push them or hold them back, but simply to guide them and to give them a plan of action." *EA 21–12-36*

"The anthropos armed his hands, and through his hands, all his living, receptive fibers, with all those tactile gestes that are adapted to grasp, to know, to master, to demonstrate and to subdue everything around him: such is the play, the biological process of development in the young anthropos. This play is the holistic blossoming of interest within any living being that is young, or has stayed young. In innumerable ways, such human behaviors are a laboratory where experience can be captured and scientifically manipulated. For the little child, naive and curious, everything is new, everything is unusual, everything is a miracle. His biological interest in everything around him has remained intact. There is a whole world—specifically, his surrounding milieu—to master and, as a consequence, to know in the true way of knowing, i.e., objectively, experientially and personally. Noting the child's biologically spontaneous interest that zooms in and out in so many directions, we tend to chide the child for being distracted. He isn't and we miss the point: more than pulled from two sides—*dis*-trac-tus—he is pulled from all sides. Interested at once and attracted by the first thing that comes along or that he sets his sights on in his universe, he continues to do so and doing so dozens of times each minute . . . ." *AA*

## Intussusception

In a second stage, Man grasps the fragmented unconscious actions of the universe on and in him with one or more of his senses, and forms himself with this information: the human converts the cosmic interactional energy in anthropological propositional energy. This conversion is simultaneously an organizing of the 'chaotic' invasion of the cosmos that will ultimately allow each unique particular individual to uniquely become the master of *his* universe. Such mastery is the outcome of a complex process of intussusception, irradiation, intellection and conduction. The reception is *intussusception*; the spreading *irradiation* and *globalisation*; the grasping of the process *intellection* and the direction towards expression, *conduction*.

"Intussusception: grasping the real, grasping the whole real, grasping the real wholly." *EA 13/11/44*

"In biological conception, two elements, ovum and sperm, once united, are one, grow as one and dynamically evolve as one. This process cannot be halted. Something analogous happens in the cosmos-anthropos interaction: it is a conception. I wanted to avoid the term conception as it was commonly used in metaphysics and I therefore opted for the term intussusception, which has basically the same meaning but with the additional advantage of refreshing the notion of geste. Intussusception means that we have received inside us the action from outside us." *EA 06/12/37* "In truth, it is no more inside than outside. We have no more interior than we have exterior. We are wholly interior, we cannot escape out of this interiority, which is why I have used the word intussusception: to receive within. What is it we receive? The ambient real." *S 12/11/51 (Labo)*

## Irradiation and globalization

"Whatever you intussuscept through any one of your mechanisms does not remain in this intussuscepting mechanism. You see with your eye? Your mechanism as a whole plays in. You hear with your ear? Your whole organism comes into play. You taste with your tongue? The entire organism plays. It is well known that one does not listen to music with one's ears only. Just as one does not see with one's eyes only. All ocular intussusception tends to irradiate, to play throughout the whole body. It is the effect of globalism. There is then already, at the very moment of intussusception, a tendency to exteriorize, given that what came into you cannot be kept in a single small corner. It has to spread throughout the entire body, so that, what I called irradiation equals globalism. Thought is never played by a single part of the body. In fact, the word globalism makes no sense at all, it is a tautology. Man can only be one, cannot be but global. There is no division in the anthropos. It is as a 'global whole' that the whole being gives itself to the w/hole." *Labo 11/03/36*

"We have a certain number of organs, not many, but we have a few. Now, although these organs mount mimemes separately, these mimemes tend to irradiate throughout the whole intussuscepting human and so to globalize. As a result, the separately mounted mimemes tend to consolidate and join up, so much so that the human play and replay is that of a homogeneous rather than a disparate player. This explains how a genius operates when experimenting in himself what he will subsequently experiment outside: he concentrates the infinitely multiple universe he is confronted with on a single point, that of the experiment at hand. And that is the secret of what I call the brilliant discovery." *EAB 21/01/48*

## Formation or the hominization of the real

### Intellection

In the physical sphere the action is mechanical and, in the biological sphere, instinctive; in the anthropological, human-specific sphere, the cosmic action becomes human or anthropological reaction, intelligent, reflective reaction: geste. Through intellection, the microcosm that I am becomes conscious of the macrocosm I have intussuscepted. "The normal human being's mechanism is in its present state indivisibly a compound—remember this word for there is no other—a compound of musculature and intellection of this musculature. The intellection of the musculature is what we call intelligence." *Labo 26/02/36*

"Intelligence is *intus-legere*: to read what is inside. It is becoming conscious, becoming aware, and that is human-specific. It is to know that something has come into me and that that thing remains there in the form of a mimeme. Mimism is first and foremost the awareness of the law of mimism.

"Intelligence is *inter-legere*: to choose among several gestes. The world is an immense chaos of interactions. But in this immense chaos of interactions comes a human being who will know how to choose from this multiplicity, the unity, I would say the unicity. That is the realm of the great discoverers: *bodies attract bodies*, and you have the Newtonian mechanics; *the earth circles the sun*, and you have the Copernican mechanics; *the child mimes all things*, and it is the even greater mechanics, greater, for anthropological, and that will one day be called the Joussean mechanics.

"Intelligence is *inter-ligare*: to link up in the form of interactions, to link the gestes that had not yet been linked. Remember the great Laplace: *Discoveries consist of bringing together ideas*—I would say facts—*that are susceptible to join but that had not been hitherto been joined.*" *EA 13/11/44*

## Conduction

"Consciousness in the human has a kind of extension. When one becomes conscious of a mechanism, one may be able at times to take charge, to direct it, to conduct it. I have called this conduction, which is the gestual word for what your metaphysical word *will*." *HE 05/11/41* For example, "What I want you to do when you are hearing me is to rethink. By this I mean that you balance what you hear me say with all that you have stored in you after it was once played in you and informed you, and can then be replayed by you at your discretion. That is what is called *will*. There comes a moment when your mastery of this entire fluid whole of spontaneous interactions once played in you is such that you are able to replay it at will, in fast or slow motion—slowing down to better observe or speeding up to better *conjoin* so that this past does not crumble into dust. That is what conscientiousness implies." *S 12/11/51 (Labo)*

"I do not know what it means, to *will*, but I do know what it means to direct a geste. The word geste has an altogether different meaning when applied to an anthropos and when applied to an anthropoid or any other being from the zoological world. Thanks to mimism, the human acting-one—acting-on—an acted-upon can in effect become the directing-one. Such *dirigism* comes about because of choice. From a multitude of possible gestes presenting themselves, one in a thousand is chosen. This chosen geste will be the guided-one, rather than the hotchpotch that could have been." *EAB 07/01/48*

## Mastery

"Controlled replay is quite rare, and difficult to achieve. If I had to truly control all I am telling you here, I would still be no further than at my first sentence. Which is why the aim of pedagogy is to mount our mechanisms in such a way that they become automatic. It was rightly said of the Roman legionaries that they carried their weapons as if they were extensions of their hands—*arma quasi manus gerebant*. The ideal soldier handles his sword with the same suppleness with which he uses his hand. A horseman and his mount are as one being. We do try, from time to time, to achieve such directed play, but it remains rare. It is what Saint Ignatius called *election*." *Labo 18/12/35*

"Man is a complexus of living and interacting gestes. He is more than an animal merely reproducing exterior actions. His gestes play out such actions by manipulating those exterior objects. This is his distinguishing feature: he is a handler of objects, and an interactional handler at that. He can take an object and put it to work on another object. The does not handle objects for the sake of beauty. His is not art for art's sake. He, anthropos, a complexus of living and interactional gestes, he handles objects in order to master the real, in order to master the earth. In this aptitude to make actions act on other actions lies his greatness. Intelligence is its own master of its own driving force. As we have seen already, and we will study this in ever more depth this year, Man is not a soul, Man is not a body. Man is a conqueror, a master of himself, who has his action in his hand." *EA 05/01/41*

"What is a Man's richness made off, and, basically, his intelligence? Of his mastery to muster his mechanisms and to concentrate them in one particular fact. Yet, even the brightest of us dies without having exhausted the thousands of gestes, the thousands of propositions that were in him and at his disposal. We are very much aware of anyone who truly masters his mechanism and who is truly in charge when waging his great battle of gestes. We are left in awe of the sharpness of his awareness and of the richness of his means of expression. That is because he has all his powers bundled in that very question that demanded proof." *HE 16/03/37*

## Communication or the exteriorization of the real

In the third stage, the cosmic explosion of action-energy turned human explosion of geste-energy exteriorizes as propositional energy. Interactional action-inter-action is unconscious. Through the human mimismic system of conscienciation, unconscious interaction becomes conscious proposition, expressed as propositional gestes: having re-made the universe in his conscientizing self, Man expresses this anthropologized cosmos. Anthropological expression is *mimismic*—Man is by nature a mimer; anthropological expression is *mimodramatic*—Man is a human compound expressing himself in global mimage; anthropological expression is *metaphoric*—Man expresses a mimismic and thus interconnected worldview.

### Anthropological expression is mimismic

*It is continuous . . .*

"Our dreams prove that we express ourselves continuously. We do so involuntarily or voluntarily. It is involuntary expression when we, anthropoi who are part of the physical and biological, unconscious sphere of the cosmos, and react by instinctive reflex; it is voluntary expression when we exercise our unique capacity to intelligize what is impressed in us and when 'I know that something has been introduced in me and that this something remains in me as a mimeme." *EA 13/11/44*

### . . . *compelling*

"Here is a most curious phenomenon: the human does not just intussuscept, he also has the extraordinary propensity to externalize, to eject what he received. Whatever was passed on to him, he wants to pass back. What was impressed in him, he wants to express. One could call this human characteristic the human's creative, fabricating tendency, which is basically no more than mimism at play. This is the subject I would like to broach this morning: the primal mechanism one might call the mechanism of exteriorization." *Labo 11/03/36*

    "Little children face the world and mime this world, or more accurately, they receive within themselves mimismically the actions done outside them, and they replay them. And it is that, human expression. More I cannot tell you, but you could never, never deny that children are beings that play. We need to stress time and again how mimism characterizes the child and manifests itself in the child in play." *Labo 08/12/37* "The play is what is real outside of us, that imposes itself on us, that is impressed within us, and energizes us to ex-press it, to re-play it, just as it was im-pressed. Do you understand this formidable process? Under the sealing pressure of what is real, a child is *im*-pressed, like soft, fluid wax, and he will *ex*-press in re-play what he has received." *Labo 18/02/34* "There is an urgency in children to replay out what the outside confusedly gave them." *EA 09/03/39* "It was the anguish of my life to wonder: why do I play? Why does everyone play? Why do little children play? I have been haunted by what I later called the law of mimism." *EA 09/03/39*

### . . . *microscopic or macroscopic*

"This play and replay is on the micro and on the macro level, as the Greeks knew for whom logos meant at once what happens within, microscopically—reason, thought—and its replay without, macroscopically—speech, language. Intussusception, the word speaks for itself, is what you receive inside you. In truth, it is no more inside than outside. We have no more interior than we have exterior. We are wholly interior; we cannot escape out of this interiority. This is why I have used the word intussusception: to receive within. What is it we receive? The ambient real." *S 12/11/51 (Labo)*

"Man does not ordinarily remain in the state of microscopic gesticulation. Man is by nature an amplifying exteriorizer. He then plays outside his inside mechanism. This explains why he invented language, or more exactly mimage. Mimage, let's not forget, is something spontaneous. A human living all on his own in the middle of a forest would make just as many gestes as if he were with other anthropoi. The fact is that he has a need to successivize his thought by letting irradiation let run its course. The most primitive of men—I would say the most spontaneous—is he who makes the most gestes, the one therefore who has kept intact his manual language, his mimage." *Labo 11/03/36*

"We cannot not express ourselves, because the real, the external actions, always replay within us invisibly or visibly. I say *invisibly* keeping in mind our normal scale of visibility. If, however we were to use a recording device that detects all these imperceptible play and replay actions, we would see that we are in a perpetual state of reception and expression. As soon as an intelligent being finds himself facing things that replay in him unconsciously, he latches on their play, and he will, consciously, use it as a tool of expression." *EA 13/03/33*

## Mimismic expression is mimodramatic

"Primordial human expression and communication is mimodramatic. Mimodramas are spontaneous, immediate expressions by the anthropos of the cosmic impressions on and in him. Thus, *prehistoric art* is neither art, nor is it prehistoric, and *primitive dances* are neither primitive, nor are they dances. The term prehistoric needs to be banned, as prelogical and primitive have been, because they spuriously divide humanity in a before and after. Primitive means spontaneous—spontaneously linked and spontaneously expressing that link. Primitive art and dances are mimodramas: mimism expressed in mimage, of which language is but a late, and a distancing manifestation.

"An event is a clew of interactions—each interaction being a variation of the basic universal formula: an-acting-one—acting-on—an-acted-upon. Caught in the human mimismic system, these interactions become gestes and propositions, gestual propositions. Mimodrama, or mimismic representation in movement, is the ordered sequencing of a cluster of gestual propositions. Genesis is a prime example of mimodramatic narrative expression. The whole of the world is explained by these mimodramas. They were labelled *mythologies,* and this prevented any further research into the matter. Those *myths* are myths either, they are explicative mimodramas that arose from the spontaneous play of human beings." *EA 09/03/39*

"The world is but a quasi-inextricable complexus of interactions that Man receives in his whole miming body and that he replays either globally, or on his lips in traditional recitations transmitted from generation to generation. Received and taken into consciousness, these interactions constitute those splendid mimodramas that attempt to explain what Man might be. This great human mechanism of explication through global mimodrama is simply splendid: the Invisible modeled Man by taking *adamâh*—soil. And he modeled the adamâh in his mirror image, or, as common speech has it: 'in his own image and likeness.' How gratifying to come across our mimismic terms again! And so we have here the modeler and the modeled in reverberation—in my parlance, that would be: potentially in a mimismological relationship. Do not call this 'myth.' Delve deeper and a splendid explication will appear for our anthropology of mimism to emulate: modelled now in mirror, in image and likeness, the adamâh is able to receive in its nostrils the Breath of the Creator. Note: the *breath*, and not our algebrozed 'spirit' from 'spiritus,' for this is concrete mimodramatic expression. The Invisible breathes his breath in the nostrils of this adamâh and it becomes a living and speaking and eating throat. Such mimodrama deserves close study: what you call spirit, what you call soul, I call nasal breath, this guttural breath that irradiates throughout the entire global mechanism of the Adam-earthling. This is not 'myth,' this is explicative mimodrama and mimodrama of such depth that our present-day psychiatrists find themselves compelled to return to it in order to understand the deficiencies of the human being's workings, be they global, oral or ocular.

"This Adam who is made of adamâh, this *Homo* who is made of *Humus*—if you allow me a little Latin wordplay—he needs somewhere to stay. No eerie Platonic Man, he is set in a landscape, one that we call to this day in our algebrozed terminology *Paradisâ*—this garden of delights that you turned into 'Paradise' without knowing what its true portent. This *Paradisâ* was a paysan's park, the loss of this primordial land to be forever talked of with nostalgia and regret. It is the subject of that epic that I return to from time to time: Milton's 'Paradise Lost.' Not that we, paysans, ever lost it! We were never chased from this earthly paradise, not we! As there are trees in this paradise, there are bound to be laws, but laws that do not refer to our Napoleonic Code Civil, article 362, but to a tree and to a fruit. This is not myth, no, this is the comportment of a paysan with regard to trees, just as we, Sarthois paysans have apples, and as paysans from other climes have bananas and others still oranges. Trees and fruit 'regained and never lost.' Because the earthling, the Man of the soil, of the land, the *terrien* in his tree-rich *terre*, he has in him something that was never studied before: mimism." *S 15/01/53* "In the beginning was mimism." *EAB 07/01/48*

## Mimismic expression is metaphoric

### Mimism and metaphor

Good teaching moves from the known to the unknown. Metaphor is an essential tool in the good teacher's toolkit. Jousse calls on three metaphors to describe mimism.

First the seal that impresses the wax and, with the seal removed, the wax expresses the imprint. Second the mirror before which the real—the cosmos, things, objects—parades fleetingly and which the mirror reflects, but, as a human mirror also stores for possible further conscious replay. Third is the metaphor Jousse borrowed from one of his revered masters, the psychologist and educationist Pierre Janet who said: 'The brain is a set of switches. The brain does not determine psychological activity; it only regulates it.' Jousse's intellection is a hitherto unexplained trigger that sets off mimage—this mimismic process that redirects a mainly unconscious influx of information towards consciousness.

In truth, mimism *is* metaphor—transfer from cosmic movement as unconscious action-interaction to anthropological movement conscious as geste-proposition. For such transfer to be possible, the real needs to be experienced as flow, a flow allowing for juxtaposition or analogy to become superposition or metaphor, through interposition or comparison. Between the action of the universe and the reaction of the human stands the switch of the human conscientizing mechanism, the gestuation that turns a phenomenon into a mimeme, *un phénomène en mimème*. The mimismic metaphoric universe is the playground of all who regained or who never lost the original paradisiacal playground: the child, the *primitive*, the *paysan*, our geniuses and artists, for all of who everything can become anything. Spontaneity, suppleness, curiosity; to model, to draw, to sculpt; play, replay, geste are among Jousse's favoured terms and his preferred verb tense is the present participle, signalling an action in process. Jousse's anthropology of mimism is a dynamic anthropology, the science of a supple human in a fluid universe.

"Man is an animal that makes comparisons. Nothing more. You call Man a reasonable animal. Well, he is reasonable only because he makes comparisons, because he is capable of classifying, in small lots, analogous things." *Labo 30/01/35*

"A child's interest is universal, that of scientist is *monoideistic*. If I were not monoideistic, I would be incapable of achieving anything at all. The true savant gets hold of just one little piece of the real and delves into it as deep as a Man's lifetime allows. That the child will do one day, but not at the start. He needs first to touch, to feel the real, the whole real, so as to be able to choose his own special field. It is such originally multiple interest mounted in him that will serve him so very well later in his comparisons, his metaphors, and his discoveries. Whence this formula of the great astronomer and celestial mechanic Laplace: 'Discoveries consist in the linking of ideas that could have been, but had not been linked before.' One can only link *ideas*—which are propositional gestes taken from the real—if one has first been in search of them. There is clearly no apparent link between an apple falling and the moon wandering through the skies. Yet, Newton, having seen an apple fall, turned towards the moon and said: 'The moon is a big apple that falls on the earth.' That is precisely what a child is looking for, unwittingly, in his multifold curiosities: on the one hand the apple falling, on the other the strange wandering of the moon. And perhaps, during a night of study, at the age of 40, 50, 60, he will feel in him this junction of two gestes that were coherent and sometimes contradictory, and he will say: 'That is the discovery: the moon is a big apple and the apple is a small moon, and they are attracted by a gravitational force, this is to say a force of weight.'" *Labo 18/12/35*

"A Man who restrains in him the power of his mimism is in breach of his duty as a human. For us humans, mimism is our sole means to acquire knowledge. Through his congenital mimism, the things Man has intussuscepted will become operational in him, even without his knowing. A child is unable to not mime the things around him. He can know the world only through intussusception and replay, and it is through his mimism and in him that the world knows itself. This is the powerful force we see at work in children playing out the world around them. Their 'play' is not what is ordinarily called 'play.' Their play is not something stuck on them from the outside, it is not something in excess, it is essentially the anthropos. Unable to be anything but a mimer, the anthropos mimes things. Having mimed once, the pull to replay will be great. That is memory and that is the law of repetition. The anthropos cannot act otherwise. Trying to prevent a child from playing is to totally ignore anthropology. It is in his play, in this, his global geste, that the child is most at ease. The anthropos plays with his whole being, with his whole mechanisms, because all his mechanisms need to operate. This is why we give ourselves over to the real with our whole body.

"Which brings us to the inescapable conclusion that, if mimism is our only true way to know, there is for us only one thing to do, which it is to apply to mimism the word *science*. To know is to mime the things as they are. It is science that went to mime the real in the various civilizations and it is science that understood that one could *know* the real only insofar as one *replayed* the real. That is the frightening scientific play and our lifetime's occupation." *Labo 06/02/35*

"A study of the vocabulary of modern science would reveal that it is in essence a gestual science, it being understood that 'geste' is not simply the geste of the preacher sending us up to heaven and down to hell, but the geste that goes into the most elusive microscopic phenomena. The gestual mechanism is quite simply the mechanism of knowledge. We can know only through metaphor, this is to say that our gestes come to play between our total human compound and the object. We will never grasp the essence of the object, never grasp the object in itself. We will ever know anything only if we receive it by way of our gestes. There is in the object something with which my geste enters into play analogically." *EA 03/03/42*

### Transubstantiation: the ultimate metaphor

Knowing is being. "When you come across someone who truly engages the real, you will be caught in the slipstream of this person's supple play and you will be entering directly the original of the play he is replaying. This is because this person's replay is directly drawn from the real, and therefore stable as all true gestual languages and mimemes are. Languages evolve at an astonishing speed from the moment their speakers move away from the original real they translate. Our present semantic evolution is astonishingly fast. Words can take on improbable meanings because, once they are no longer the mimismic replay of the characteristic thing, they enter the domain of convention and arbitrariness. On the contrary, when one 'mimes' a particular animal, miming one or another of its characteristic actions, we are bound to mime it as it is: an-acting-one—acting-on- an-acted-upon. We cannot change this interaction, we cannot equivocate, we are glued to the real and the real is glued in us.

"The lesson to be learned here is that all mimers are objective before the real and this point is crucial. Indeed, if we accept that science, that knowledge is an *adequatio mentis et rei*—the correspondence of mind and thing, of the known thing and the knowing object—then we must conclude that it is at this stage of human expression, the stage of mimismic 'language,' of gestual manual-corporeal expression, of mimage, was the stage were this adage was verified and realized. What indeed is an object? It is a geste. What is my knowledge of this object? It is the geste redone as exactly as possible without change, without slant, without atrophy. True knowledge would be for you to be able to recognize the object when it is in me. That is the true science, the true *adequatio mentis et rei* the thing and intellect coinciding." "True knowledge is to be the thing and to see the thing, to be yourself and to see yourself. It is when sequencing our gestes in this way, and we do this either unconsciously or consciously, that we discover our capacity to *distinguish*, if not to parcel, this unfolding of things. If we simply let the interactions of the universe replay in us, we see, feel, mime, *the sun parching the plant, the plant absorbing water, water moistening the soil, the soil shaping in undulating hills* . . . and so on and on and we find ourselves taken up in an immense interactional play, and giving ourselves free reign, the entire universe comes into play in us in a ceaseless dance of Shiva signifying, dare I say, Man's comprehension of the world." *EA 06/03/33*

"Not ever, not in an eternity will I know what you are; not ever, not in an eternity will you know what your children have in their human compound, never, never! It is impossible to understand one another from human being to human being. Impossible! If you tell me: 'I do not understand you,' my response will be that I find it extraordinary that you able to convey to me that you do not understand me. We are mutually impenetrable, yet, mimism is the anthropological angle that allows us to overcome this impenetrability. What I need do is to circumvent the difficulty by becoming the other. I need to *know* the other—in the Semitic sense of the word—by cohering with the other in all my fibers. It is the great anthropological operation as defined in the Bible: 'Adam knew his wife,' which is re-enacted when the Prophet stretches himself out over the young child and puts his mouth on the youth's mouth, his hands over his hands, his body on his body. It is that, to know. To know is to coincide.

"Which is what we do by mimism. We take an object with all our human recording devices—our eyes, our ears, our hands . . .—and we intussuscept this object. It is more powerful even than knowing biblically, it is knowing inwardly. The power of the words we use is quite beyond our grasp. To know is that, to know is not only making to coincide, it is making to interpenetrate: this, B, must be in A. To know is becoming the other." *Labo 08/12/37*

"And the finale is splendid:

'They will be two—a single flesh.'

"Not just a face-to-face, but a union. And in the Aramaic Targum, as recaptured by Ieshua—one more proof that he did not refer to the Hebrew text but to the Aramaic text:

'They will be two—in one single flesh.'

"The opposition is splendid: 'They will be *two* in *one* single flesh.'

"It would be more accurate to translate as: 'They will each of them be in a single flesh.' That is this union which might be called a transubstantiation." *EA 06/03/44*

## Metaphor and the Invisible

For those people and peoples who accept the existence of the invisible, the only means of expressing this invisible is through the visible: they sublimate the visible gestes of the world, transpose them, make them into metaphors. Metaphor is the transport of one order of gestes into another order of gestes. The unknown is expressed by the known, the visible transferred into the invisible.

"Man, everywhere, is tormented by the invisible. Why is it that we find Man everywhere dissatisfied with the mountains, dissatisfied with the rivers, dissatisfied with the trees? The real is beautiful, and rich with science, and yet, Man has forever been dissatisfied with the visible and thought it necessary to explain the visible by the Invisible." *HE 20/11/34* "This is why anthropologists need to move from ethnic milieu to ethnic milieu and to scrutinize the very depths of the frightening sincerity with which Man engages with the powers of the Invisible. A human who wants to enter the invisible, who wants to enter the invisible world, has no other means than to use his mimemes *metaphorically*, this is to say by a transfer of gestes. Theologians and spiritual directors are unhappy because of this impossibility for them to be informed by the object of their science. When as an anthropologist I embark on the study of the anthropos, I place one before me; and when it is the natural, spontaneous human, I want to study, I go to where the Amerindian lives and I observe him quietly.' When, however, an anthropos wants to study God, he cannot place God before him and tell him: 'Thrust your mimemes on me'; when he wants to study angels, he cannot appear before the assembled celestial court and ask: 'O angel, inform me. Let your mimemes flow into me.' Here smiles the anthropologist, because, whenever great theologians want to express the formidable problem of the Inaccessible, of the Invisible, they have to turn to us, anthropologists, to get their mimemes.'" *Labo 11/12/35*

"It is around Breath, around invisible and therefore mysterious breath—invisible for we see its effects only—that Humanity has built its most tragic mimodramatics." *S 27/01/37* "These stories are not *myths*; they are attempts at explaining the Invisible. You might think that all liturgies are outdated, but I am not so sure, or, more exactly, I am quite sure that they will not be outdated for as long as there is one human being alive who tries to express bodily the Breath of the Invisible." *S 27/01/37* "Palestinians leave us, with our visible pragmatists' mindsets, perplexed because, having drawn their concrete gestes from the visible world, they at once sublimate them and have them operate in the invisible world." *HE 21/01/36* "They could obviously do no more than what all peoples who want to express the Invisible, which is to sublimate the visible things. The only way for them to do so, as Palestinians, was to sublimate what they considered to be their most noble mechanism: the pedagogical mechanism of the Tôrâh." *HE 24/03/36*

"Here you see the true reach of anthropological mechanics. We lacked the humility to admit: that other peoples have thought too, and have thought with this wonderful tool [metaphor] that children use spontaneously, as poets do—poets being those among us who still try to remain tied in to the real—and as do all those peoples who are wholly in contact with the real. It is the intelligent being who embraces the visible world utterly and who, through a sublime leap in the Invisible, expresses with utmost concretism that what his senses could not fathom. Herein, I think, lies Man's greatness: to make, by means of his senses, things so elevated that it enables him to grasp, and to incarnate as far as possible, a whole invisible world." *EA 13/03/33*

# CHAPTER 3

# The Mimismic Worldview: On Science and Religion, Style and Civilization

"There are aspects of human mechanics that we have ignored."

S 02/02/56

THE SCOPE OF A Jousse lecture is often much broader than its title would at first suggest. In *The difficulty with ethnic translations*, the lecture from which the following lines are extracted, the immediate topic is that of mistranslations of texts and ignorance of the original contexts causing an originally coherent system of thought and expression to appear incoherent and even absurd. How this happened with the transmission of the Aramaic Palestinian Ieshuan tradition is illustrated in lecture 7, *infra*. To Jousse, one of the main reasons for the accelerating dechristianization of society in his time was due to an algebrozed teaching and consequent erosion of the message that buttresses Western civilization. The lecture being given at the École Pratique des Hautes Études, in a lecture series on the history of Christianity, Jousse takes as his starting point the recent encyclical *Divino Afflante Spiritu* of 30 September 1943. This papal message encourages biblical research in the original languages of the texts and their social, cultural and historical context, ad Jousse could only feel vindicated: this is what he has been militating for ceaselessly, in his 1925 publication *The oral style*, in the follow-up sustained conference program, *inter alia* at the Pontifical Institute in Rome, and in his lectures since 1931.

"I am asked, at times: 'Do you convert any of your listeners?' What would I convert them to? To that Catholicism of yours you yourself do not understand the first word of and from which I have distanced myself in horror? My aim is to make my listeners aware of the formidable question of Man's attitude towards the real. This is the very first and all-important conversion everyone needs to effect who is presently shaken by this immense cataclysm that is called a change of civilization. This is the conversion we all have to *first* impose on ourselves, *each of us*. Before converting others, I have tried to convert myself and it is this conversion you hear from me, three times a week. It is a tragic emprise, this human conversion. Anthropology leads us inevitably to ask ourselves if we have truly understood what constitutes the basis of our civilization: Catholicism. And my answer is, frankly, no. And it is because we do not understand this that in this document here, the Pope underlines forcefully the need for a new study of style. You know, don't you, that if there is anyone who has put global style, both in its oral and in its written forms, at the forefront of Palestinian studies, is I, the anthropologist who is speaking to you here." *HE 09/02/44*

"To address an issue, one should start at its base. The construction of a church does not start with the steeple." *Labo 23/02/45* Similarly, discussion about a religion should start with examining the soil out of which it grew. Conversely, "If faith has to be brought to others, it should be in the form of a civilization. It may eventually be taken beyond civilization at some later stage." *EA 10/03/42* "What the young people present here before me need do, is to remake in themselves the new Man and that new Man is the traditional Man, the Man who, building on his deep-rooted civilization, reaches out towards others so as to achieve a more perfect realization of himself through brotherly interchange." *EA 16/06/47* "A change in civilization does not happen overnight and we will no doubt have to go to a great many struggles and upheavals before reaching some measure of stability through rethinking civilization from its anthropological base." *HE 24/01/45*

## Religion, "the science of the invisible" *Labo 19/01/38*

### Introduction: the invisible, an anthropological constant

It is an anthropological fact that "Be Man, as has been maintained, the normal, the biologically normal development of the anthropoid, or, as is my deep-held belief, a unique creature in the universe, we find him *tormented* by the invisible. Why is it that we find human beings everywhere dissatisfied with the mountains, dissatisfied with the rivers, dissatisfied with the trees? However beautiful the real and rich with science, we find Man dissatisfied with the visible and in need to explain the things visible by things invisible." *HE 20/11/34* "You are my witnesses here: until now I have spoken to you of nothing but things recordable, this is to say, things one can measure, count, observe—I have spoken of nothing but the visible world. But if you admit scientifically that there are certain ethnic milieus that believe as strongly,

I would say more strongly even in the invisible world, you will be able to bring logically into play all of the human's expressive gestes. When dealing with anthropological matters, this is a matter of fundamental importance! Mankind is not one in its behavior, and this to the chagrin and bewilderment of not a few individuals." *EA 30/01/33* Today, "no-one denies the power of science, how many do deny the power of what is called religion, and what I call the science of the Invisible?" *Labo 19/01/38* "Can religion be studied scientifically? One has, in the very first instance, to know how a human being operates. Man is a religious animal. It cannot be otherwise because the anthropos needs explanation, and religion gives him explanations in line with his milieu. Please hear me right: *in line with his milieu.*" *EA 17/03/42* Which is why, "as anthropologist, I move from ethnic milieu to ethnic milieu to observe and research the very depths Man's frighteningly sincere interplay with the powers of the invisible." *EA 30/01/39* How do we set out to answer the fundamental question, "the formidable question of Man's attitude toward the real"? *HE 09/02/44*

## Of two explicative systems: equational science and revelational science

"Our Western civilization draws from antiquity a twofold heritage: on the one side, there is the experimental Greek milieu, and on the other side, there is the revelationist Palestinian milieu. Both sides lay claim on the real, this is to say on science. Because of a most curious vivisection, we have failed to pursue our research in the direction of the Palestinians and retained from them no more than a whiff of emotion that we call faith, religion. On the other hand, we analysed in increasing depth all that we inherited from the Greek ethnic milieu and that is what we now consider to be true science. The Greek technique happens to be in absolute opposition to the Palestinian technique. The general direction of Greek research methodology is observation and it is in accordance with these observations that modern science perfects itself incrementally. In the Palestinian ethnic milieu, the method followed is not observation, but what I could call revelation. Confronted by nature, the Greek tries to scrutinize it ever more objectively, whereas the Palestinian tries to grasp the revelation it conceals. When then the scientists of our ethnic milieu pose the problem: 'Can science and religion be reconciled?,' I, as anthropologist, I reply: 'The question is wrongly put. Do you understand what you are talking about?'" *HE 31/01/45*

"Of the two great explanatory systems of the world, one, the grand theory of universal gravitation, is aligned to the Greek experimental milieu.

*Before* this grand theory of universal gravitation, however, there was a theory even larger in its explanation: the theory of universal Insufflation. If we understand universal gravitation, our macroscopic instruments will allow us to calculate the ellipses, calculate the motions of the spheres and so on. Similarly, if in the world of the child, in the world of the spontaneous Man, we understand the theory of universal insufflation, a host of hitherto puzzling problems start to look profoundly logical. The teachings of this theory of universal insufflation are still with us and will possibly never die, because of its extraordinary depth. Extraordinary depth indeed: the depth of the whole Unknown. I told you in my previous lecture how we live ever more in a world of mystery. The theory of universal insufflation has mystery as its basis. So coherent is this great explicative system that a better one has not yet been found." *EA 13/03/39*          .

Let us address the problem differently and let us "take the system as it stands before us. How it measures up to the greatness of human thought, that we will have to discuss later. Yet, we must concede that, for as far as human greatness is concerned, we cannot find totally wanting he who discovered universal gravitation! We must concede that we cannot, for as far human greatness is concerned, we cannot find totally wanting he who conceived and teaches universal insufflation!" *EA 13/03/39*

## Changing the method

### All science is ephemeral

"The real has no bounds and the positions of the science of fifty years ago are not the positions of the science of today. Today, true scientists no longer dare to make any assertions at all, for we know all too well that the truth is like water flowing through our hands." *EA 30/01/* "All science is indeed ephemeral: it is obvious that a thousand years hence, and much sooner even, people will smile warily at our anthropology, smile at our biology, at our psychology, smile at what we are presently saying, and fortunately so! Science can only progress when moving from the lesser known to the better known—we have long since ceased to dream of knowing anything fully. Present-day science is no more than a closer approximation of a real that will remain forever unknown." *Labo 19/01/38* "We, humans, spend our lives in a fog. What is the universe, what is matter? What is life? On the latter question, "A number of geniuses spent their lifetimes tackling this unknown, one of them, Pasteur, did so, less than a century ago. [Pasteur held that] life can only arise from life, but are his results the final word on the matter? No scientist would dare to say that they are. We have not been able, *yet*, to create life from inanimate matter. More we cannot say under the present circumstances. Will we ever find conditions conducive to inanimate matter bringing forth life? We are in a fog, and we can neither confirm nor deny. True science teaches us modesty. We do not do skepsis, nowadays, we do work, which is altogether different. We deny nothing. We affirm nothing. We continue to search and we pose our hands on this fog that helps us to move further. That is all. If we cannot speak of anything because we do not know the be-all and end-all of anything, we still have to play at finding some explanation. We must bring gestes into play. If we do not, we will remain at zero, zero, zero." *EA 13/03/39*

Theories do set in the collective mind, comportment and vocabulary. Our Western modern society has opted for the grand theory of universal gravitation and to arrive today in this particular society with any other explanatory system is bound to meet with skepsis or ridicule. Yet, a theory such as the theory of universal insufflation "does no more deserve to be met with the gales of laughter than, in a few thousand years and sooner, even, our present-day explicative system of universal gravitation." *EA 13/03/39* "Our era is an era of experimental science. We want to understand and to understand according to the norms of our milieu. As things stand, I happen to be the first researcher to try to establish the link between what we were taught in algebrized terms and modern explicative science. There is a coherent and profound logic [in this tradition] that we were never made to understand. Because it was gestual, and we preferred to remain in algebrosis." Where the original system drew on the very depths of the anthropos, "we today live with residue of residue. What we handle is residue of explicative gestes." *EA 13/03/39*


*From static to dynamic anthropology*

"As a young artillery captain, I chose between Mount Wilson, where celestial mechanics are studied, and the Indians who offered me, in their gestes, the primordial expression. I returned from the United States an anthropologist, not an astronomer. There are aspects of human mechanics we have ignored." *S 02/02/56* Instead of plumbing the depts. of the skies, Jousse chose to plumb the depths of the human being. He would, however, remain a scientist, and apply the rigorous scientific research principles of the hard sciences to the human science of anthropology. He needed to change the method: "I had set myself a singularly bold task. At twenty, my work was done. I think discoverers discover when very young. I however needed to find the most appropriate environment, the most apposite, for the best possible exposition and reception of the discovery. Thus, immediately after the war, on my return from the United States where I had for two years been training American generals, colonels and commandants, and after having studied in their reserves the techniques of expression used by the Indian tribes, sure now, absolutely sure that Man is but a complexus of gestes, I arrived in 1922, one morning at 5 o'clock, in one of the train stations of Paris, facing this immense receptacle of thought awakening. The memory of my mother was with me. And there I arrived, little Sarthois paysan, bringing a wholly new method to people who thought with diametrically opposite methods than the one I came with." *EA 12/01/41*

He had indeed set himself "a singularly bold task": "Pasteur, my master and guide in scientific research methodology has been one of the greatest benefactors of humanity by proceeding to disinfect living organisms. Following his lead, dwarf on the shoulders of a giant, and relying on him to see further in the future, my ambition was to reach even higher. I took on not just individual organisms but entire social bodies." *EA 25/01/41* Jousse was going to change anthropology by changing its method and, in doing so, he was to challenge the entire prevailing academic and social culture of his time. More broadly even, he was to propound no less than a change of civilization. Metaphysics and psychism, based on the premise and invention of Man divided into a body and a soul, had to make way for observable and accessible mimism with its premise of Man as an indivisible human compound: "Man, the anthropos is an interactionally miming animal. This starting point will allow us to surge way beyond those who went with psychism. When facing an anthropos, I am confronted, not with a body, not with a soul, but with a human compound. Mimism, a *humane compound*, is a complexus of gestes, and therefore essentially dynamic." *EA 12/01/41* A Geste is a human compound expressing its interaction with the world it *receives*, *mimes* and *intelligizes*. The anthropos is his cosmos, a cosmos he hominizes.

"Confronted for centuries with the formidable complexity of the physical universe, the masters of celestial mechanics endeavored to find what had always been suspected: the single and unifying law. Today everything is understood to submit to such a single unifying law, from the ellipses in which the stars gravitate to the strange curbs inscribed on our micro-photographic recorders by the smallest of atoms when we bombard them in our laboratories. Yet, confronted with the anthropological universe, we had to wait till these very last years for anyone to even try—to just try—to discover the single unifying law that would allow us to grasp, order and possibly explain the even greater complexity of the human gestes. Why is that so?

In my previous lectures, sustained by your faithful and continued support, I have taken a close look at the anthropos—not unlike Newton focusing on the apple and 'always thinking about it.'

"In the past, the anthropos was looked at and studied by paleontologists as a prehistoric skeleton and, by comparative anatomists, as a series of anatomically aligned skeletons. In reaction to these approaches, I founded what I have called: the anthropology of geste. Geste is something that is in essence alive. What else is a dead person if not a person who no longer makes gestes. It was a bold stroke to utter the word that would put life into anthropology: the *geste*. I was bold enough and I changed the method. Instead of looking at alignments of skeleton-anthropoi, I took eternal anthropos in its guise of the small child, the then totally unknown anthropos-child. Children had been left in the care of nurses and people dabbling in psychology. What I learned, and what I taught you here is how to *observe* the anthropos. That is how I discovered the law that is now as authoritative in psychiatry as it is in psychology, in the sciences of language and writing: human mimism." *EA 09/11/36*

## *An insider methodology*

Equational or revelational, "all science is an attempt at explanation by this anthropos who perpetually rises, invariably forgets and lapses, rises again towards more real, and again falters and falls and rises and faces yet again, after thousands of years of interval, the very same problem." *S 27/01/37* Yet, "How, at some given moment, Palestinians faced, understood and behaved when confronted with the immense cosmic mechanism, remains still most interesting." *HE 22/05/34* "For a long time, I held the belief that all the revelationist civilizations were unscientific. But I had to accept the evidence: they are extremely scientific and logical!" *S 13/01/38* They are scientific: "When I am told: 'Your work is not scientific.' I reply: 'Scientific is that what grasps the most real at a given moment and explains the greatest number of things.'" *S 27/01/37* They are logical: "How can I define logic in function of my anthropology? I would say that logic is the smooth progress of intelligent continuity." *HE 08/08/45*

Coherence, however, can only be recognized from the inside. "Methodology is about developing an investigation of the real in itself, and about adapting this investigation to a particular ethnic milieu. Such a milieu is always infinitely complex and it is not enough for the investigation to be right; what is necessary is for us to have before us people who resonate with the method because they are aware of it, understand it, and are therefore able to apply it appropriately." *HE 05/05/36* "If you do not place yourself inside the mechanism of a specific system that is considered to be explicative, you are bound to say: 'But what is all this?' *EA 13/03/39*

How to judge a system? If we define system as a unified interacting whole—an interactional cosmos—then coherence should be the norm against which to measure any explanatory system's reliability and validity. For such an assessment to be fair and correct, the system needs to be taken as is, in its wholeness and on its own terms.


## The theory of universal insufflation

### *The scientific believer*

"I created anthropology, which is to say, the science of mimism." *S 14/01/54* "I, as anthropologist, work as an atheist, in the etymological sense of the word: as someone who does not take divinity into account. Let us be very clear about my way of tackling problems: here, in this lecture hall, I do not do religion." *EA 24/02/44* "My position as scientist: as an objective anthropologist, is that I observe, I record, I verbalise." *HE 10/11/43* "Before you here, I am not irreligious but I am unbelieving, which is not the same. I am religious and a non-believer in the sense that I try to know, and it is this desire to know that inspires me to undertake this research each and every person should undertake." *HE 02/04/40* "I happily make mine the well-known saying that 'a little bit science diverts one from religion. A lot of science maintains you there'—maintains one *in*, mind you, not takes one *back* to. I do not really believe in conversions because I believe one is born into a religion. All my studies have been about increasing my knowledge and understanding of what I have received at the maternal hearth. My studies are about becoming ever more conscious of the formidable mechanisms that are bound up in the traditional teaching of my mother. That is what you saw me do at the School of Anthropology and my audience there are Muslims or Judaists and from whatever other confession, because that is what it is about, it is, at heart, about understanding how a mother transmits to her child a tradition that is beyond her. Do you see that this is how a person of a traditional civilization rediscovers himself? It is for this reason that I, whenever I meet someone of a different faith, I ask that person questions and their answers have invariably been singularly enlightening for me." *EAB 03/03/48* "I am scientific even in the habit I wear." *EA 13/03/39*

"A religion is a system of explicative gestes. This is why, at the origin, there was no separation between religion and science. The great builders of religion were great builders of explicative systems. Moses was a savant in his milieu and in his time, Confucius was a great savant in his milieu and in his time, the Buddha was a great savant in his milieu and in his time. It is you, who created laity, you are the regressive ones. We, who are global, we see things as a totality, we are, I venture, in *totalitarism*, we cannot separate science and religion." *EA 24/02/44* "I do not know the meaning of this vivisection between science and religion." *EA 28/02/44*

"Faith is not something blind, it is a scientific thing, first." *S 12/11/51* "Faith is a science *first*." *Labo 23/03/38* "Faith, which is religious scientific intelligence." *HE 26/05/43* "The habit I wear confuses sometimes, which is a pity because it diminishes the role of the priest. A priest should master all the great techniques, mathematics, ethnology, stylistics, astronomy, *above all* anthropology; a priest must be all that and *in anthropology especially*, no-one should surpass the priest scientifically. And I do wear this habit while being able to speak on a par nearly with the best minds of anthropological science. My position is not an easy one to defend because the circles of theologues, our science is always put to use for the purpose of converting people, but that is not something I am made for; what I am made for is to be with you and like you, I search. My habit of course tells you that I have chosen. Yes, *I made my choice*. I do not however feel satisfied with that little science that I have and I therefore I continue to work always, always, always to bring ever more clarity in to this great this great thing on which I spent my life." *HE 06/02/40* "I never felt shaken in my faith by anything whatsoever." *S 09/02/42* "Everything anthropological is our concern. This cassock I wear is a robe of clarity, not an obscurantist cover-up. We are scientific believers. We are not afraid of science. And we have rejected, left and right, whoever tried to oppose our march towards the light." *EA 10/02/42* "Either you chose science-based faith, which is mine, or you chose the easy-way faith, which is that of other people." *HE 06/12/44*

### *An explicative system built on "universal breath"*

"What we are taught about revelationist civilization is fundamentally flawed by prejudices which the modern explicative science of mimism has to confront head-on. And what is it that I bring here? If I am afforded a few more years, what will make my name known? This: 'Jousse and human mimism.'" *S 27/01/37* The religion "we are taught in algebrized terms" is Christianity. Successive translations, often mistranslations, and transplantations into foreign soils can make any once true, and thus coherent system look incoherent, any once cogent logic, illogical; metaphors, once luminous, opaque.

On an all-encompassing theory of Breath, of Insufflation, an entire tradition was built, as a whole, coherently. The first task of the anthropology, which Jousse calls a modern explicative science, is to restore the system to its original coherence.

"Once you studied elementary and higher mathematics, you are able to tackle the great celestial mechanics. You here have done your elementary and superior mathematics of human mechanics, so let us see how the great gesticulators and gestualizers have explained the world. This explanation is perfectly coherent when we take as our point of departure the notion of a permanent intussusception of what is outside of us. A child considers that all is alive outside him, because all is alive in him, and because he has the sensation, *a sensation one should never lose,* that he will only know the things from outside him by bringing them into him. We will never be able to know that what is outside of us. We can only know that what we have to a greater or lesser extent intussuscepted. Children have this sensation deeply imbedded in them, played and replayed. All is alive in them because all replays; all is truly explicated because all is truly in them developed. Things will be 'explicated' as a child develops and as he develops the 'imbrications,' the complexities that have been received in him.

"When a child, or any other spontaneous being, sees something behaving strangely, something like this piece of paper here before you, for example; I now perform this gesture of blowing about air; and the paper moves. How very curious. Why does this paper move? If you have a theory about air, you bring your theory about air into play. This air now, where is this air? If you were to need ether in order to get an understanding of one or other phenomenon, you will make use of ether. Someone comes along, however, someone like Einstein, who tells you: 'We don't need this ether.' If the existence of air as tool of transmission is one explanation, in the example of the movement of the shreds of paper, it is not the only one: breath might be another. All our great laws are derived from things as simple as this, as simple as Newton's apple. Just as the rubbing of amber was needed for the discovery of electricity, so is the human breath on the piece of paper necessary for us to feel that some extremely curious phenomenon is happening: *it plays under the breath.* The entire formidable mechanics of the universe can be ordered and explained by this simple geste of breath—breath is everywhere. The words *spirit* and *spiritual* that you bandy about, it is I ask you *spiritus,* but *spiritus* means breath. Breath is in all things, incorporated as it were, because it is not breath by itself. You cannot see my breath. Breath by itself does not exist. Yet, if this thing here moves, it is because it has in it, breath. It has breath. So, we are calling on Breath, Breath marked out as being all-powerful. And being all-powerful, it will be a Breath causing

everything; it will be a Breath ruling everything; it will be a Breath reward-
ing everything." *EA 13/03/39* "It is around breath, breath mysterious because
invisible—breath of which we see the effects only—it is around breath that
humanity has built its most tragic mimodramas." *S 27/01/37*

"When, before entering his career of improviser, an improvising rhythmer [an oral composer] goes and spends a wake in a cave that is reputed
to receive the breath of the invisible—in our algebrozed language 'inspiration'—this man believes in miracle. He well knows that when he will later
proffer his improvisations, they will not come from him. Of this he is as
sure as of the light of day. You may well counter: 'This is a fallacy: it is what
he believes.' Now, that is your way of believing; his is wholly different. This
is exactly the wrong attitude that we have adopted for half century or so. It
is I the anthropologist speaking here, not the theologian. Only through the
observation of their attitude before the Invisible will we come to begin to
understand these peoples, their gestes, their histories. Many of their stories
are so wholly penetrated by the Invisible that they can only be understood in
that light." *HE 05/06/34* "Their stories are not myths, no, they are attempts at
explanation, and as we will see later, attempts at explication of the Invisible.
I am not as assured as you are that liturgies are obsolete, or rather, I am sure
that they will never be obsolete as long as there is even a single Man alive
who tries to express the breath of the Invisible with his body." *S 27/01/37*

### *The Invisible incarnate—"I made my choice." HE 06/02/40*

"It is, at heart, about understanding how a mother transmits to her child a
tradition that is beyond her." *EAB 03/03/48*

Jousse called his anthropology of mimism a modern explicative science, a scientific explication of religion and of civilization, a system that
is whole: "The great law of mimism extends from Man to God" *S 12/02/53*
"Man is an interactional miming animal. What does he mime? The world,
and God, even." *S 12/03/53* The anthropologist and scientific believer
Jousse comes to the conclusion that "[t]rue Christianity transcends any
ethnic particularity to such an extent that it seems to well up spontaneously from the inmost anthropological depths." *S 03/03/55* This "inmost
anthropological depth," the inmost depth of humanity, is mimism: "In the
beginning was mimism. In the beginning was rhythm. In the beginning was
rhythmic mimism. Here we reach, one might say, the very depths of living anthropology." *EAB 07/01/48* However, true Christianity is Ieshuaism
before *Christo-grecism*, this is to say, Christianity before its emigration to
the Greek cultural milieu, the Christianity of its founder, "the anthropos

Ieshua, to give him his Aramaic name; Ieshua, Galilean; Ieshua, paysan."
*HE 09/12/42* Ieshuaism participates in the paysanism of the "mimodramatic
and rhythmo-catechistic civilizations that do not vivisect the sacred and the
profane." *HE 01/03/44*

"I am not into converting anyone, I am a pathfinder, I bring light, and
it is up to you to judge by the facts." *HE 22/03/44* Each human is a unique
private individual and "we receive the real only *ad modum recipientis*." *HE*
*24/01/45*—in the manner of the receiver. Moreover, "one is generally of the
religion of one's mother. In truth, one knows the visible and invisible world
only through one's mother." *S 19/01/56* "Ordinarily, ninety-nine times out
of a hundred one is modeled by the theo-mimers of one's milieu. Born
in the Amerindian milieu, you would have been fashioned by the Indian
theo-mimers; born in China, you would have had the theo-mimers or theo-
mimists and theologians of China or India or Arab or whoever, you see?
And this training starts from early childhood, in the family." *Labo 23/02/38*

"A very simple example [of living tradition] is what I sense every
morning at 5 o'clock, when I say what is commonly called mass—that I call
the Palestinian mimodrama of the Bread and of the Wine." *EA 12/12/49*
"At that moment come to me, from the uttermost depths of the Palestinian
milieu, the true explanations of all that I say, of all that I do. From under
every word I pronounce, Aramaic rises. All the gestes I make are the gestes
of traditional Israel for many thousands of years." *HE 15/01/35* "It is the
formidable transubstantiation of the teaching Word that one eats whilst eating the Teacher." *EA 23/02/48* "What we have here is truly what we can call
a *priest*, this is to say *he who creates life*, as, tomorrow morning, with the
exact same certainty, I will take the death matter of bread and wine and say:
'This is my Body. This is my Blood.' What is most extraordinary is that I am
wholly convinced of the reality of this. Yet, I am not a simpleton. Call this a
residue of ancient dogmas if you wish. But with all my intelligence, which is
on a par with yours, I can profess, humble as is my custom: 'I believe, and I
would give my flesh and blood for it, that I am in the presence of transubstantiation.'" *EAB 03/03/53*

"In Rabbi Ieshua of Nazareth, there is undeniably a Semitic echo, but
there is also an extraordinarily personal echo of genius. As my study of
him proceeds, I have reached the point where I cannot but endorse what
one of his Jewish listeners said of him: 'No, never did a Man speak as this
Man speaks.' As an anthropologist, I put the accent on the word Man, but
I do find in these words a traditional resonance that prolongs my work as
anthropologist so that, in the end, under the anthropologist you will find
the believer." *HE 15/05/34* "I am not concerned here with knowing if something is real in itself. I so believe in this, by virtue of my habit, that I have

endeavored to know the logic of the faith bequeathed to me." *HE 02/04/40* "Ieshua the Galilean was powerful enough to transubstantiate the bread in to his flesh and the wine into his blood. He will be equally powerful enough to take the metaphoric formulas we studied last time and to fill them with reality. He will realize the ethnic metaphors of the manducation and of the bibition. That is where I want to arrive at after a life-long study of the facts, the anthropological facts, not the dogmas. What the dogmas are I do not as yet know, what the ethnic facts are, those I do know." *HE 22/03/44*

The last phase of mimage is the phase of sublimation of Man, when Man becomes becomes clearly and wholly conscious of his unique function et signification, which is to humanize the universe by con-scientizing the universe and so to divinize himself. In this ultimate transubstantiation, Man grasps the ultimate truth, which is that his mimism is in mirror and in echo of the primordial divine mimism, that he is the recreator of the creation: "In the mimodrama of the creation, divine mimism humanized Man. In the mimodrama of the Communion, human mimism divinized Man." *HE 10/11/43*

This then is Jousse's itinerary, his human mimism gone full circle, the ultimate mimism of the transubstantiation of the Host—human mimism grounded in the divine; the science of mimism grounding faith in science. *Human mimism* is thus not a pleonasm: within the cosmos, mimism is a human-specific trait through which the human mirrors and echoes, or re-flects and voices the original, divine Creation. This was already inchoate in Jousse's very first publication, *The oral style*. In its concluding sentence, Jousse speaks to us of his " . . . scientific research, as yet so little advanced, into the mysterious word of Mankind, that frail, yet wonderful echo, of the eternal creative Word!"

## Mimism and style

### Introduction: "The style is the Man himself"

Style is the gauge of the cosmos-anthropos connectedness. Style is when cosmos and anthropos coincide, when human *ex*pression matches cosmic *im*pression. Style is the measure of this oneness. As he did with Aristotle's proposition, Jousse rekindles Buffon's aphorism: "Le style est de l'homme même"—"The style is the Man himself." Style signifies mastery. In the mea-sure that a human understands his universe, he harmonizes with it, becomes one with it.

"Style is the flow of mimemes that pour in us. We may not always be conscious of these mimemes but we have a duty to bring them into our consciousness. That is what being human is about. Consciousness may become so acute that the conscientizing process no longer impedes the spontaneous flow of gestes. That should be our aim: to attain this wonderful and powerful mastery summed up as *The Style is the Man himself.*" *EA 01/02/37*

### The style

"The style is the man. It is the whole man giving himself wholly to the real, the man as a whole receiving and replaying the real. It is that, style." *HE 12/02/41*

"Style is the Man who took the universe in his sphere so fully that he is capable of putting it in triphase form and of replaying it, whatever the circumstance: I am the master of myself as of the universe. That I am, and that I want to be . . ." *EA 09/01/45*

### The Man himself

"But what does that mean, the Man? What is 'Man'? Man is this uninterrupted series of mimemes taken from the real that flows in him:

"Anthropos never is anything more than that. You, I, from that very first time we opened our mouth to bawl to life, till the last rale that will close our mouth for the great silence of death, that is all we are. It is that, the man. Nothing too admirable, indeed, but something we need to be aware of. And those mimemes, those mimismic gestes, what are they? They are the replay of those things we have taken in us, those things that we have received in us. That is what they are, and that only. So, Buffon's definition needs some redefinition: 'Style is the often unconscious flow of mimemes in us that we need to bring into our consciousness. It is that, Man. At times, our consciousness of this influx of mimemes will be so acute that the flow of gestes will be spontaneous, yet conscious. That is the goal we should set ourselves: to let the mechanisms freely operate and to be all the while conscious of them operating; to be always at once handled and handler; to be always at once vanquished and victor." *EA 01/03/37*

*The style is the Man himself*

"I have a thorough knowledge of the French language. I have, for thirty years, silently worked at mastering all the terms of the French vocabulary and I can assure you that my French vocabulary is so fluid and adaptable in me that never does a word pass my lips that has not be been uttered willingly. My answer then, when I am rebuked for being occasionally a bit harsh with some or other philologist or metaphysician, my answer is unambiguous: 'I commit mortal sins only deliberately. There are, when I am concerned, never any attenuating circumstances. I am always guilty and I plead guilty because I am the master of my tool. That is the degree of awareness a child should be taught as early as possible and it is that, style. 'The style is the man' refers to a human who has gained such mastery over his mimismic mechanism that he is in complete possession of it, and who has trained himself subsequently in capping his mimemes with algebraic expressions appropriate to his particular ethnic environment. The more spontaneous and conscious a human's gestes, the more truly will he be the master of himself and of others." *EA 01/03/37* "I am the master of myself as of the universe." *EA 12/05/47*

# Of three styles

"Irradiation of our gestes in our human compound is global, manual and oral. There are, therefore, three styles: corporeal style, manual style and oral style." *S 31/01/52* Primordial corporeal-manual style transformed in oral style, and manual and oral style were projected in the form of written style, of graphic style.

## *Corporeal-manual style*

"Corporeal-manual style is expressive. Man is indeed essentially an animal that expresses and that is expressed. Man cannot be in the passive, or dare I say impassive stage the anthropoid finds itself in. Where the young anthropoid wriggles, the young human child plays—meaning that he expresses himself and is expressed in all sorts of things. It is *ex*-pression, for, by the process of intussusception and mimism, the objects press-*out*-of us their own images. Manual style then is expressive, and, when the expressive mechanism comes in operation, consciousness sets in, and with consciousness comes what sets humanity apart: creation.

"Corporeal-manual style becomes creative. This is what happened in the caves of Montignac, twenty-five thousand years ago. Men entrusted with the provision of food for their companions created the bison, create the horse, created the various beings that had to provide food. This is still the case today among those peoples we call primitive and savage and who are in fact infinitely more alive and more intelligent than we are in their mastery of the real. This expressive manual-corporeal style then, is creative.

"Manual-corporeal style can also be rememorative. Think of the admirable binary mimodrama projected on one of the walls at Montignac in which we see a hunter plunging his spear in a bison, and the bison with his horn attacking the assailant. This is beyond the stage of creation, this is the stage of rememoration, so much so that we find the hunter's name planted on the corpse of the bison in the form of a grouse. That is his name.

### Oral style

"Being inherently lazy, humanity found global expression too unwieldy and replaced it with laryngo-buccal expression. Cinemimism—mimism of the whole body—was abandoned for phonomimism, which is mimism through sound. Oral style replaced global style and used our auricular and our laryngo-buccal mechanisms rather than the great mimodramatic mechanism commonly called dance, but which is quite simply global creation or global rememoration. Creation was now by sound, and there came about creators in the etymological sense of the word: they cried the object out of nothingness. Expressive oral style thus became creative style that in turn became rememorative style. In this oral style we come across historical recitations just as before we had historical mimodramas. They are our epics that are recitations evoking the deeds of the ancestors and also the deeds of the gods, which are commonly called theologies.

### Written style

"Manual style and oral style manifest in graphic expression. This may be the mimoplasticism of a child expressing a bird, not by mouth, but by seizing prime matter clay and by modelling it with his hands into a small bird that could take off. For that is what should normally happen when the person kneading the clay has the Power. Which is what we witness in the prehistoric caves where those who model animals are wary of modelling human beings. This is indeed why, in the primordial caves, we do not come across humans modelled in the likeness of the modeller. Man was afraid of his fellow human. To make the statue of a god is to incarnate the god. A statue is not inert. That is why a modeller of an Invisible incarnated the invisible, why the drawer of the invisible incarnated the Invisible.

"At some stage however, due to some fatal degradation, these painted mimograms will be used and become ideograms, as was the case in Egypt. It is, I dare say, a 'theory', a suite of gestes. They were however so dangerously alive to them that, in the so-called ideograms found in the pharaonic tombs, dangerous animals appear, like the lion, that are cut in half: they are alive, these lions, and they need to be made harmless. Anthropology explains this evolution from mimograms to ideograms with a host of facts. Reading all that has been published in connection with the laws of expression I am teaching will take you a lifetime. The materials are countless, but unclassified and not ordered *according to a unifying law*. That is what I did in my first manual of *Oral Style*, which is a synthesis of sorts: manual style, oral style and written style." *HE 24/01/45*

## Oral style

### *From global style to oral style*

"I mentioned a number of doctoral theses written these last three years on oral style. The focus I think, should henceforth be more and more closely on global style. There, I think, lies the true solution. Before being oral, the geste is global. Oral style is only a particular form of global style." *S 18/06/31* "The oral style is simply the transposition on the laryngo-buccal organs of the global mechanisms, and the global mechanisms in turn are the reverberations and mimemes of the interactions of the ambient world. That is my contribution. And it has not been easy to preserve these mechanisms all alive and fresh. There was always the threat that they would be wrested from Life." *EA 26/01/48*

"An object that has a form is liable to have a sound too, and very soon this sound will represent the global characteristic geste of that object. At that stage, there is a double mechanism: a global, manual and corporeal mechanism and an oral, a laryngo-buccal mechanism. The former soon yields to the latter, dwindles and ultimately disappears. When corporeal gesticulation becomes laryngo-buccal gesticulation, mimograms transpose into pure graphic expression, into some sort of algebra. The end result will be humans spending their days, from age five till age eighty, with pen and ink, blackening sheets of paper, as is already happening with a few among you who have never seen the real, never saw things, never looked at things and who don't care much anyway. The results are for anyone to see. The problems I raise here remain forever unsolved because nothing ever that concerns them is put as a problem. To such people, their page of writing is the be-all and end-all of everything and turning to them for solutions is futile.

"Whatever this whittling away of human expression, there are fortunately still a few peoples who have preserved a modicum of life, peoples who do not go the whole way of the metaphysical and graphic sloth we are witness to. It is to these peoples we will turn to find out if human expression has taken form on the human lips—on the laryngo-buccal gestes—in the same way it did in the whole body and in the hands. This is why the studies I have initiated need to be taken further, into more oral-style ethnic milieus. I identified this third style as *the oral style*—an expression that met with extraordinary success and that generated a great many debates, which is all the more curious for those who engaged in them not having bothered to familiarize themselves with the topic." *HE 05/12/33*

### Origin of the term oral style

"I was often asked the question: 'How did you hit upon this idea of the *oral style* that is famous now the world over?' My immediate answer is that I did not hit upon this idea because I never had ideas, I leave that to the metaphysicians. However, I had the *mimeme* of the oral style. It has been my extraordinary fortune to be born in a family that remained unchanged for thousands of years. It is not so much that I came upon the idea of the oral style as that a Gallic tradition transmitted to me the mimeme of the oral style. The expression oral style was only a most exact verbalization of a phenomenon that our classical studies had left wholly blank and untouched.

"My first task was to adopt Pasteur's approach and to disinfect the vocabulary that I was about to use. When I became interested in logical human expression, I found that the books I had before me were infected by the following treble terminological catastrophe: in the beginning, Man expressed himself through dance, music and poetry. From the very start I had to make it clear that here, we do not do dance; here, we do not do music; here we do not do poetry. What it is then that we do? Something altogether distinct from this residue.

"In our present ethnic milieu, making rhythmic gestes has no discernable logical or didactic aim at all. If, on the contrary, we act out our interactional mimemes as the Amerindians still do to this day, our expression becomes wholly logical. Moreover, whenever these global gestes grow into sound, our terms will prove to be concrete and visual too, but that does not make them poetic. When these interactional phonemes happen on the human mouth, they will be rhythmic and they will be melodic—they cannot be otherwise—but that does not make them musical. Music is altogether different from didactic rhythmo-melody. Poetry is altogether different from phonetic expression of vocalic mimemes. Dance is altogether different from the rhythmic expression of interactional mimemes. It took enormous efforts to wean my listeners of the old technical terms that clog their handbooks." *EA 26/01/48*

## Mimismic oral style

"How does the human being, placed at the heart of action of the universe, manage to conserve the memory of these actions within him, and to transmit this memory faithfully to his descendants, from generation to generation?" *EA 03/04/33* "There is in fact only one approach possible, which is the angle of human globalism. Anthropology should grasp Man as a whole living being, expressing himself with this sort of consistency that I have called the law of mimism, the law of balancing, the law of stereotypy by ethnic formulas, and the law of transmission in oral-style milieus." *HE 17/01/39*

The cosmos plays into the anthropos. The anthropos replays the intussuscepted cosmos. Situated in time and in space, all Man's re-play is necessarily distributed and sequenced, i.e., rhythmed. Rhythm manifests in the human bilateral body, and thus bilaterally. To master his cosmos, Man sets himself at its center and divides continuous time in time measured, with past and future parallel to the centre; he divides space in a treble bilateralism: left-right/up-down/front-back; he creates spatiotemporal rhythmic and bilateral formulas that mould his propositions for ease of reception, memorization and transmission. With repetition, patterns or formulas take shape which make easier further storage and classification of mimemes, and hence their retrieval. Thus comes into being a style, a mode of expression obeying basic universal laws of human expression: mimism, rhythmism, bilateralism and formulism. This is the global-oral style, the tool of traditional memory. It is the style of the verbo-motors, of those for whom human ex-pression is movement: corporeal, manual, laryngo-buccal or oral-verbal movement.

## The laws of mimismic expression

### *Rhythmism*

The action of the universe is continuous, and the cosmic energy flows uninterrupted into the human being. This flux of actions provokes a reflux of reactions. It is this incessant movement of the cosmos-anthropos interaction that man needs to canalize in order to master it. Rhythm is a mechanism of distribution of the flow of continuous time into measured time. Rhythm stems the flow of intussusceptions so that the human can understand the self and the cosmos.

The tool of solidification, man finds in himself: it is rhythm—a canalization, a dyking up, and a taming. Rhythm provides both the flux that energises reception and integration, and the logic, the order, with which man stores and conserves the mimemes formed by his intussuscepted impressions. Rhythm will allow him subsequently to preserve and to transmit them. He replays them to build himself up as an individual—because, as he ex-presses them, they im-press back into him. He replays them in order to transmit them to other human beings—as individuals or as members of a community. The origin and purpose of rhythm therefore is practical—it serves to take in oneself and to conserve—and communicative and pedagogical—it serves to ex-press and transmit. The mimismic play of the anthropos in the cosmos expresses itself in time; time is rhythm, *rhythmos*, flow. Rhythmically, this is to say, temporally. "In manual-style Man, fluidity is thought at work: the geste, with its fluidity, allows the multiple meanings of things to be gasped. Fluidity however, also renders them fragile and transitory. That is why man quickly realized that the liquid bronze of his geste can be solidified by the insertion of rhythm. Rhythm hardens the human geste, fixing its suppleness in unalterable form." *EA 19-03-34*

"When man, thanks to the development of his mimism, constructed his language, he noticed that he possessed an extremely supple, living, anthropological metal: he discovered the liquid metal of his supple and adaptable geste—the human geste is a liquid metal. Thus he sensed that the suppleness and fluidity of his thought matched that of the objects and creatures surrounding him. He realized however that he needed to harden his thought at a given point. He decided that he could not follow the Greek philosopher: *panta rei*, everything flows. No! I cannot let everything flow; sometimes, I will have to seize—a precise, expressive word—to seize myself up again, to retake possession of myself, to re-play, one-on-one. How can this be achieved? By rhythm. Rhythm quenches the human geste and turns it into steel. To me, limiting rhythm to the domain of aesthetic music is to grossly diminish us, humans. For millennia past, Man took it upon himself to mount thousands of gestes, bit by bit, a geste at a time. At some stage, whilst trying to embrace the real by rendering his gestes as supple as possible, Man felt that he had within him, within his fluid mimism, something that would allow this suppleness to firm up and to become unalterable. I refuse to see this marvelous power as no more than an artificial embellishment, a superficial cloak thrown over some thought. If you take away the rhythm that unifies and stabilizes humanity's acquisitions, what will we be left with? This is why, when venturing through the various ethnic milieus, I am so keen to gather the first concrete realisations of the word, in the form of those spontaneous and stabilised balancings which are the binaries and ternaries that give us the proverbs." *HE 15–05-34*

### Bilateralism

Space equally needs to be distributed if it is to be mastered. Man puts himself at the center and orders space according to his own construct which is multiply two-sided or bilateral: left-right, up-down, front-back. Objective, cosmological and unconscious mimism already implies the binary operation of "action-reaction." Subjective, anthropological, conscious mimism implies the binary operation of "play-replay." Expressive mimism is similarly bilateral because the human being uses his bilateral body as a tool in order to move and express himself.

"Balancing is so universal because it facilitates gestual and oral expression. Bilateral Man expresses himself in his structure all the more easily for following the fundamental laws of human gesticulation." *S 04/06/31* "The world is, as it were, bilateralized, because Man is bilateral. Like a new Atlas, Man seized, and balanced, the whole universe: *fas* to the right, *nefas* to the left—good and bad. 'And he will place the chosen at his right and the damned at his left.' What a formidable thing, this hand balancing bilaterally." *S 19/11/51* "See how a mother cradles her child, unwittingly in conformity with her bilateralism. This is because we are two-sided: left and right, front and back." *S 10/12/51 (Labo)*

"The Tôrâh is large, immense, full of fruit, but its balancings have not been sufficiently mastered, and one cannot carry it if one is not sufficiently trained, not equipped as are the Palestinian rabbis. Then a Clever One came, and it is Solomon who made the balanced Mâshâl:

"And he made ears for it
"and it began to be carried by its ears.

"This, then, was the splendid solution out of which emerged this marvelous style, which is both audible and portable." *HE 07/05/40*

### Formulism

To master his universe, man orders it in measured time and measured space. This spatiotemporal ordering gives form to the indiscriminate messages he receives from the cosmos. By miming the message, or massaging it into a form according to his own nature and structure, he makes it his own and makes it possible to conserve, to remember and to recite: the formula is a facilitating tool for conservation, memorization and recitation. Propositions, or units of thought, are made to be carried forth easily and faithfully. The formula allows for this portage, this trans-portage, this trans-mission.

"Homer composed and improvised by propositions. Propositions, but made to what purpose? They are made to be carried. In these milieus, the unit of thought is the proposition which, once properly put together, will always be the same for all the individuals of the ethnic milieu and will be easily and faithfully carried forth." *EA 25/02/35*

## Civilization

### Introduction: the laboratory of awareness
### —of mimism and algebrosis

Jousse's lectures are a laboratory of awareness, "where Man becomes aware of Man and creates awareness of Man. Man is now no longer 'this unknown' for he becomes his own discoverer. One only knows well oneself. To know oneself well, however, one needs to observe oneself well. The true laboratory is an observatory. It is an observatory of the self. And this observatory is a laboratory because it is hard work to learn how to see oneself." *HE 10/11/43* "We are trying to see and understand, apart from any religious consideration, that the fundamental question is to know one-self, by oneself, in oneself." *S 19/03/53* "I have shown you how this laboratory of oneself, in oneself and by oneself taught me the great anthropological law of mimism." *S 26/02/53* "My aim is to make my listeners aware of the formidable question of Man's attitude towards the real. This is the very first and all-important conversion everyone needs to effect who is presently shaken by this immense cataclysm that is called a change of civilization. It is this, the conversion we all have to impose on ourselves, each of us. Before converting others, I have tried to convert myself and it is this conversion you hear from me, three times a week. It is a tragic emprise, this human conversion." *HE 09/02/44* "It is not religion I am concerning myself with here. I am concerned purely with civilization." *EA 18/01/43*

Originally, the anthropos-cosmos rapport is that of a universe *impress*-ing the human being—the human compound—and the human *expressing* the universe, either miming with his whole body—*corpor*age, miming with the hands—*manual*age, miming with the phonatory organs—*langu*age— or by projecting his expression on a fixed exterior support—any form of -graphy. Whatever the means, from mimeme to grapheme, anthropologi-cal expression remains organically linked to cosmic impression; remains a *mim*age—*mimo*dramatism, *mimo*plasticism, *mimo*phonetism, *mimo*gra-phism; remains a mimer-anthropos in interaction with a mimed-cosmos.

Over thousands of years, mimismic expression algebrized. Algebra being "a procedure, as you know, that consists in using signs without con-cern for their value: 'the signs signify at will.'" *EA 14/12/42* Algebrism might turn into *algebrosis* in which "signs can mean anything as there is no longer any contact with the real. However, this absence of contact is morbid." *EA 14/12/42* Algebrosis is the vivisection of the anthropos from the cosmos, and not just of individuals, but of civilizations, as the title of the lecture from which the latter quotation is drawn explicits: *Algebrosis and the death of civi-lizations*. Mimism is about the anthropos constructing his self, mimeme by mimeme, out of the cosmos, and anthropoi building the collective self that is called civilization, collective mimeme by collective mimeme. Jousse as-cribes "the immense difficulty we have today to express ourselves, to under-stand each other." *HE 09/02/44* to our choice of civilization: having opted for language rather than mimage, our civilization, dissociated and algebrized, "suffers at every turn from these dissociations and these algebrizations, suf-fers from these permanent contradictions." *EA 23/01/33*

"I never had but one thought, mimism and its algebrization." *S 14/12/33* "How did we arrive at this algebrization of human thought? Where did we begin and how have we journeyed in order to impoverish human thought to the point of saying: 'or x.' But x what? That was the great problem that challenged me when I was twenty." *S 01/02/34* "What I do tell you is that from the moment we left our mother's womb, we are no longer ourselves. What is it then that draws this iron curtain between our true, deep self and the us in search of ourselves? It is the social milieu and singularly, language." *S 10/01/52* "The anthropology of algebrization leads us from the mimeme to the algebreme. The mimeme invariably tries to seize the thing, as it is and attempts, for as far as possible, to play out the real in its full richness. Laziness came and, dispensing with a mechanism too costly in energy, too unwieldy in its global replay, chose to rely on the lighter laryngo-buccal organism. Sound, I hold, has been a catastrophe for us humans. Sound has detached the human from the gestes of the real. Because of sound, Man became intoxicated with himself. Sound turned Man into a sacred egoist. Man's interest was no longer in finding out about the things but rather about himself. The real lost a contemplator—we were left with only an auditor, and for all that, with an auditor who listened to himself." *EA 11/02/35* Global mimage, whole-body or corporeal geste, was reduced to laryngo-buccal mimage, which is language or the geste of the *langue* or tongue, and this oral geste would set us on the path to the further reduction of the movement, of the geste, to writing. "Writing was mimography first, but we went from death mimographism to the even deader algebroseme, and so we arrived at that one puny thing called the alphabet." *EA 29/03/43* "We lost the great expressive geste. We are left with words that are pure algebremes." *EA 30/01/39* "We have become mineralized." *EAB 14/01/48*

"Our present-day classical culture is dead. What I demand is a living and life-giving culture, and one that goes much further and deeper than language, one that goes to the primordial expressive geste. Under each of our words we need to find the geste. For the anthropology of mimism is gestual and actioning." *EA 30/01/39* "It was quite rightly said: 'Once you have seen Jousse, you understand him. If you have not seen him, you do not understand him.' This is because my teaching is simply my geste on which I put terms that are as precise and exact as possible. You can grasp this precision and exactness only by seeing the underlying geste." *EA 20/11/44* "This is nothing but an application of the law of mimism which will arise whenever you come to me with a question: 'What will this yield us as gestes?'" *HE 11/06/41*

"Spontaneous anthropos hardly exists any more among us. Fortunately, not all Men are in our algebrozed and artificial stage. Observation of the anthropos in the various ethnic milieus enables us to see what wells up from the very depths of spontaneous anthropos and to apply it in our approach to the child, rather than to rely on quick fix gimmicks." *EA 27/01/36* "Confronted with anthropologically pure beings in other ethnic milieus, we are struck by the sharpness with which they perceive, engage and express things. This I had become aware of since my early childhood where I lived in contact with the Sarthois paysan milieu." *EA 23/01/33* Ever since, "I never had but one single idea: mimism and its alteration." *S 14/12/33* "The poles ± *spontaneous* ↔*algebrozed* sum up my study of the anthropos, and what the anthropology of mimism is about." *EA 21/11/38* This scale measuring spontaneity and algebrosis concretizes "the formidable question of the human's comportment before the real." *HE 09/02/44*

## Mimismic civilization and algebraic civilization

"Man is a human compound! Whence the absolute necessity to initiate proper research in psychology as is done at the School of Anthropology and the like, institutions that are equipped and geared towards that type of research. Unless they are able to develop their own methods, this is the path researchers need to follow. If problems are not posed in their proper perspective, everything is at risk of distorting at the root. This is why I prepared today's lecture in touch with those so-called primitive civilizations and with our own civilization, that I call dissociated and algebrized, and suffering, for this very reason, at every turn from its dissociations and algebrizations, suffering from its permanent contradictions. Anthropology can help us resolve the immense problems our dissociated and dissociating ethnic milieu is confronted with on a daily basis, provided it applies the latest methodology of dynamic anthropology in its study of these so-called primitive milieus." *EA 23/01/33*

"All civilizations started off with laws, or guidances that steered the people in a particular direction. This applies to all ethnic milieus. I would say that we, in our milieu, *materialized*. Instead of being preoccupied with gestual—gestual, not spiritual—civilization, we focused increasingly on technology, and that is how material civilizations came about. Presently, our concern is with devising ever faster cars, air-planes that taunt the sound barriers, methods to blow up the world with atoms. This is what our genius is set to work at. Other geniuses set themselves altogether different goals! They are the great founding fathers of civilization: Confucius, Mahomet, the Buddha, Moses, Ieshua . . . They aided people to better realize their potential and to even surpass themselves. In our colonies, not everyone went down on all fours when we arrived with automobiles, airplanes and the like. I well understand why they were not in awe of those. Maybe there is an infinitely better way to be human than by constructing an airplane, be it the fastest in the world. And something much more difficult to achieve too.

"As a young artillery captain, I chose between Mount Wilson, where celestial mechanics are studied, and the Indians who offered me, in their gestes, the primordial expression. I returned from the United States an anthropologist, not an astronomer. There are aspects of human mechanics we have ignored. Mr Thiam, sitting here before me, I am not bringing him an airplane, I am bringing him *himself*. I am not going to make him French. I want to fraternize with his Sudanese tradition, I, of Sarthois stock. I do not want to convert him with Greco-Latinism, I want to try to make him understand Ieshua the Galilean, who is so close to him in his ethnic mechanisms. I am saying to Mr. Thiam: if you want to study Ieshua and be baptized, you have *in you* everything needed to become fully conscious of this formidable mimodrama of this *immersion* that is called baptism; of this formidable mimodrama of the *manducation of the word* that ends in the *manducation of the teacher*, in the paysan bread and wine. And you have *in you* everything else too. To convert a Malinké, study him, first, and, then, later, the Other. But one needs to start with him in order to arrive at the Other." *S 02/02/56*

"Enough has been said about evolution, progressive evolution, regressive evolution. What it is truly about is evolution in depth. We become human insofar as we become more conscious of the richness that is us: 'Become what you are.' We are earthlings because the norm should be the paysan mother who gives birth to her child in a pays, in a particular land of a particular soil." *S 10/01/52*

## The Gallo-Galilean civilization

"I am in no way distanced from the material civilization of railways, today, of airplanes, tomorrow, and of transatlantic flights and rockets to go to the moon, the day after tomorrow. All this should however not prevent us from thinking of our earth, and of their earth, the earth of those we are presently colonizing, because Man, everywhere, will always and foremost be an Earthling. And what about those waters, those great rivers like the Mississippi? When I found myself before the Mississippi, I was filled with wonder, but of a lesser wonder than before the so incomparably limpid Sarthe river. I speak of waters—forgive me, but to me, the most beautiful thoughts are not unlike those proud poplars that border the Sarthe and that reflect in its waters. Go visit the bridge of Beaumont-sur-Sarthe or the bridge at Fresnay, and see the great poplars. You might well learn there more than you ever will from all your civil-law hand-books, because there, analogical mimism will reveal itself to you in its entirety. It is the land, the problem we have to deal with: the land, the pays, the soil, for it is they that model the paysan who lives on it and who works it." *S 19/01/56*

True Christianity is "Ieshuaism, which is Christianity before Ieshua became Hellenized to 'Christos.' Christianity must be taught and taught scientifically because, secular or clerical, you, French people, you belong to this Gallo-Galilean civilization. Just as Muslims depend on Mohamed and Chinese depend on Confucius, you, like it or not, you depend on the paysan-Rabbi Ieshua the Galilean. That is what I taught you, whatever your thinking, secular or not. That is what I taught you, because that is our first premise: civilization: to do Ieshuaism, but Ieshuaism after having studied our own deep-rooted Gallic civilization. And that Gallic civilization was this great civilization that the sceptic Julius Caesar deemed invincible because this civilization, he wrote, 'believed in the immortality of the soul.'" *S 22/03/45*

The Gallo-Galilean civilization is the momentous convergence of two paysanisms, ironically brought together in the slipstream of the same military oppressor: "[T]he Gallic paysan milieu and the Galilean paysan milieu [which] are strangely analogous, however much geographically remote. Maybe it is precisely because of this surprising analogy in their limpid mimismic transparency that these two paysan ethnic milieus have miraculously mutually interpenetrated to so create and spread the sublime mimismic gestuality which is the Gallo-Galilean civilization." *HE 10/11/43*

"The unconscious is everything a child receives from birth onwards, unknowingly. It is everything the Sarthe gave me without me knowing what it was I received. Until death, there is a perpetual and universal intussusception. Everything is received unconsciously and will become subconsciously rich in direct proportion to what I have received." *EA 30/11/50* "What I have always done, personally, is to observe the real and nothing but the real. The aim of my professorial lectures was to bring the real into consciousness. It is indeed so that, whatever the topic under discussion, from the moment Man is concerned, every topic and its related contents need to refer to the one overriding, essential and primordial operation of human mimism. The overarching primacy of mimism is the better observable where the human being has remained natural and spontaneous and thus remained in the sphere of fundamental mimismic play and replay. In such an environment, there is no need for us to contrive and distort the normal inner workings of society in order to link then to the central driving mechanism. It is ignorance of the one great fundamental anthropological law and its ramifications in all spheres of human life that leads to contrivance and distortion. Solutions to human problems are never more than particular instances of general human mechanics.

"This principle is well illustrated by all the questions posed by memory—which is the tireless replay of mimemes—and of rhythm—which is the energetic and facilitating propulsion of the replayed mimemes. Man is an ephemeral tradition of such mimismic play, and humanity the forever verified, rectified and redefined tradition of all such individual manifestations. The world is a continuous mimodrama the various acts of which are played out by various ethnic milieus, seemingly independent from each other, but in reality profoundly dependent on anthropological mimism. This dependence of particular ethnic expressions on general anthropological mimism is most alive and obvious in ethnicized milieus where spontaneous mimismic gestes escaped paralysis. This is why anthropological research went out into the immense ethnic laboratory to discover privileged milieus where *pays* and *paysan* still mutually reflect and echo. Willingly or not, the anthropos is always ethnicized: he does not live in the Platonic world of ideas. The anthropological, however, always survives under the ethnic, and it is up to the anthropologist to choose, concretely, the lesser ethnicized societies. My choice fell on two ethnic milieus that are strangely analogous, their geographical remoteness notwithstanding: the Gallic paysan milieu and the Galilean paysan milieu." *HE 10/11/43* "I have found Palestine in Sarthe, in my Sarthois maternal hearth. I was brought up by a mother who knew by heart the extraordinary innovation of the great Palestinian, and particularly Galilean paysan, Ieshua of Nazareth. For as far as I am concerned, these two paysan civilizations clearly had to be put in parallel." *HE 10/11/43*

"[My allegiance is to] Ieshua the Galilean, my master; with my mother, my only master." *S 22/01/53* This twofold allegiance to a Gallo-Galilean paysan civilization finds its concrete expression in a twofold transubstantiation. First: "What do you have in you? In you. That is the crux of the matter. What I have brought here is what I learned in my age-old, maternal Sarthe. My mother incarnated in me and my mother is all I ever taught. But it is that, a Man's depth. A Man is but what his mother is." *S 08/03/58* Second: "I very early on understood what my dear collaborator Professor Goguel told me: 'One understands Ieshua only insofar as one increasingly becomes Ieshuan.' And I dare say that I have been Ieshuan from my mother's womb." *S 03/03/55*

## The path ahead—confraternization

Marcel Jousse was a veteran of World War I, the recipient of the Legion of honor and the Croix de Guerre for exceptional bravery. To him as to his to his fellow combatants, the military defeat, two decades later, and the subsequent occupation of their country by the foreign power they had helped defeat, was the betrayal of a civilization they had paid for with blood and life. Jousse's response to the debacle was twofold. At the beginning of the occupation, he interrupted his normal lecture program and inserted a series of conferences on the theme "Be yourself"; immediately after the liberation, in another series of lectures on "The anthropology of language and colonization," he challenged his listeners to reflect on the irony of their country, just freed from five years of occupation, still occupying a host of foreign lands. "You went to overseas countries and you went there with your paper, with your dictionaries, with your ignorance of living, global and miming Man. And you wondered why some of the people there confronted you, for being *themselves,* they felt superior to you. That is why I tell you, yet again, that to *begin* by throwing these people in your algebrozed and dead mechanisms is the wrong way to go. They should be introduced to your civilization only much, very much later, once they have gained awareness of their superiority—of *their* superiority, mind you, not yours. You should introduce them to your civilization only when you are able to tell them, in all sincerity: 'Your superiority differs from mine. Your superiority is *analogical* to mine.' That is the point! Everything being analogical. Each individual being analogical too, for you are not me and I am not you. And this is why I forever return to the word *confraternization.*" *S 17/02/55*

"For twenty years now I have been doing here before this one thing, this thing only, that what used to be called 'prelogism'—I have been systematically 'prelogical.' Told: 'This manual language is the language of the savages,' I replied: 'It is the manual language of primordial pure Man!' Told: 'That is the memory of the savages!' I replied: 'These are memories that are active and effective!' And I could go on and prove to you that all those human mechanisms despised by you manage to achieve the 'Explication in the sciences,' as one of our present-day savants termed it. What all this entails I will explain to you next year in a series of lectures I called 'The Ennoblement in the sciences.' That is indeed what we will be doing: instead of killing off all these various civilizations, we will ennoble them by making them conscious of their individuality. And before us will rise, not savages brutalized under our whips and forced to supply us with cane sugar and cotton, but human beings, beings neither white nor black nor Greco-Latinized, but beings who will be nothing but themselves and who will bring us, who agonize under the weight of our overweening verbosity, a transfusion of Blood, of Life and of Geste." *EA 17/06/46*

"If a concluding sentence were needed, I would add a sentence of thanks. When I started these lectures at the École des Hautes Études of the Sorbonne, I was not worried, but a little curious, rather, as to who my listeners would be. Some people should have been seated here in the front row, who had asked me anthropological explanations, philologists who write in journals of apologetics aimed at converting the unbelievers. That those people shone by their absence did not overly surprise me, as it was within the logic of their habitual behavior. What the young people present here before me need do, is to remake in themselves the new Man and that new Man is the traditional Man, the Man who, building on his deep-rooted civilization, reaches out towards others so as to achieve a more perfect realization of himself through brotherly interchange." *EA 01/03/48*

# PART 2

# Marcel Jousse

*Seven Oral Lectures on Mimism*

# Introduction

## On Reading Marcel Jousse's
## Oral Lectures

MARCEL JOUSSE TAUGHT AT three institutions of higher learning in Paris, from 1931 until 1957: the University of Paris (*Sorbonne*, S), the School of Anthropology (*École d'anthropologie*, EA), and the School for advanced applied studies (*École Pratique des Hautes Études*, HE), as well as in his own Laboratory of rhythmo-pedagogy (Labo). In the latter he teaches future Kindergarten teachers, at the other institutions the lectures are public, with specialised focus—biblical studies at Hautes-Études, pedagogics at the Sorbonne and anthropology at the School of Anthropology. Each teaching year at each of the venues has a general theme in which feature on average fifteen (S, Labo), twenty (EA), or twenty-five (EHE) lectures.

Most of these thousand-odd lectures were not written out but rather performed. An exemplary verbo-motor, in direct contact with his varied audiences, Jousse took his cue from a skeleton plan, with contextualizing introductions taken from whatever was current: a book just read, newspaper articles, posters, a recent conversation. He had the foresight to have professional stenographic recordings made which Gabrielle Baron, his lifelong assistant, later typed out. Now digitized, they are made available on two CD's by the Marcel Jousse Association.

The chasm between the spoken word and the written work is a major theme of Jousse:

> When you read me, you no longer have my voice, you no longer have my whole breathing and vibrating being. It is a fallacy to think that one speaks as one writes, and that one writes as one speaks. I was often told by listeners: 'What you told us today was most interesting. Will your lecture be available soon, in a week or two, perhaps?' Well, yes, in ten or fifteen years maybe! Some of my ideas I tested out for up to twenty-five years before I had

them published. Writing is a wholly different exercise, person to person contact is lost and although thought is cast and creation achieved, every reader will have his own interpretation. It was always said that a disciple is a traitor of sorts, as he replays the master's output through his own mechanisms. I am indeed baffled at times when I am shown articles on my thought—baffled to see how this here became that there. Each reader creates his own truth. Yet, it at that very point perhaps that we begin to live and survive, when our thought has been played out by each of the individuals in their image and likeness. It is interesting that there is more than a language to shape each and every individual's unique attitude. We are not cars on an assembly line. Each individual fashions his own truth. *S 22/02/34*

## The seven selected lectures

Each of the lectures chosen illustrates one or more facets of Jousse's anthropology, methodology and terminology, with mimism, mimage and oral style as overarching themes. Being set in a new context, the selected lectures have been given, in their presentation, titles that reflect the theme they illustrate. The original title has been kept in the translation proper.

### *Lecture 1 On method*

In *On scientific discovery*, Jousse retraces his own itinerary as a scientist. His method is autoethnographical, i.e., he uses self-observation as science, an approach which is a matter of methodological principle. If, in traditional scientific research, it is a categorical imperative that subjectivity and science are mutually exclusive, Jousse's scientific imperative is no less categorical as he holds that a researcher's own experience is his most reliable and even exclusive original source of information: "People who heard me speak said: 'But he always only talks about himself!' Whom should I talk about? What can you talk about? Can you escape from this bag of skin you are locked in?" *S 31/01/52* "Intussusception, the word speaks for itself, is what you receive inside you. In truth, it is no more inside than outside. We have no more interior than we have exterior. We are wholly interior; we cannot escape out of this interiority, which is why I have used the word intussusception: to receive within. What is it that we receive? The ambient real." *S 12/11/51 (Labo)* This ambient real from which he is inseparable, is the research field of the human-as-researcher. We are, each of us, our very own exterior, our own ambient real, anthropologically interiorised and particularised. Passively or actively, we are under "the propelling power of mimism." *Labo 08/12/37*

Mimism means the anthropos and the cosmos coinciding, I and the universe cohering, spontaneously and instinctively or deliberately and intelligently. Joussean research is autoethnographic as it uses the researcher's life experience to understand the experience of self, of an entire group and ultimately of humanity. *The rhythmic and mnemotechnical oral style among the verbo-motors*, Jousse's first and exemplary scientific study, thus has as its point of departure his own experience of the living orality of his Sarthois childhood, analysed and enlarged, through his primary and secondary research, from its ethnic base to the status of anthropological phenomenon.

## *Lecture 2 On the anthropology of mimism*

This lecture summarizes Jousse's teachings of the first part of the year 1931. In this series of lectures on the theme *Geste in ethnic psychology and in pedagogic psychology*, Jousse outlines his anthropology of mimism.

In the regrettable absence of any film recording children's gestuality in all its complexity and in its seamless continuity, Jousse records the awakening of mimism in a child, drawing on a few mimismic gestes that show just how basic and inherent mimism is to the human being. Children are his main research subject because—at least before they are being socialized, algebrized and algebrozed—they embody the spontaneous human being, mirroring their environment without distortion.

Learning through mimism, which is immediate learning by miming gestures, is too soon followed by alphabetization and writing, which is algebrism or socially mediated learning. The movement away from mimismic play to the alphabet is not an isolated matter concerning only individuals: it is a matter of choice of civilization. We, algebrozed people, went to civilize spontaneous, concrete, mimismic people. It is time for us to go and learn from them what is the human's natural expression and the human's natural relationship with his environment. This is why, to do research, in rhythm e.g., one needs to go out of our algebrozed civilization to meet spontaneous peoples in whom rhythmicity is still alive. Research should be done both in the ethnic laboratory and in the artificial laboratory, but in the ethnic laboratory first, in order to get the basics right.

*Lecture 3 On the pedagogy of mimism*

The pedagogy of mimism emanates from the law of mimism: the human should operate according to the law of the universe and the human child should be allowed to operate accordingly, this is to say, in the nature of things. Left to his spontaneity, the child will be in tune with the universe, and as the universe is in incessant movement, the child too will be in movement, and that child is then indeed a *perpetuum mobile*. The child is energy, in the strongest original sense of the term: a force in action, in flow—in *rhythmos*. We are, all of us, rhythm, living-being rhythm, biological rhythm, rhythm that is at once regular and supple.

The child is a natural born mimer, a natural born rhythmer: the child intussuscepts—takes in and makes it his own—and expresses all that is impressed in him. And here arises the major difficulty: society canalises, and often paralyses this natural, incessant rhythmic expression, resulting in a stifling process, exacerbated by writing and by the book, which mediate at best, and alienate at worst, from the real. So it is that many, indeed most children study without learning, their gestes atrophied and thus also the expression of their mimemes, and thus also their memory. In pathological cases, there is no longer any replay possible as the geste has been terminally arrested in algebrosis. In contrast, peoples who have remained spontaneous still have the capacity to *dance* the real and through these *dances*—more accurately *rhythmo-mimisms*—and through their *animism*—more accurately *pangestualism*—the whole universe can manifest in play which the anthropos can replay. Jousse pleads with society for an education that will *form* individuals instead of *de-forming* them by dis-individualizing them through verbigeration. Mimismic pedagogy, a pedagogy not of words but of life.

*Lecture 4 On algebrosis*

What happens to children individually happens to whole societies and even a whole civilization: mimism turns into algebrosis and algebrosis is the death knell of a civilization. Nothing illustrates this more potently than what happens in the algebrozing process of our main tool of communication, language.

When a people is shocked out of its language, and this language is phonetically, grammatically and semantically broken up, and indeed smashed, by military, political and religious conquest, this language no longer voices the self of its speakers. The process is one of dissociation of the human being from his own real. Such language, in the very mouths of its indigenous speakers, now *mouths* not their own real, but foreign cultural practices, beliefs and values. This is how the metaphors—by which a people live—die, and their comparisons no longer compare and test words against reality. Human expression then no longer leads to communication, but to vain verbiage divorced from the real. This is what happens when artificial bourgeois city society replaces natural paysan life.

This lecture should be read with its context in mind: in 1942, France is occupied. How could this have been allowed to happen? To Jousse, because age-old established and proven values were betrayed from within. In the early part of the twentieth century, France abandoned *paysanism* for *citadinism*—the land for the city—and *mimage* for *language*—the immediate person to person communication for the mediated word written—abandoned its intrinsic traditional values, just as Gaul had done in the early first century. Jousse premonition in February 1940 of the consequences of such abandonment was to become reality barely four months later:

> We are now in 1940, and have no idea of what is going to happen. If for example Hitler invades us—not something I am looking forward to—a state as monstrous as the Roman Empire will come into being. The Roman Empire has been the bloody mushroom that pushed its way throughout the world and was so successful that we today proudly proclaim ourselves Greco-Latins. We should not put too much blame on those who came to crush us, seeing that we were only too happy and proud even to have been defeated two thousand years ago. Read the research done on the subject, read Camille Jullian's eight volumes, and you will see that the Gauls did what some of us did when they wired at once their congratulations too Hitler at the time of Munich. The telegrams had arrived and France had not even been invaded yet. If Hitler moves to Paris in 1940, people in their numbers everywhere will hoist their swastikas, start German schools and name it the Germano-French movement. If there are still French left, that is! I am hammering the point, because our present circumstances are ideal for us to understand what an anthropological and ethnological mechanism means. Great empires arose this way and great empires also fell apart. Empires do not last. The French people may well disappear, just as the Gallic people disappeared. *HE 13/02/40*

*Lectures 5 to 7 On the worldview of mimism*

These lectures expand on three fundamentals of the worldview of mimism: the human conscientizes an unconscious universe; this humanized and conscientized universe is an interconnected universe; and in this universe, the visible and the invisible too interconnect.

## Lecture 5 On the hominizing geste. Mimism and metaphor

The whole universe is one mass of juxtaposed and interlinked actions: the universe is analogical and interactional. Within this cosmos, the anthropos is acted upon and reacts, ceaselessly. The cosmos' action is unconscious, the anthropos' reaction potentially conscious. Analogy is juxta-position, metaphor trans-position. If "Man is an animal that makes comparisons" *S 14/01/32*—and in the present lecture Jousse calls comparison a *shy metaphor*—then Man changes an analogical universe into a metaphorical universe: intelligent Man intervenes in the juxtaposed universe, and operates a change from (analogical) position to (metaphorical) re-position. In the process of mimism, the anthropos intussuscepts, intelligizes, conducts—such is his path to mastery of himself, of the other, of the cosmos. The human being has the capacity to change a passive acceptance of an analogical cosmos by actively recombining the elements of the cosmos and so changing the original formula. An unconscious cosmic interaction becomes a conscious anthropological proposition. The juxtaposed flux of the unconscious interactional cosmos has become conscious, intelligized, propositional.

The anthropos-anthropos relationship mirrors the cosmos-anthropos relationship. No bodies of impressions in any two human beings are equal. Each unique particular is a unique particular set of mimismic intussusceptions, called mimemes. How then is communication possible between anthropoi? If mimism renders us mutually impenetrable, it also offers the means by which the difficulty can be overcome, through analogy.

The first stage of the mimismic process is intussusception, which is not a passive reception but an adjustment of the external real to my internal real. Similarly, a human being can adjust his particular real to the real of the other: I can adjust my propositional gestes to his propositional gestes, I can, ultimately, and ideally, adjust to the point of becoming the other. The better I mime the thing I intussuscept, the closer I get to the *original*, to the *source;* the greater my rapport and rapprochement with it—the better I understand it. Understanding is identifying with. The less my real is action, and the more it becomes geste, the more my cosmos is hominized. The more it is transported, i.e., metaphorized from the cosmos into the anthropos—metaphor = transport—the more I move from the biological to the anthropological sphere. The exterior becomes the interior. I become the thing that I see.

## LECTURE 6 ON AN INTERCONNECTED UNIVERSE. MIMISM AND COMPARISON

Through the human's mimismic capacity, the juxtaposed (analogical) flux of the cosmos becomes an interposed (metaphorical) solidness that can be acted upon. An unconscious interactional fluid cosmos has become a conscious formulaic propositional anthropos.

"Man's stroke of genius was to have become clearly aware of the mimeme that spontaneously welled up in his moulded musculature. This mimeme is indeed nothing but the reverberation of the characteristic or transitory geste of the object in the human compound." *EA 06/03/33* "Intelligence is the awareness of mimism. I am intelligent when something has taken form in me and I become aware that it is taken form in me: I am the kitten that crunches the mouse. I feel myself playing this in myself despite myself." *Labo 06/02/35* "True knowledge is to be the thing and to see the thing, to be yourself and to see yourself. And there, in this sequence of gestes that we make either unconsciously or consciously, we notice that we are able to distinguish, if not to parcel, this unfolding of things. Let's replay in us the interactions of the universe and we will—see or feel—we will mime the sun parching the plant, the plant absorbing water, water moisten the soil, the soil shaping in undulating hills. And so on and on and we will find ourselves taken up in this immense interactional play, and if we let ourselves go the entire universe will come into play in us in an incessant dance of Shiva signifying, dare I say, Man's comprehension of the world.

"Geste at once stabilizes and represents the movement. Gestual mimismic language is the very language of the spontaneous human being and of the human in the fullness of his living richness and in the fullness of his living truth. Unfortunately, we entered the study of language with our predetermined idea of what human language should be. Language however did not call on our present-day ignorance before taking form on human lips. Language shaped itself. Our task is to examine how things happened anthropologically and to avoid restricting them, *a posteriori*, to the confines of our narrow and limited knowledge. If we view the passing world in its three-phase gestuality, we will discover human science and human memory and human logic." *EA 06/03/33* "Which is why, when we compare our perception and understanding of expression with those of these concrete civilizations, we find ourselves metaphorically still in the primary grades." *EA 14/03/38*

> When you come across someone who truly engages the real, when the supple plasticity of his play allows you to trace back to the original play the very thing he is replaying, you yourself, through his intercession, come in contact with what he is tracing in his play. This explains why those gestual languages, those gestual mimemes are concrete, this is to say, modeling the real. From the moment you tear away from the real, languages evolve at a formidable speed and change from century to century. Our present semantic evolution is astonishingly fast. Words can take on improbable meanings simply because they are no longer the mimismic replay of the characteristic thing. We are in the domain of convention and arbitrariness. If, on the contrary, we were to 'mime' a particular animal, if we had to mime the geste he does, if we had to mime the geste the object makes on which the acting one acts, we would find ourselves incapable of changing this interaction, we would be unable to equivocate, because we would be bonded with the real and the real would be bonded in us.
>
> All mimers are objective before the real: that is what we come to understand here and it is of crucial importance. If we accept that science, that knowledge is an *adequatio mentis et rei*—the correspondence of mind and thing, of the known thing and the knowing object—then we must conclude that it is at this stage of human expression, the stage of mimismic "language" or gestual manual-corporeal expression, that this adage was verified and realized.
>
> What is an object? A geste. What is my knowledge of this object? It is the geste redone as exactly as possible without change, without slant, without atrophy. The ideal would be for you to be able to recognize the object when it is in me. That is the true science, the true *adequatio mentis et rei*. All peoples that are at that stage are peoples for whom the exterior world exists. They have noticed and they know all the gestes of the things, and it is disconcerting to hear Professor Lévy-Bruhl talk of pre-logical mentality: "Look, they have no abstract ideas." Abstract ideas? Abstract ideas that consist of talking about anything without saying anything, without any knowledge of anything? Heaven guard us against that sort of abstract idea! These people do not have words to say "tree" in general. Why do you think they should care about the tree in general, seeing that a "tree in general" does not exist in reality? There is *this* tree that is an

oak tree, or a pine tree, or a maple tree. They will not tell you "the animal that munches the tree," but they will tell you: "This animal, or the squirrel" chews in this particular squirrels' way of chewing such tree, such conifer, this type of maple, which is mimed in the characteristic geste of the extension of its branches or the shape of its leaf. I have no need for that sort of vague idea you want to portray to me as superior knowledge of the real. You call this generalization, I rather call it vague and inconsistent distortion. *EA 13/03/33*

## Lecture 7 On ethnic liturgies

This lecture deals with mimism and the invisible, and turns the tables around as to who is civilized and who is not. What is civilization? Marcel Jousse's anthropology of mimism responds to a question of Charles Darwin and to Darwin's suggested answers.

From Charles Darwin, *The Voyage of the Beagle* (1839), chapter 11, paragraph 5:

> They are excellent mimics: as often as we coughed or yawned, or made any odd motion, they immediately imitated us. Some of our party began to squint and look awry; but one of the young Fuegians (whose whole face was painted black, excepting a white band across his eyes) succeeded in making far more hideous grimaces. They could repeat with perfect correctness each word in any sentence we addressed them, and they remembered such words for some time. Yet we Europeans all know how difficult it is to distinguish apart the foreign sounds in a foreign language. Which of us for instance, could follow an American Indian through a sentence of more than three words? All savages appear to possess, to an uncommon degree, this power of mimicry. I was told, almost in the same words, of the same ludicrous habit among the Caffres; the Australians, likewise, have long been notorious for being able to imitate and describe the gait of any man, so that he may be recognized. How can this faculty be explained? Is it a consequence of the more practiced habits of perception and keener senses, common to all men in a savage state, as compared with those long civilized?[1]

From Marcel Jousse, lecture at the School of Anthropology, 23 January 1933:

1. Charles Darwin, *The Voyage of the Beagle*, National Geographic Adventure Classics (Washington, DC: National Geographic Society, 2004) 183.

When problems are not put in their proper perspective, ev-erything becomes fundamentally skewed. When preparing for this lecture, I decided to put in parallel the so-called primitive civilizations and our own civilization that I call dissociated and algebrized, and suffering constantly from these dissociations and algebrizations, from these permanent contradictions. As is often the case, the very same individuals who launch campaigns for the preservation of the humanities in our schools, are also those who are the first to protest when one tries to instill life into teaching techniques and other education related fields. Let us just for once be clear about things! If the humanities are so precious, so formative and so educational, is it because they are dead, bookish humanities, and just good enough to let one pass exams? Or should they enhance life by adding life, something only life can do? One cannot breathe life into dead words on a page. This forever stiff skeleton needs to be resuscitated, its desiccated and mummified muscles need to be brought to life and play by confronting them with living beings. That is what anthropology is about: these peoples, when studied through the latest methods of dynamic anthropology, can provide us with laws capable of solving the huge problems posed at every turn by our own dissociated and dissociating ethnic milieu.

# The Methodology of Mimism

## *Marcel Jousse on His Scientific Itinerary*

### Outline

Introduction: *Homo faber*, the most
intelligent being of the creation

*Conception and elaboration*

Childhood

*My mother's cantilenas*

*The cantilenas of the old women*

*The children's mimismic play*

Early studies

*Lessons memorized through song*

*Prompting the initial word, and balancing*

*Meeting the mummy*

Classical studies

*On Homeric and biblical formulas*

*On Greek roots and algebra*

*On Champollion's grammar*

## Confirmation

Reading

*The tripartite plan*

*Physiology*

Conversations with . . .

*Psychology, ethnography*

*Colonial officers*

*Explorers*

*Missionaries*

Travels to . . .

*The Amerindians from the reserves*

*Selected informants*

*Indian reserves*

## Publication

Interviews with . . .

*Delacroix*

*Père de Grandmaison*

*Père Descoqs*

Immediate responses from . . .

*Medical doctors*

*Psychologists*

*Old biblical scholars*

Eight years later . . .

*Psychiatrists and anthropologists*

*Educationists*

*The young biblical scholars*

## Conclusion: Joining academic disciplines

# Lecture

# On scientific discovery

*L'Invention scientifique* S 01/02/34

## Introduction

*Homo faber,* the most intelligent being of the creation

The Human is the most intelligent of all living beings as he alone is truly a maker of tools.

As I pointed out in my previous lecture, the human being had for a very long time an obsessive pre-occupation with the making of tools to grasp and understand the real. Even before he seized the first stone to use it as a weapon, we saw him modelling, within himself, his tools for action, by creating this extraordinary thing that we might call the invisible energetic tool.

We also saw the progressive development of tools, from the tool mounted in the musculature of the human body to the construction of a multitude of admirable machines that record Man's words and gestures, such as the phonograph, the cinematograph and the full range of currently used laboratory tools.

In the light of this, I thought that it would be interesting, if not to you then at least to me, to do a kind of retrospective of what this research into the invention and discovery of tools for the mastery of *the real* could mean to the researcher himself.

Fellow researchers have asked me quite often: "But how did you arrive at this synthesis of the anthropology of geste and rhythm?" Now, to detail in public all the ins and outs of the steps necessary to develop something that holds together would be quite a task, but it might be interesting nevertheless to set out what someone in no way out of the ordinary managed to achieve simply by dint of observation.

What I would like to show then, in this lecture, is how someone with perhaps just some sharper gift of observation was able to discover what others had not yet found. I want to describe to you the three phases of the development of my investigation into the psychology of geste and rhythm.

They are:

- The elaboration of the research tools, and we will see that this development is an unconscious process. We so often tell ourselves, after the fact: "I remember clearly that I noticed this or that." Mostly however, proper awareness comes only later. This intussusception of things is therefore unconscious.

- The verification of the soundness of the living research tools.

- The presentation of these tools so that others can adjust them to their individual use.


## Elaboration

In this first phase of this process, we will examine successively:

- early childhood

- first studies

- classical studies


### *Early childhood*

I agree with Napoleon that this phase starts long before the birth of the child. Napoleon, who knew all about people, said: "A child is formed in his mother twenty years before his birth."

I have often told you here that I owe any contribution that I have made to my mother. It is truly thanks to the linguistic, I might say experimental training my mother gave me, that I am able to contribute anything new.

As soon I was I born, cantilenas were sung over my cradle.


#### My mother's cantilenas

My mother had an extraordinary memory. Being orphan, she was brought up by her totally illiterate grandmother who taught her the whole repertoire of ancient cantilenas of the Sarthe region. As she taught these to my mother orally, my mother never saw these cantilenas in any written form. I came to consciousness amid the rocking motions of these cantilenas, and up to this day, whenever I let myself go, it is those first rocking movements that I experience all over again within myself.

It is amazing how those very first experiences of rhythm influence an entire life. I certainly owe my hypersensitivity to the whole question of rhythm, to this training that happened even before the awakening of my consciousness. Those songs that rocked me then, indubitably informed the entire infinitesimally minute system that constitutes my receptive fibres. Lamartine, you may know, said that, often, when he fell asleep, he was rocked by the rhythm of the recitation of lines of verse.

I have felt this sensation of rocking almost all of the time, and even now, as I speak to you, I still experience this sensation. My sentences balance, in spite of me. I do not claim to speak well, the stenography rolls recorded here make that clear enough, alas, but what I do know is that, in the end, my sentences always balance correctly, because since earliest childhood I have been used to this *rocking* of a sentence that ends well. My mother was extremely demanding on the point that a sentence should be phrased impeccably, right to its end.

The stenographers who work in the Chamber of Deputies are quite critical about the performance of the various extemporizers within the Chamber. It appears that those who finish their sentences are a very rare breed. It is always easy to start a sentence, but extremely difficult to finish it, unless one has, since earliest infancy, become used to balance one's sentences. There is a kind of first movement, a kind of first easy balancing to start off with, but it is very difficult to follow through and to finish the sentence with the same quality of balance as at the beginning. It is for this reason that I believe in the importance of balanced rhythm for the formation of the child's powers of expression. We do not pay sufficient attention to this.

When one studies the rhythmic schemas of Homer, one realizes very quickly that each is made of two balancings. This is equally obvious in Palestinian oral style and in something even more complex: in the elaboration of the rhetorical period by the professional Greek speechwriters. One always senses a consciousness, a concern for the balance of each statement, because the Greek period was conceived for oral delivery. These orators did nothing more than develop, in an overly bookish fashion perhaps, this balanced utterance. The beautiful Greek rhetorical period, the truly beautiful oratory period is simply nothing more than a permanent perfect balancing.

A sentence that does not balance, not only hinders one's breathing, as Flaubert said, it hinders the whole organism. A man speaks with the most conviction when he is able to seize his audience and rock them, as a mother rocks her child.

We, human beings, are most sensitive to sweetness, softness and at the same time to the pattern and the balance in human utterances.

Let us not forget that we are first physiological beings. Yes, we are psychological as well, but, essentially, we are balancing and undulating physiological beings.

This is, I believe, the source of the sensation of rhythmed balancing in me. I may fail to put it properly into practice, but what is imperfect is of my doing, while what is perfect comes, I am convinced, from this rocking throughout my childhood.

As I grew older, and maybe because I had become accustomed to this perpetual melody—I say melody because I do not like music much—I realized that I was raised, as it were, by melody. People often tell me: "You must like music very much." In fact, I like music as I like algebra, but melody is infinitely more to my taste, in much the same way that I have a greater affinity for concrete language.

Which brings me to what has always been my greatest problem: how did we arrive at this algebrization of human thought? Where did we begin and how have we journeyed in order to impoverish human thought to the point of saying: "or x." Now, x what? That was the great problem that challenged me when I was twenty and to which I will come back to this later.

Throughout my childhood, however, I did not pose myself so many questions. I learned from what happened around me.

## THE CANTILENAS OF THE OLD WOMEN

I was then five or six years old when my mother took me to an evening gathering. This gathering of peasants, nearly all of whom were illiterate, took place on a farm near Beaumont-sur-Sarthe. Much of the work that I have subsequently undertaken definitely came about because I have had personal contact with illiterate peasants. In psychology, we have erred principally because we have looked only at lettered people. As a result, we have created a psychology of lettered people and we created mental faculties that mirror our own. That this is a serious mistake becomes all too clear when one reads the works of Lévy-Bruhl: his concept of *prelogicality* is a lettered person's one-eyed perspective.

We will always tend to regard as inferior people who are not yet *algebrized* as we are. Can one truly say that to be concrete is inferior? Quite the opposite in my view. Understand how contact with illiterate and intelligent peasants could awaken the interest of a child who has only just begun to learn to read after having memorised a good deal.

I started to go to pre-primary school when I was four years and a few months old. At that time, I could not read, but I already knew a great many things by heart that I had learned through psalmody and melody. You will find evidence of this in my pedagogic system. True psychology, like true anthropology, consists of nothing more than developing oneself—in a more organized form perhaps than in ordinary life, but knowing and developing oneself is essentially what constitutes psychology.

These evening gatherings of the peasants generally took place during winter. They came together to eat chestnuts *with sweet cider* as the song goes, and as the peasants got more and more into the swing of things, they would get up and chant psalmodies. Formed by the cantilenas of my mother, I could feel the deep rhythmization of all these peasants. Theirs was not so much chant or song as a kind of melodic singsong. At that time, they all knew large numbers of these melodic singsongs, which they no longer know these days because they go to school, but at that early time, practically the only people who had formal instruction were the most prominent farmers.

The people, or more specifically, the women, who knew the greatest number of those balanced recitations were the old grandmothers. They were extremely interesting to observe, because they were very concerned with accuracy. Thus when someone began to intone one of these chants and dared to introduce a variation, one or other of the old ladies (and I can once more see good old mother Guespin in her corner) would reprimand the reciter and say: "It's not that word, but this!."

We find this concern for accuracy in the oral tradition everywhere. When I read the fine works of Mr Henri Basset on the literature of the Berbers, I underlined in each chapter this tendency of the old women to demand word-for-word accuracy: "That is not how it is recited."

Clearly, this demand for accuracy in the tradition was most striking, but what was also amazing was the sum of things learned. Memory! We no longer have any idea of its capabilities! When I simply strung together like beads the series of texts that make up my first study on *The rhythmic and mnemotechical oral style among the verbo-motors*, the philologists cried out: "But, it is absolutely impossible that human memory should have such powers." This they claimed because they themselves were totally deprived of memory, having lived in milieus totally deprived of memory.

This is an example of how a person's training can dictate their reaction to something new. We should not assume that we judge on the basis of facts, we judge on the basis of who and what we are.

It is thus, in our own image and likeness, that we have created the sciences of psychology and pedagogy, with catastrophic results. Only when it reflects the experience *of all human beings* will we be able to create a true educational psychology. Our present experience is extremely narrow seeing that it goes no further than ourselves. Had we all been raised in milieus more open to memory, scientific problems would have been very differently posed.

The fact is that these people, these philologists, have from the very beginning lived only with the printed word. They have gone from their schoolbooks to this or that somewhat larger book, from matriculation to bachelor›s degree or doctorate. How could they have the slightest notion of what the training and formation of the human memory means, having had no personal experience of it themselves?

Our education has been designed and formulated by people who hail from this exclusively bookish formation and training, or, if they were not so trained, they dare not admit it. Indeed, it is striking how in our society people feel somehow ashamed to say that they have lived in an illiterate milieu.

How wrong! Illiterates can be formidably intelligent. It is among them that I acquired my taste for observing the real. When I was very little, I used to go for walks with these peasants whom I have loved so much—and whom I revisit regularly in order to keep a check on my experimental method—I marveled even then at their practical knowledge. It goes without saying that they could not decline *rosa*, rose, but they could identify different types of wheat, corn, barley and oats, and they knew the various kinds of good and harmful herbs. They referred to them using the sorts of picturesque names that we, in our bookish civilization, use in poems. This is life as it is lived in close contact with soil, sap, wind and sky. This is what constitutes the genuine education of the living concrete individual, in contact with actual objects.

Never forget that a child's interest is gripped much more by the name of a plant that he can see than by a word that is written on a piece of paper and that does not correspond to anything living.

I still remember those flowers we called *tall morning-glory*, a kind of volubilis that closed at night and opened in the morning—a little rural drama all of its own. When in my lectures you hear me cite this or that example as coming from nature, I am indebted to these illiterate peasants. They accustomed me to be wary of the fine speeches of those who speak brilliantly about everything, but who know nothing. Peasants smile quietly to themselves in the presence of fine talkers of this ilk. Beware: these people are extremely perceptive.

What I have just told you, I will tell you again, with reference to people called *primitives* and *savages*—those great Indians of the Americas who re-gard us with cold contempt. They allowed themselves to be fatally crushed in the United States, there being, unfortunately, no other recourse! If only it could be understood how rich, these people, in physical sensations and intussusceptions of actual things! Alas, we always chose to ignore this. We judge people by the thickness of the books they have written, when they should be understood based on the quantity of real that they have grasped. Because people who have genuinely discovered something, have nearly always done so because they have put their books aside in order to deal with reality itself. I will reiterate, and repeatedly, that my first scientific training was my contact with the peasants of Beaumont-sur-Sarthe.

### THE CHILDREN'S MIMISMIC PLAY

Something that struck me just as forcefully was to see how children play at everything: I still have all those children's games in my muscles. I was haunted by the question: Why do children play at everything? They are given ink, a pen, an alphabet, and yet these children drop, the alphabet, and the written page, in order to go and play at all sorts of things—like little savages.

I have ever seen, all along, children consistently trying to escape all our bookish constraints in order to play at everything. Do not be surprised then when I state:

*In the beginning was the rhythmo-mimismic gesture.*

Indeed, in the beginning, that is all I have ever seen.

Pedagogues I met all told me: "But you are right! This is the kind of method to truly educate and form a child." It is all this that unfolded in me. All my explanations here are a mere commentary on my intussusceptions as a child, which I went subsequently to verify the world over. Unfortunately, whatever pleasure I took in listening to my mother singing her cantilenas, I would unavoidably end up doing what everyone else did: to learn to write, and to learn to read books.

### *Early studies*

What struck me was the contrast between how lessons were taught inside the classroom, and how children behaved outside the classroom. Made, inside, to learn our lessons in total silence, once outside, all my little playmates and I learned our lessons in a far livelier way! I can still hear and I still have in my ears and muscles, those balancing psalmodies of us young pupils learning our lessons! Why, I ask you, does a child left to himself go completely counter to the method he is taught by inside the classroom? At school, the child is made to learn in silence. He is not allowed to talk. "In class one should hear a pin drop." Yet, that self-same child, schooled to silence, once out of the room, rhythmically psalmodizes his lessons into memory. This strange fact has always intrigued me, and continues to do so.

We will need to return to this matter. Why indeed force the child to learn his lesson in a whisper when you are going to require him to repeat it aloud? That, in my view, shows an ignorance of basic psychology. It is not unlike trying to learn to play the piano on an instrument that produces no sound. It has struck me very forcibly that children *instinctively* memorize their lessons by chanting them out aloud.

## Prompting the first word

Another detail that similarly struck me, one that I mention in all my writings, is the start of a feeling, a sensing, of the *propositional geste* as a whole. When one of us had to recite, but had not learned his lesson very well, a little friend sitting behind with his book open would prompt the initial word of the sentence or line of verse:

> *Oui, je viens dans son temple adorer l'Éternel . . .*

Silence. Then, one heard the "Holy Spirit" prompt discreetly:
"*Je viens . . .*" and the recitation would pick up again:

> Je viens *selon l'usage antique et solennel. . .*

> [Yes, I come to worship God here in his shrine /following our
> old and solemn custom . . .]

And so it went on . . . This law of facilitation is so effective that a number of ethnic milieus put it to regular use. As I had occasion to show you before, the main proof we have that the Prologue of John originates from a Semitic, oral, rather than a Greek, written, milieu, are those famous *link-words* or *clamp-words* that facilitate the recitation:

> *In principio erat* Verbum *In the beginning was the* Word

> *Et* verbum erat apud Deum *and the* Word was *with* God

> *Et* Deus erat Verbum *and* God *was the* Word

It is the very same *prompting* technique by which one breathes to oneself the initial word of each succeeding phrase.

As you see, the child knows spontaneously, instinctively, how to use prompting.

So then, why not use it as an aid to memorization in the composition of the texts children are meant to learn? This is not happening for one only reason: those writing the learning materials are ignorant of the real laws of human psychology. As things stand, children are punished and sent to the corner when the real culprits are mostly the teachers.

This apparently insignificant act of prompting is proof of a basic mimismic creed, to wit that a proposition is set off from the start. Not the word, but the phrase is the yardstick, so much so that when the start is given, one goes automatically to the end, often not any further, admittedly, but the sentence as a whole is a given.

## The balancing

This practice of prompting goes with another practice that equally struck me, one that at the time I did not understand either, but registered all the same. Children, I noticed, always sway to keep their recitation going. It is most curious. I remember how, in a class on galvanoplasty, one of my comrades, a charming fellow, but lazy as a sloth, recited his lesson, balancing the proposition rhythmically: "The galvano, the galvano, the galvanoplasty, the galvano, the galvano, the galvanoplasty . . ." That is as far as he got. He had been telling himself: "If I can get the balancing to start, it will go on to the end." It did not, but he had at least the principle right.

That is how the child learns. Observe how he sways. Equally, observe the Jews at the ancient walls of the Temple of Jerusalem, still balancing their famous laments! Go and observe how one recites the Koran, everywhere: balanced and psalmodied. People often say of public speakers: "They look like performing bears." This is because they strive to shape their phrases whilst simultaneously *balancing their muscles*.

I go through life an interested spectator: I watch, I observe. The laws of physiology are at play all the time. We obviously do not realize this, since we are all subject to those same laws! After all, this is only to be expected: the inmates of the same prison eventually cease to see one another.

To the child that I was, all of this remained in an inchoate state, so to speak. What professor Ombredane recorded in his third volume of the new *Treatise of Psychology* of Dr Dumas, are my childhood experiences and feelings as a four to ten years old.

## Meeting the mummy

A great event took place in my life during that period, an event I have already briefly alluded to. I fell in love with an Egyptian mummy. This was, so to speak, my first and only love, even to this day. I have loved, and continue to love, with a deep abiding love, an Egyptian mummy. Here is how this love-at-first-sight hit me.

On Thursdays, my mother used to go to Le Mans, and when I had been very good, she would take me with her. As I was keen to know everything, she took me to the museum, to see the mummy about which the schoolmaster had told us. If you are in Le Mans, go to the Préfecture museum, and there you will see my beloved. You enter a large room, then another to the left, and there, in a large, rather curious box, is an Egyptian priestess, immobile, serene, neatly embalmed. I stayed there, rooted to the spot, and I said to maman: "Go do your shopping and leave me here, you can pick me up later." I stood there for two hours maybe, motionless in front of this small dead face, and small desiccated body, with her two hands crossed on her chest. The sight had an extraordinary effect on me, because there were small rigid drawings that formed a sort of miniature procession all around the sarcophagus. An idea came into my mind that was to haunt me subsequently, and continues to haunt me: all these little drawings painted all around, had they once been alive, like that little priestess lying there all embalmed? Were they not all alive once, those frozen characters, as in the games children play? Was there not, going on all around this stiff embalmed figure, a complex game involving people who gestured as children do?

This association haunted me: what we had there were signs that were dead, but that had once been alive, just as that little priestess was dead, but had once lived. I have been truly haunted by that. The outcome of that meeting is obvious: if I am here, it is because of my beloved, that small Egyptian mummy.

### Classical studies

Then came the time when I was made to do what all truly good people do: I went to high school and was plunged in conjugations, declensions and all that comes with it, as you know.

### THE GREEK ROOTS

I had the good fortune to be taught by extremely intelligent teachers, who made me start learning Greek through a little book that I still have on my table: Maunoury's *Petite anthologie ou recueil de fables, descriptions, épigrammes, pensées, contenant les racines de la langue grecque* [Short anthology or collection of fables, descriptions, epigrams, thoughts, comprising the roots of the Greek language]. My teachers, truly remarkable men, told me:

"A person knows Greek well only if he has learned it through its roots. It is therefore necessary to learn the roots first." So I learned Greek through its roots.

At one stage, I said to myself: "How strange! These Greek roots always look like vocal gestures of a sort. For each sound there is a meaning: *to grasp*, *to scratch*, or *push*, etc., exactly like those little gestures, or drawings, that I saw around the mummy's sarcophagus."

Might not the association of those little *drawings* also apply to *words*? What I was dimly groping after, without being able to work it out, was the important principle we will explore later, that language is in the first place mimage. When projected, language is mimo-drama; taken down as spoken, language is phono-gram.

Two ideas began to fuse in me, unwittingly and their fusion lead to the first two stages of expression that I teach at present at the *École d'Anthropologie*. There is first the stage *of manual-corporeal style,* which is living expressive geste or mimodrama that projects itself in mimismic silhouettes. Given stable form on a surface, mimodramas results in mimo-grams, or drawings. In the second stage, these gestes become oral, laryngo-buccal roots, that develop into means of interactive communication. That is the stage of *oral style*. Both these stages of concrete expression end in a process of algebrization, in *written style*.

I could not see that far ahead though, at the time. I merely sensed that there was something profound going on that I would have to work at and get to know. Once I had become accustomed to the Greek roots, I was made to learn Homer by heart. That was entirely sensible, since I believe the only good way of familiarizing oneself with a language is to learn texts in that language by heart.

## ALGEBRA

At the time I came into contact with Greek roots, I started studying algebra. How different the concretism of those Greek roots, which were *gestes*— movements—and this algebra, which did not mean anything at all anymore and functioned merely as formulation for its own sake. In algebra, one used letters that could mean anything one wanted them to mean.

A problem was taking shape in me which, later, when I was twenty years old, I thought of publishing as an essay *From concretism to algebriza-tion*, the first thesis subject that came to my lips, so to speak. My exposé here is no more than a continuation of this title. What I am dealing with is the shift from mimismic geste to algebra, a problem we might broach together, fifteen or twenty years hence: How do human beings arrive at all these algebraic formulations that are so disconcerting to our imaginations?

People who tried to review Einstein's works ended up writing absurdities, because they tried to render as concretism something that is essentially algebrism.

It is this shift from the one phase to the other that is so interesting. Children however should not be prematurely forced into the algebraic phase. They should be allowed to explore the phase of concretism for as long as possible.

## On Homeric and biblical formulas

What does the child learn when he is with his mother? Not words, for, as I told you, his mother speaks to him in short and concrete sentences: "Bring me the watch," "Keep still, sit down, lie down, leave me alone." The word, per se, is in no way spontaneous, but the sentence is. One expresses oneself in brief complete units of sense, in short sentences, what I later called *propositional gestes*.

That came as another revelation me. I felt that we come across formulations that are always the same. This confirmed what I had heard on the lips of my mother. When I heard her sing the cantilenas of the Sarthe, nearly identical same formulas were repeated time and again.

This feeling, this experience, of the formulaic unit of sense, which I later called the formula or *cliché*, I *first* felt in the cantilenas of the Sarthe. I felt it later in the Gospels. When I was still a child, I was extremely intrigued by the person who is my lifelong study: Jesus of Nazareth. Not, curiously, as God. What interested me in Jesus was the man, and not in the shape of those garish sculptures painted in red, blue, and green with their twisted poses. I was never in the slightest interested in those things. No, what drew me to Jesus of Nazareth, was what he brought about, as recited by my mother.

Every evening, my mother sang, psalmodied to me, a parable. She knew her Gospel wholly by heart. Here again, you will find her influence on my studies and research. I still sense her dear voice, not in my ears, but in my mouth, and because of this sensibility, the repeated incidence of formulas struck me: formulas in the recitations of the cantilenas, formulas in the recitations of the Gospels, and in the compositions of Homer, formulas.

Still a child, I would ask a teacher who knew Hebrew well: "What language did Jesus speak?" He told me: "I'm not exactly sure. In the seminary, they told us he spoke Greek, perhaps even Latin. Others, however, say it was perhaps Syro-Chaldaic. I know that one finds it in the Targum." Because of my eagerness to learn, he said to me: "If you like we can work at this together." Thus it was that I began then and there to scan the formulas of the Canticle of Job (if one can call it a canticle) and to study the Aramaic Targum. I have gone on doing so to this day. Had I been killed in the 1914 war, one would have found one of those Aramaic Targum in my pocket. I have persisted in this in an attempt to have the actual language of Jesus in my mouth. Jesus of Nazareth has always been my true scientific obsession.

Through all those recitations I came to feel that there was something similar to the holophrastic compositions of Homer, that all those original reciters of the Old and New Testaments had expressed themselves in formulas, and that, further, there was something in these recitations which resembled the recitations of the old Sarthe grandmothers. That is how there developed in me, bit by bit, what has become the *Oral Style* which an entire young generation is presently studying.

## On rhythmed compositions

When I was required to write compositions in Latin, the sense of rhythm guided me to the extent that, instead of writing my Latin verse lines on Sunday, I took the subject on Saturday with me to the four o'clock study period, in my mouth, not in my head, and not in my eyes (as I don't see anything in my mind's eye), and then, in the evening, before going to sleep, I would rhyme thirty, forty, fifty Latin verse-lines that I composed spontaneously in my mouth. All that practice and experience has developed an extremely pronounced sense of rhythm in me, so much so that I can recite Greek and Latin verses in a rhythmo-melodic form only. To read Virgil or Homer without putting it to a dactylic melody is insufferable to me.

It is much the same for French rhythm. I remember having submitted several French compositions, and even a philosophical dissertation—in verse! I wrote and write the verses very easily, because they dictate themselves in me, in my rhythming throat. Which is why my class mates called me *Virgil* because verse poured, so to speak, spontaneously from my throat.

I was then not at all surprised, later, to find that certain ethnic milieus, like the Palestinians, situated the center of life in the throat, in the *néfèsh* (that we call the soul), and not in the head, but always in the throat which is to them the site of psychological condensation, as it were.

## On the grammar of Champollion

It was at that time during the holidays that I tried to procure a book we had been told about: Champollion's grammar. One could say that my love for the Egyptian mommy compelled me to read this book that a teacher managed to find for me. I must admit that I did not understand it all then, although there was one particular term that I found most revealing: *the mimismic characters.*

If you have some day the chance to page through this Egyptian grammar—an admirably printed book, by the way—you will see how this term strikes one throughout. This *mimismic character* was waiting obediently there, so to speak, in an embryonic state, waiting to be fitted into the complete explanatory system I was to develop later as *mimism.*

## Verification

The material for my system was ready to hand. All that remained was to put it in order. From that time on, I have felt that I needed to parcel my life's work. I have always been preoccupied with one idea only: *mimism* and its algebrization.

So, between the ages of fifteen and twenty, I gradually distinguished the three phases of human expression, namely corporeal-manual style, oral style and written style—with algebra following on. From that point onwards, all my studies have converged on the issue of *the styles of human expression*: I have included therein all the operations of the savants, the *mimismic characters* of my Egyptian mummy, the mimograms (that I did not yet call mimograms) and the oral style in which I put all the recitations of my mother, all the Gospels of my mother, all the cantilenas of the old grand-mothers and of the Sarthe peasants. Later on, I had to tackle algebra and all that is associated with the mechanics of human communication.

## *Readings*

At this point, I set myself to read. My reading was organized in accordance with those three phases. I never write. I have not a single note. No one should entertain the notion, at some future date, of ordering my notes. I never take down references, but my fingers remember.

When I need to find a text—let us say that I need to find a passage, I know that I will find it at such-or-such a place on the page—and oddly, it is my hands that find the page. My memory resides in my fingers. All four walls of my room are covered with books. Yet, any night I can locate the book I need, and the passage I am looking for.

I carry it all inside me. I do not take notes. The great difficulty in constructing any new understanding lies precisely in the fact that one is overwhelmed by notes. You know yourselves how the abundance of notes crushes you, once you turn. How does one get these notes at the ready?

Simple! Bring them to life in yourself! They will link up by themselves. On a walk, on horseback when I was an officer, or later on foot, ideas often joined up quite unexpectedly, *because they were alive in me.* One discovers things not by dint of filing-cards, but by living gestes. It is the same when I speak. I could not speak from cards, but my plan is there, all the same, wholly organized.

I have lived my whole life on that basis. My life is sectioned like those big steel bridges. From the moment I am faced with a book, my reading falls into these divisions that are alive in me. Not only did it give me a very powerful memory, it also organized all my observations and reading.

*Verification* by reading began from the moment that my research plan was established. I chose to study *physiology*, in the hope that it would explain to me all the laws of mimism, and *psychology*, which would give me the intellectual grounding to this mimism, as it were.

It was thus that I came in contact with Pierre Janet's *Psychology of behaviour* and with Bergson's *Schème moteur.* By way of *verification,* it is clear that I owe the most to these two men.

Readings on ethnography provided me with all I needed to assemble the various phases of manual, oral, and written expression. I stored all this away inside me, not higgledy-piggledy, but in accordance with my tripartite plan, and the parts eventually illuminated one another.

*Conversations with . . .*

My reading helped me better to understand my conversations with colonial officers. I belonged to the artillery and many of these officers had been either among the Arabs, or among the Malagasy, or in some or other manual-style or oral-style civilization. I greatly profited from these conversations.

I also met with a number of explorers from central Africa who shared with me their interactions with populations that were most interesting from the oral tradition point of view. Missionaries too, although they did not know the underlying laws, provided me with facts about manual style and oral style.

*Travels to . . .*

At this point, when all was complete in me, I was sent on a military assignment to the United States, and there I was able to gather documents of primary significance and worth from among the Amerindians. I came face to face with the manual style in all its splendour. Only in this civilization could manual style be studied in the full richness of its expression. It is there that living human expression should be studied, and studied now, for it is fast disappearing.

My method, as you see, is similar to that used by Rousselot in experimental phonetics: do not digress, do not wander; to succeed, concentrate on a few representative individuals. This I did when I went to the reserves where I had the opportunity to meet, and concentrate on a few individuals who allowed for in-depth study. Later I made contact with some Indian chiefs who made themselves available and who gave me access to some of the reserves where I could see for myself all that was left still of this language of gestes which is so little known, and of their mimographic writing.

In this way I was able to observe the *living* connection that exists between the mimismic gestes of the ancient Egyptians, the Chinese, the Sumerians, and the Amerindians.

## Publication

When all this monumental work had been completed, in 1923, I needed to present it as a book.

*Interviews with . . .*

It was then that I went to see Professor Delacroix who has been an intellectual father to me and who told me: "Your ideas are very interesting, but very novel. I think it would be useful for you to prime your milieu so that they understand you."

At that point I also met Father Grandmaison and Father Descoqs, director of the *Revue de Philosophie*. That is how I published in the *Archives de Philosophie* in 1924, a study, really no more than an outline of my work, a study made of quotations loaned from the principal books that I have read on the question. In all, I had read some five thousand works.

I have selected from the authors that I read, sentences, or parts of sentences that coincided *with my discovery of the real*. In the reading of the book, you will clearly detect my underlying plan expressed, for the most part, in the words of other people. No-one can claim: "It is not true." The references are all there.

### Immediate responses from . . .

Today I no longer need to use this method to be accepted and understood. All I have to do is to make contact with those people who are predisposed to continue with my research. The medical doctors have understood me best. Dr Morlaâs has been one of the first to link this whole question of the mimismic geste to apraxia. After him came Dr Ombredane with links between the mimismic geste and aphasia. Later, a great many younger people investigated the oral-style tradition in their doctoral theses.

### Eight years later . . .

In the beginning, obviously, it people were shocked when I studied *Rabbi Ieshua of Nazareth* in an ethnographic and anthropological form. Everyone was so used to talk of him from a purely religious point of view. Currently however, the focus is entirely on the oral-style approach. A glance at the latest studies by younger researchers on this question will show you that the whole question is being revisited from this life-restoring angle.

## Conclusion: Joining various disciplines

Can you see what my method has been at heart? I have simply put into relief all that I have learned from my birth until the age of eight. That is all I ever do. What I am doing here is no more than explain to you my childhood experiences.

In today's lecture, I have simply illustrated the final sentence of our teaching program signed by Dr Morlaâs: *The aim of the anthropological studies of Marcel Jousse is to search for a link between the disciplines of psychology, ethnology and pedagogy.*

As you can see, my life is very simple. It is turned towards one goal only, *the study of life* as it manifests itself through mimism. Mimism that is dominated by thought, for not only is Man a maker of tools, but from these tools, he fashions living and durable thought. Of such thought, you will be the master builders through a pedagogy of life.

# The Anthropology of Mimism

## *Marcel Jousse on His First Year of Lectures on the Anthropology of Mimism*

## Outline

### Introduction: the biological film and its substitution

[*To compensate for the absence of a biological film, of a "movie" on movement in the human's life and education, Jousse gathers a number of facts proving the importance of movement in the development of the human child and in human societies.*]

### Mimism in the child

The awakening of mimism in the child

From mimismic play to the alphabet

From concretism to algebrism

From mimismic play to the alphabet

From concretism to algebrism

[*Three instances that illustrate how in our society child development and education move from concrete to algebraic expression, from mimism to algebrism*].

## Ethnic laboratory and artificial laboratory

### *Rhythmism*

[*Scientific research done, first, on concrete, or mimismic and on abstractive or algebraic expression in the ethnic laboratory, from life, and, second, in the artificial laboratory, through instruments. Both forms of research into rhythmo-mimism validate each other.*]

Amerindian rhythm, Bulgarian rhythm, medieval rhythm: o*bservation in the ethnic laboratory*

The rhythm of energetic explosions: o*bservation in the instrumental laboratory*

### *Mimism or the mimismic play*

Mimism of spontaneous people

Algebrozed and rhythmo-mimismic dance

The interactional geste: *all mimismic expression is three-phase interactional*

### *Concretism (evolution of rhythmo-mimismic or concrete expression)*

Mimographism

Phonomimism

Phonographism

The oral style

The written style

## Conclusion: lessons to be learned from spontaneous peoples

In education and life, and need to record fast as we are wiping out this heritage. This can only be achieved through collaboration.

## Lecture

## An outline of the psychology of geste

*Esquisse de la psychologie du geste S 03/12/31*

Being a student of Pierre Janet, I have, in last year's lectures, tried to apply to the study of geste the psychological, objective and adaptive method of my master. At the start of this year, again following his example, I would like to give you an overview of what we have covered thus far.

We have, above all, studied the child with the aim of observing how gestes are mounted in this small human compound that appeared before us as a whole. We found that this child revealed itself to us, almost at once, as a prolific, manifold gesticulator.

### The biological film and its substitution

I suggested at the time the following experiment: let us take a motor-camera to record on film this little gesticulator in order for us to analyze afterwards, at will and in slow motion, the complexity of his movements. Imagine how instructive a filmed document would be for anthropology, of a human being recorded from his first sigh to his last breath. Research in child psychology has yet to make sufficient use of cinema. I think this is wrong and I will try to remedy the absence of such *biographical film*, if I can call it so, by bringing together and organizing methodically the largest possible number of partial and scattered observations. This dotted line of stepping-stones should enable us to follow the unreeling of the child's spontaneous gesticulation. Failing this, it just flits by, soon to be forgotten.

### The awakening of mimism in the child

If we were to observe a child day by day, week by week, month by month, we would see how he develops, from all points of view, but especially from the point of view of geste. At the very early stage, we see how he tries hard to focus—with his eyes first, but soon his head too takes part in this primary action and the child begins to receive, instinctively, the gestes imposed on him by the features of the face that bends over him. The child smiles when he sees his mother smile. No need to tell him

*Begin to know your mother with a smile, little boy!*

No such command is necessary, for the smile plays out all by itself.

Later on, the child begins to express, which is to play out, to mime, not only the face of its mother but also her other gestes and those of anyone around. Within a few years, the child has become a consummate mimer.

What we are witnessing is an anthropological phenomenon of extraordinary importance and one that needs extensive study: the child's play, the metamorphosis of the child, through geste, in everything the child has seen. The child becomes the dog he sees running, becomes the bird he sees flying, becomes the mouse he sees scampering about, becomes the tree he sees spreading out. The child becomes the whole universe! He is this scary mimer, this tease I described to you last year. Lurking in a corner of the lounge, on the lookout for the tics of the people present, he will replay these tics before our wondering and surprised eyes, the very next day, with disconcerting accuracy. Why does he do that? He does this because he is gifted with the mimism that is inherent in human nature. Remove mimism and you remove the education of the child, his curiosity and his willingness to be taught. This is why I quoted at the time Aristotle to you:

> Man is the greatest mimer of all animals
> and it is through mimism that he acquires his earliest
> knowledge.

## From mimismic play to the alphabet

The child, then, is a living being keen to grasp everything, a being who, to express himself, makes use of all the concrete expressions that he draws from the surrounding real. Then, alas, arrives the social milieu that gets a hold on him, paralyzes him by tearing him away from his play. From now on, he will no longer be catching the countless expressions of the real through his congenital mimism and draw on it to his advantage. The expressions of the real are henceforth kept in check, hardened and frozen, and the child is made to squat before his alphabet. That was the subject of my first lecture, last year: *Concrete expression and algebraic expression in language and education.*

In that lecture, we observed the child, the child viewing all things in the light of life: *life* on the outside and *life* on the inside; the child *dancing* for the simple reason that all things move; everything dancing without him and, above all, dancing within him. It is this many-tentacled child that we plonk before a page of writing and, slowly, bit by bit, his curiosity about things ebbs away, his curiosity of all gestes of things moving whittles. For years to come the child is dumped before an algebra, for it is a fearsome algebra, this alphabet of ours. All too often I receive calls from distraught mothers of so-called deficient children, mothers who tell me: "It is impossible to teach this child to read . . . it is impossible to teach this child numbers."

I told you last year how a number of educators understood the process of alteration. They first put before the child three pieces of fruit—three apples, let us say. That was concrete reality indeed. The child then calculated on its fingers the number of apples. From this simple point of departure, the teacher proceeded to turn this concrete thing into an algorithm, which gave us:

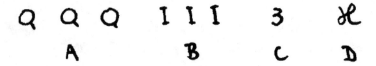

Many children will be able to go from A to B who will not be able to go to stage C.

Then, putting the numeracy question aside, the exercise wades into extreme alteration by taking any random number and assigning to it any random, purely conventional value, saying: "Let . . . be x." From A to x, there are quite a number of stages that will leave behind quite a number of children.

### From concretism to algebrism

This is a major law we are dealing with here: the passage from concretism to algebrism.

Ethnology tells us that algebra appeared very late among thinking people. Man indeed has great trouble to extricate himself from the concrete. The concrete is in any case always abs-tracted—taken out from—the intelligized concrete real in order to become a solely functional symbol.

All our efforts should aim at elevating our children from the concrete stage wherein we find them to the algebrized stage of our present civilization and science. However, how do we go about this? If we look around us, objectively, we have to ask ourselves: how can we possibly observe the *spontaneous* nature of any individual of our society when they have from their infancy been wrenched from their spontaneity and desiccated in an algebra that is no doubt useful and necessary for a particular type of research, but that is extremely impoverishing for the study of global concrete psychology?

That was my first lecture and it is at this point that the choice of laboratory arises.

## Ethnic laboratory and artificial laboratory

In my second lecture last year, I said that we have two types of laboratory at our disposal: the artificial laboratory and the ethnic, the scientifically used ethnic laboratory. Here is how this applies to the study of rhythm, by way of example.

### Rhythmism

It is quite a challenge, in the study of rhythm—of the various types of rhythm—to deal with people who have been a-rhythmic for twenty, thirty, forty, fifty years. Indeed, the rhythmicity that was no doubt potentially present at the beginning, was stunted in its development and wilted into inexistence.

Reading quite recently a study on musical rhythm, I couldn't but wonder at how superficially rhythmic phenomena are analyzed presently. The reason is simple: to the people dealing with rhythm, rhythm is not something vital, it is nothing but an add-on, something superimposed, something seen on a printed page, with musical notations that in no way correspond to the spontaneous rhythmicity that we can find elsewhere.

I told you how much I admire laboratory work. My master Rousselot used laboratory work to great profit and I am convinced that the study of rhythm will only progress when subjected to thorough investigation in a laboratory by means of recording apparatus.

However, in our environment, the choice of subjects can become a matter of contestation: where do we find them? I proposed last year that we take our research into rhythm into other civilizations, to civilizations where rhythmicity, and therefore dance, is the people's daily bread. Explorers and ethnologists unfailingly mention in their records how in these societies, dance and rhythmic chant accompany work, rest, marches: how rhythmicity is everywhere, all the time.

Unfortunately, those ethnologists who crossed over into such civilizations and who became well aware of the importance of rhythm, had no training in rhythmicity. This is why their records leave us with a quick translation here and some quick approximate notation of melody there, with no regard for the minutiae of rhythmic variation in the particular ethnic language concerned. We sense, when reading these reports, that an immense

research field lays open before us, and one that needs to be harvested immediately because our invasive civilization penetrates everywhere and levels
everything. The ethnologist Paul Rivet told me just two months ago: "We
need to speed up our ethnographic research because in fifty years' time, the
entire world will be dressed in cap and coat."

There is no doubt that all these living, spontaneous manifestations
of rhythm are disappearing fast. I based my methodology on those ethnic
milieus that are much more spontaneous than we are (they are spontaneous, not primitive, not savage). No sooner have we established true contact
with these people—having learned to speak their language or at least having
become comfortable with them—and we realize that we are dealing with
very subtle beings who have at times a very refined sense of this matters of
rhythm. The feeling for beauty is universal and the esthetic of these dances
and dancers has not eluded those so-called savage people.

### Amerindian rhythm

Princess ZitKala-Sha I remember telling me—I was with a Sioux tribe in the
United States then: "You cannot perceive us as anything but savages, you,
Europeans, given the way you study us." What I propose and what is needed,
is an insider method. Instead of judging those peoples from our point of
view, we need to try to understand them on their terms.

### Bulgarian rhythm

This ethnic laboratory method is yet a quasi-unexplored treasure chest.
Admittedly, there appears from time to time an objective study on rhythm,
such as, recently, Mr. Youseff's Sorbonne University thesis on the rhythm
of popular Bulgarian chant. Students in rhythm will find this study all the
more interesting for being undertaken by a native researcher, himself a Bulgarian, who mixed with the singers of his milieu. Thus his sense of sense of
even the most curious rhythms of these so-called popular Bulgarian songs
predated his research into their peculiarities.

Paul Valéry shaped our own sense of the aesthetic. Now, I very much
like Paul Valéry, but Paul Valéry does not have a monopoly on beauty. There
is, in these spontaneous milieus, a s beauty that is much more concrete, I
would say, a beauty much closer to life. A thesis as that of Mr. Youseff is
a godsend to us, and one that will be of great help for us to understand
such beauty. Here we have a young researcher trained in up-to-date research

methods who analyses, within himself, what others of his milieu enact spontaneously, without analysis.

## MEDIEVAL RHYTHM

Wouldn't it be interesting if we could equally grasp from within, our own famous medieval authors of epics, those authors who rhythmed spontaneously in octosyllables, balancing with a tendency to march in rhythmic steps from eight to eight syllables? As things stand, we will only be able to reconstruct those rhythms second hand, from dead texts, and even then, only after having for years analyzed proper living rhythms. Although those dead texts will be given a second breath, new life and spontaneity, by the very fact of having been processed through the conscious organism of the researcher.

The range of problems I raise here arise from my wish and will to study the expression of life from life itself.

So far then our ethnic laboratory and its subjects.

## THE RHYTHM OF ENERGETIC EXPLOSIONS

What about the artificial laboratory apparatus that we will point at these people?

Our tools will reveal to us the great law of life, or, better put, of the beat of life.

Let us examine a repeated geste. Let us ask any one human being to articulate in the recording machine the syllable PA—PA—PA—PA—PA—PA—PA, specifying that this syllable be articulated with the same intensity. No rendering of this syllable will have the exact same intensity. After any two or three syllables, there will be some sort of explosion, and, where the person thought he articulated each syllable with equal intensity, we will find that, in fact, an energetic explosion occurred on some syllables. It is that, the beat of life: energetic rhythm.

As any living being, Man is an accumulator of energy, an energy that sets off at biologically equivalent intervals. Not mathematically equal, mind you: rhythm is not the repeat of a biological phenomenon at equivalent intervals—there will never be mathematically equal intervals in life. The recording apparatus will show us equivalence, not equality. Therefore, someone who explodes in a particular rhythm will have this rhythm explode in a variety of sub-rhythms in accordance with the size of the specific member of the body involved in the explosion. Thus, the rhythmic explosion of a person walking is not the same as the rhythmic explosion of someone snapping his fingers, blinking an eye, or speaking.

What we have here are multiple interpenetrated gestures, but gestures that will tend to superimpose one upon the other, in fact, to add up. This is why children who balance while they recite also tend to stomp on the floor, in time with the explosion of the intensive syllable on their lips. Just yesterday I asked children to recite in anapestic rhythm the following sentence—it concerns the Gauls who, it is said *loved combat and beautiful words*—"Ils aimaient les combats et les belles paroles."

I noticed how a child rhythmed as follows:

v v—v v—v v—v v—v

Ils aimaient les combats et les belles paroles

*They loved combat and beautiful words*

and his whole body danced in tune with his mouth.

Children have not yet acquired the puerile and respectable civility that we set as the norm of our civilization. It is therefore in the child that we will be able to grasp this energetic explosion of life. It is this explosion that will thrust forward each of his gestes. It is this thrust that gives rhythm to each of his gesticulations.

### The mimismic play

This *mimismic* gesticulation will progressively take over the whole of the spontaneous being. Children's mimismic gestes are countless. Left to their gushing spontaneity, children observe the things that surround them and allow these things to mould them. Ask a child to tell you what he has seen. He will not just tell you, he will make a play of it and mime all that he has seen: "Yes there was a large horse (geste) and the soldier jumped on the horse (geste) and the horse went off galloping (geste) and then, a large man, with his walking stick (geste again) hit the dog (mimismic geste) . . ." This mimismic gesticulation is most interesting, and were we to follow it through, we would find out what true mimism was like, before being congealed by our social pettinesses.

Our children, unfortunately, are soon deprived of the right to mime. They are told: "Keep quiet, do not mock people in this way, it is very naughty" and slowly the child's mimism dies off, and the child becomes someone very good, very proper, with eyes lowered and gestures none. In our civilization, a child is perfect only insofar as he is immobile and fossilized.

What an odd notion of what an ideal child should be! How odd this pedagogics of death! This small living, moving, dancing subject is turned into an impeccably marmoreal object: a statue. O ye pedagogues! Look at a well-run class: it resembles the lecture hall I have before me here. I admire you all here because you are grown-ups, but if you were six, five, four years old, I wouldn't admire you, I would pity you . . . What I would expect from you is for you to be as impossibly full of life and bounce then, as you are now well-behaved and perfectly immobile.

What I would expect from five-year olds would be that little boy sitting behind that little girl and pulling the bow in her plaits some four or five times, at least. I would expect, when two people left a few moments ago, all those little heads to turn to see what is going on. Movement, you see, is so much more interesting than immobility. I hold with that great expression of the Jews in the desert: "Make us Gods who walk before us." Children want things living and moving—and what is the first thing *you* do? You immobilize them and immobilize yourselves.

However, our teachers may indeed be very well-behaved, and it might not be considered very pedagogic these days to make gestures, we remain unable to kill our desire for movement: we go out to listen to public speakers, to see dancers, to hear people speak with their whole body at the cinema. I just read that there are, worldwide, some fifty million people who, every night, sit down to watch films. Why would this be? Simply because the immobile things that we could find in books are less interesting than films that replay gestes. Who among us here knew *Ben Hur* before they saw the film? Even now, what we want is things that move and do.

In a few years' time, the book might well be the film. Through the film, the demand for moving, dancing, gesticulating literature will inexorably increase. What is it that we ask from the book—I fine topic I propose for this year's lecture progam . . .—what we ask from the book is things that *suggest* . . .

O, suggestion, dear Father Bremond, suggestion! Is that not what we ask from your so cherished literature? That it suggests, that it makes us see. As some literature professor is bound to expectorate: "Look at this sentence! How it makes the thing visible." What happens, obviously, is quite simply that there is, underlying this particular sentence printed in algebraic characters, a power that has us act and react, that has us see and hear and play out the *suggested* thing. Such is the compelling need for movement still alive in us!

## Mimism of spontaneous people

Whereas our conventions kill our inherent need for spontaneity, other peoples have made of this instinctive spontaneous gesticulation their traditional expression. In the Amerindian tribes, you will find people communicating through bodily dancing mimic gesticulation alone. We studied last year this language of gestes that reproduces each of the essential gestures of animals, plants, waterways, clouds, and indeed all things that Man intussuscepts and plays out. The mimismic faculty is such that two beings who never met before are able to understand each other solely through the boundless mimismic gestual fluidity of their body. Were it possible to have a human being fluid and flexible as an amoeba, we would see this man liquefy and, as Valéry has it, turn amazingly hard and incomparably supple. Spontaneous people grasp, reproduce, and concretely mime, in all their subtlety, every one of the finest gestures of nature, those very gestures we do no longer even notice.

Dictionaries are being drawn up to record the mimismic expressions still practiced among the Amerindians, in Australia and also, derived from a very old substratum, in a now polished form, in the dances of Java, the Malabar coast, the prophets of Israel . . . As for Greece, I refer you to Lucian's dialogue on dance.

## Algebrozed dance and rhythmo-mimics

Such *mimismic dance* appears to us as much exaggerated in its expression, because we have become accustomed to a sort of *promenade à deux* under a chandelier. We should not call those subtle expressive mimismic gesticulations *dances* in our sense of the term. We need to call them *rhythmo-mimics* or *global recitations of great traditional gestes*. For indeed, in this kind of gestual poems, all the gods parade before us. Research has begun on this and none too soon, for within half a century all these marvels will have disappeared.

## Interactional mimism

Now, if mimism truly is the doing of thinking people, then research cannot be satisfied with juxtaposing gestes and records that, however fine-tuned, consist of nothing but unconnected scraps of information. What we need to realize, and I made you aware of this last year, is that we are dealing with people who have a systemic grasp of the real through observation and replay of the fundamental cosmic formula: *an acting one—acting on—an acted upon.* As I told you then, this means, for example, that an old man is mimed as *one who totters*, and so we have the concrete formulaic figure of *a tottering one—ticking off—a sucking one*: an old man ticks off a child.

A host of gestes translate the verb *ticking off*, depending of what precise action is meant. The richness of such gestual expression comes as a surprise to us, because we have to rely on the reduced *oral* expression (*langu*-age) of this *gestual* expression.

The most important consideration for us is that such gestual expression is truly intelligent: it is a proposition, and it is thought, this *tottering one ticking of the sucking one*. Such propositional geste is the primary tool of all human science.

## Concretism

Every action of the universe needs to be formulaically intussuscepted and replayed as *an acting one—acting upon—an acted on*: the squirrel climbs the tree (all this finely played out), the horse eats this or that specific grass (I insist on: *this or that* specific *grass*). These people were deemed to be incapable of abstraction. The fact is rather that they have no interest or use for our notion of the *general*. What does interest them is the concrete, mimismic, gestual form of this particular plant having this particular form, color, curve; this particular pointed way of projecting itself in the air. Every detail was observed and taken note of. The world was but an immense drama intussuscepted by *the miming one* and rendered by him in beauty and intelligence.

That is the lesson these ethnic spontaneous milieus teach us and it is that that we need urgently to record on film. Urgently, because tribes disappear every year, and with each of them disappears a world of marvelous expressive mimismic expressions.

At this point, we are able to understand the true power of the geste when this geste is traditionally developed, when it is truly rendered by a human being who makes of his geste a tool of logic, of demonstration and of beauty too, for the aesthetic is never absent from intelligent life.

### MIMO-GRAPHISM

The question now arises: what kind of writing for peoples who express their thoughts gestually? The answer is simple: look at the shadow thrown on the blackboard here, on the wall; one only needs to seize upon the gesticulator's characteristic geste at the precise moment of the expression and to draw it on the wall of the cave or on the plane surface of the bark of a tree. Every single creature then, gesticulated by the mimer, can project itself in a characteristic form, and we have writing, called pictograms and hieroglyphs. They should rather be called mimograms, for what is truly recorded is not the *idea* of a bird being written, but the characteristic geste of the bird being projected. The man who turned himself gestually into a bird is rendered by the bird. There is no metaphysical confusion here, the like of: "I have the idea of a bird, and because I have the idea of a bird I am drawing a bird." No, nothing of the sort: what is projected is the geste itself.

Mimography, when properly developed, is able to reproduce just about any and every interaction. No doubt however that the challenge will always remain of how to project statically something that is moving and dynamic.

## Phono-mimism

During global gestual mimismic replay, the human tends to simultaneously replay the characteristic sound of the thing that is being replayed. This is another aspect of mimism: phonomimism.

A sound heard by the ears is replayed spontaneously by our lips. This is why children reproduce quasi-unwittingly the sounds they hear on their mother's lips. This is how transmission of language happens before the age of reason. A child does not know the sound has to be reproduced. Quite simply, the child hears the sound and it echoes on his lips, just as happens when he finely traces the thing by his mimismic geste. If the thing mimicked has a sound, this sound too will be mimicked simultaneously, and we have an onomatopoeia of sorts. If the thing makes no sound, a sound may be reproduced that is analogical to the geste. When the geste is hard, harsh, a corresponding hard, harsh vocal emission will accompany the effort suggested by the global gesticulation.

The phonation of sounded mimicry needs to be studied in those peoples who still have the sensation of miming *vocally* the things they mime *bodily*. Thanks to the talking film, wholly unexpected work could be undertaken. What seemed to be an artistic endeavor may be put to good scientific use.

As soon as sound develops as a facilitating tool, mimismic geste falls by the wayside. As and when civilizations develop, the global, the corporeal geste trails off and sound takes over. We will come across this law again in the mimogram.

## Phono-graphism

The notion of an ox was first expressed by miming an ox's horns. For a fish, the fish was mimed with its scales and its particularities. When sound arrived, what was mimed corporeally was now vocally pronounced and sound replaced manual mimicry. Thus, for example, the sound A L P H would designate an ox. Research by a Chicago professor shows the ancient mimographic characters, as well as their pronunciation and development up to our time. Through graphic evolution and graphic inversion, this figuration of the ox became our present A, the original having turned half-circle, and we had, first ∀ and then ⊅ and ultimately A.

What precisely our alphabet owes mimography warrants further research as and when we come into contact with those civilizations that still use mimography as writing.

## Oral style

When human expression moves to the laryngo-buccal muscles, our manual style will be replicated and become oral style. Oral style too balances and obeys the same laws as manual style.

From a pedagogical point of view, we need to find out how these physiological laws can be of use in our context. First, we note that oral style is always sung, that it is always naturally melodic. Then, listening to these spontaneous people, we notice that the balancing of their body keeps the propositional gestes in equilibrium, creating a kind of binary, at times ternary verse-line, a form of dance.

I remember a Sioux dance in the United States. One felt how the balancing of the melody and the balancing of the words fell in line with the balancing of the whole body. This accords with Monsieur Youseff's thesis where he states: "In order to study the rhythm of the popular Bulgarian chant, we need to know the dance that dictates this rhythm." If we are mindful of this globalism, we will be able to feel the origin of what has become our own poetry.

All these oral literatures are rhythmed literatures. At the beginning of all civilizations "dance, music and poetry went together," we are told. This is so because at the time, the spontaneous human being as a whole exteriorized his traditional intussusceptions.

The children of such milieus who learn the traditions from their parents receive them in the manner they had been handed down, which is, wholly, globally. I refer you to the fine studies of Milman Parry who researched this question and who has shown how this improvisation happened through formulas transmitted to professional rhythmers. This explains why Homer has been the historian, the theologian, the savant of his time.

## WRITTEN STYLE

When it became necessary to transmit this global oral style to civilizations that no longer made use of this rhythmo-melodic balancing, and when the "writing reed" made its appearance, gestual rhythmicity slowly dwindled away. There is ample proof of this evolution in the transition of our epics to the novel, of the songs of the aedes—the traditional Greek singers—to Herodotus, the first historian. I will deal with this question later this year. Rhythm is broken . . . we no longer need rhythm to sustain our gestes, we no longer need rhythm as an aid to memory, for memory is the sum of our gestes used for the ease of transmission.

# Conclusion: Lessons to be learned
## from spontaneous people

This oral-style pedagogical psychology then, in the end, raises the question: of what use can the linguistic and literary phenomena we have just discovered be to us in the short term, given that we no longer are in this era of dance, of rhythmo-melody, but in the era of writing and of the printed book? I intend to tackle this problem, and resolve it, this year.

What I believe is that literature could be given new life if studied from a new angle, which would be from the point of view of the psychology of geste. Monsieur Youseff's study is a methodology that could be broadened to include the examination of a number of problems of style. This is why I have given this year's lecture series the title: The psychology of geste and stylistic psychology.

I have here before me specialists in a considerable number of disciplines. I believe that we could investigate how my findings, as I presented them to you, might be applied in the fields of pedagogics, of psycho-pathology and of literature. We have the data, what needs to be done is to find a specialized application in each particular field of study, something that has already been done in outline in the research I mentioned, and already admirably achieved even by some of you who are here present.

# The Pedagogy of Mimism

## *Mimismic Pedagogy, a Pedagogy Not of Words But of Life*

### Outline

#### Introduction: the metaphysical vocabulary used in books on education

Soul

Thought

Ideas

Images

Imagination

Lies

The *idée-force* (the energetic idea)

### Intussusception of mimemes

Unconscious spontaneous intussusception

Conscious spontaneous intussusception

Attentive and interested intussusception

—verbalization of intussuscepted mimemes

—verbigeration of empty words . . .

## Conservation of mimemes

Unconscious replay of mimemes

Conscious replay of mimemes

Replay of remounted mimemes

## Controlled replay of mimemes

Speed

Justness

Suppleness

## Conclusion: a pedagogy of things, not of words

## Lecture

## Mimism and the memory of the child

*Le mimisme et la mémoire de l'enfant. EA 02/12/35*

## Introduction: The metaphysical vocabulary used in books on education

If you are as wickedly curious as I am, and read the books on education that are published every month, you may have noticed that every page seems studded with a host of words which, when I was younger and studying philosophy, I considered to be very sophisticated. Words such as *association of ideas—abstraction—memory—images -imagination—judgment* . . . and so many more of that ilk . . . When the child reaches high school, he finds himself faced with this fancy series of words and says to himself: 'Our teachers must know what all these extraordinary words mean.'

I remember that when I was studying philosophy, my greatest ambition was to understand the meaning of all these grand words. As I was already experimenting even then, I told myself, "Perhaps, if I could become a professor, occupy a chair, and talk about all these words to other people, perhaps I might discover their meaning."

Ladies and Gentlemen, all that ambitious pride of mine has come to this: I am now a professor, I have a professorial chair, but alas, I am compelled to confess to you that I do not yet know what all these words mean! . . . And what makes it worse is that the people who use them, know no better than I do, might know even less than I do, because they have never asked themselves the questions I have, and they have never made a study of these things, whereas I have spent a life-time trying to understand what all these words mean, and in particular the meaning of that very frequently used word: *memory*.

This is why I am focusing on this subject today, for it is particularly pertinent in the light of all that I have said thus far.

What is memory?

Methinks, it is only a word, in the same way that *association of ideas, abstraction, judgment* are just words . . . *Memory* is no more than a word. Why? Because when all is said and done, it amounts to absolutely nothing more than something that has never really been studied until now. Of all the philosophers, only one—and he was not even a philosopher—Fouillée, had an intuition about this. He wrote a book this intuition: the *Idée-force*—the energetic idea. At the time, that word made my day. I said to myself: Ah! The idea! At least I will know what it is that I am looking for. I am looking for a thing called *idea* just as the character Jérôme Patureau did when he sought a social condition, I will know what it is because an *idea* has *power* . . . There is an *idée-force*!

Sometime later I noticed that there actually is no substance to this thing, that the *idea* is actually nothing, and I even realized that we don't have *ideas* at all. Then, what about the e second member of the hyphenated word, this word *power*? I asked myself how it was possible that *ideas*—which do not exist—can have *power*. After many years of patient observation, I discovered that we humans were born with one capacity only: this great law of *mimism*, which we have studied in previous years.

We have in ourselves only mimemes. They are in us, how? Through this curious mechanism that we will now study:

   - through their reception and intussusception

   - through their registration and conservation

   - through their replay and ex-pression

## The intussusception of mimemes

You know that the aim of science has always been to simplify. What is not simple is generally not true. Those among you who have studied the history of the sciences, and, in particular, the history of astronomy, will remember how the whole mechanics proposed by the predecessors of Copernicus was improbable. There was talk about epicycles and eccentrics. There was an entire overwhelming terminology. Why? Because they thought: "The human is the greatest entity in the universe! Man is the center of the world; therefore, the rest of creation was designed with man in mind. So, we will have everything turning around Man." And the sun, the moon, the planets, the stars, were all made to rotate in a marvellous round dance, and the astronomers were satisfied seeing that they were at the heart of this sidereal operation. This system was overly complicated.

Now enters in this distinguished scientific fold a maverick, the kind of problematic character that turns up from time to time, and takes a devilish delight in telling the other savants that their words mean nothing. Disquieting, troublesome and odd, Copernicus appeared and said: "Would it not be rather amusing if, instead of epicycles and eccentrics, one was to declare the exact opposite . . . if, instead of putting the earth at the center, we were to place the sun at the center and have the earth move, walk around the sun like the other planets . . ." It set the cat nicely amongst the pigeons in the firmament of those whose own personal worlds centered on the famous words: *epicycles* and *eccentrics*!

When I suggested that our entire psychological terminology should go the way of the *epicycles* and the *eccentrics*, there was no comparable commotion, and consequently this whole convoluted terminology continues to be used for another twenty, thirty, fifty, for even a hundred years . . . it is terribly difficult to change the vocabulary of a social milieu. Note, by the way, that Copernicus's discovery has not changed our day-Today vocabulary in the slightest: the sun *rises*, the sun *sets* . . . It is so easy to think (or rather not to think) by using the same words that were used long before we came along. This is precisely what we find in our philosophical treatises: words are facile. Words make it possible for us to go on talking meaninglessly about

*abstraction, association of ideas, images, idées-forces, memory, judgment . . .*
And there are masses more where these came from.

Currently, however, we no longer have the right, neither scientifically nor anthropologically, to use this litany of words—which I now quietly erase from the blackboard, and which I wish I could erase as easily from all books that deal with the child. For, indeed, it is with those words that the child is carved up. When astronomers jump the track with their inert formulas, it has impact neither on the path of the moon, nor of the sun, nor of Jupiter, Mars or any of the other planets. But it makes a significant and serious difference when teachers place themselves in front of the child and tell us, or tell the child, which is more or less the same thing: "I will cultivate your memory, dear child, I will cultivate your imagination," when, in fact, these teachers do not want to cultivate the child's imagination, but his memory. Even if, as we will see later on, it is not altogether clear to me how *imagination* and *memory* differ, the fact remains such confused terminology perverts our young science of education.

Schools were created *made to measure*. Made to measure—the immeasurable. Please! With all your old nonsensical, meaningless vocabulary, are you really measuring your children? You do not look at your children. You look at their words, and with these words, you analyse your children's faculties. Those Faculties of Psychology!

None of that withstands rigorous examination.

### Unconscious spontaneous intussusception

We saw, last time we met, that a normal human being has eyes that open. When these eyes open on the reality of the world around them, they receive unknowingly and unwittingly—and I would say even unwillingly—the gestes of the ambient universe. There is no more to it than that.

What has actually happened in that process? It is possible for us to be entirely unaware of what is actually happening. Indeed, for many years, the child opens his eyes, or rather his eyes open for him, because he doesn't have to *will* them open. Eyes are made to be open (except during sleep) and they *open*—to the universe. Thus the child receives into him this entire ocular mechanism that we have studied in the previous lecture: this capacity to mimismic the movement of what it sees, to have the spontaneous irradiation of what it sees and makes its arms wave and its body move. The child does not *want* to play; the child does not *want* to amuse itself with this or that: it is what is inside the child that *wants to amuse itself in* him, that wants to play at something. What is that the child is moved by a mechanism that has been mounted in him. He does not play, he *is being played*, he *is being operated upon.*

We will see later on that this is still the case with us. Do you believe that the positions of my tongue are actually willed by me? If they were, I would not be able to express myself. Do you really believe that when I want to pronounce one or another syllable, I consciously place my tongue at the very end of my palate? This notwithstanding, I have trained myself, for twenty years—and perhaps longer—to engage these terrible things called audiences. In so doing, I have trained myself *to do what the child does* when the child receives impressions through his eyes—and therefore through his *ocular* mechanism, and therefore through irradiation into his *manual* mechanism, and therefore in his *corporeal* mechanism—I have trained myself to let all this operate in me, *without* my conscious control or knowledge. I feel inclined to say: I cannot *not* speak. He who has not integrated all these mechanisms at the level of the unconscious will never be able to speak. It has to be logical in me, it has to be regular in me, I have to aim at accuracy in my use of the French language.

What happens to the child is similar. The child is admirably played upon. A child's spontaneous play is so much more beautiful than the myriad little mechanical toys that we will be tossing down the chimneys at Christmas in a few weeks' time. His playing with his muscles will enthral him much more than any array of toys. To wit: the little children who receive overly expensive toys, will, more often than not, abandon these sophisticated toys and take their dad's walking stick and start *playing horse* with it, even though they might have just have been given a beautiful mechanical horse. This is because the mechanical horse does not allow the child the freedom or opportunity to play with his whole body. All these mimemes that are mounted in him need to play, but they cannot do so through the mechanisms of a mechanical horse! This is on a par with you wanting me to arrive here with beautifully pre-prepared and perfectly printed sentences, which I would simply operate like a mechanical horse! I, however, I am not a mechanical horse; I am a living horse and one that needs to express itself in full play.

What is needed in teaching is Life that arouses the lust for Life. However, wherever you look presently, people are busy creating inert, dead educational toys. I remember a pre-primary schoolteacher who once told me: "What you give us is not yet rounded off, completed and finalized. When are you eventually going to develop a method?"—But what is this thing called a *method*? It is like having little dominoes, and eventually having the kind of collection of little things that Madame Montessori has. Good grief! Is that what is going to be the result for the child! For heaven's sake, leave that kind of inert operation to the elderly who play cards and dominoes when they are ninety, but don't make your three to seven-year-old children play at cards, at lotto, at dominoes! Give them *real* things to play with! Yet, it is the former that one aspires to achieve. That is what we are invited to observe in the pre-schools when we are shown the educational revolution that has been taking place over the last ten years.

Let me frankly tell you that all these present-day gimmicks are worse even than what I was subjected to in my time. At least, in my time, there were no pretensions, whereas now there is the pretence that we are overhauling education! Overhauling it with what? To overhaul something, one has to be familiar with that thing's inner mechanisms. Not one educationalist has yet bothered to study anthropology, which is why I feel it is incumbent on me to press forcefully for anthropology to be included in education. I say: "You have no right to touch the child. What you are doing there is quite simply the very negation of the anthropos. You know neither what you are talking about nor what you are dealing with."

I know I am on the right path because I have observed, and done nothing but observe. What this observation reveals to me, in the intussusception of these ocular mimemes that irradiate as manual and corporeal mimemes, an *unconscious spontaneity*.

We underestimate the rich extent of our capacities. This is why Man is able to discover in himself, throughout his lifetime, things that were impressed into him at the age of two, of three, of four.

You have read of, or you have experienced, such instances yourself. Finding yourself in some spot, you thought you had never been in before, a replay begins: "It looks to me as if I recognize this corner of this field here. There was a little path there . . . it seems to me, but where? . . . Ah! There it is!" You were only two years old when your mother took you there, yet the mimeme was mounted in you. This becomes obvious when, during a lecture on the mechanics of childhood memories, your hand suddenly begins to tremble because, deep inside you, some forgotten memory stirs. You might not have been more than two years old, but that day, you tried to jump over a small ditch, the effort was too much for you, you fell and seeing that her little tot could no longer walk by himself, your mother carried you for miles on her back . . . "It's true! It was there, at that spot!"

Why do I remember this? I have no idea, but I know that when I need to recall something, the recollection that was *entered* and *interred* more than forty years ago, rises to the surface. It is there *in waiting*, waiting for the appropriate time. And there, from the depths of forty years ago, the geste replays. We are none of us any more than that. We are all no more than intussuscepted *gestes*, *mimemes*. Just as I will have seen the caretaker pass by a number of times during my lecture, my mimemes will be mounted in me, and at one or another time, my mechanism will replay.

We have deep within us the embedded and embodied potential from which the gestes well up, and it is this that makes us feel empowered, that makes us feel that we can achieve anything—as the Latin saying goes: *possunt quia posse videntur*—they are capable because they seem to be capable. That is precisely why it is necessary to have been spontaneously enriched with mimemes in the first place. That and no more than that.

I reject the entire current terminology because all boils down to the simple fact that *Man is a complexus of mimemes*. That is all the human is. True, these mimemes can be specified in a great many ways, but the bottom line is that mimemes are all we have and all that we are. We all know this all too well. On my way to this lecture, I caught myself looking somewhat anew at the numerous posters in Paris, and it struck me that all along the metro tunnels there are nothing but mimodramas. There is that small boy with his small pout standing in front of a hot chocolate drink (of some b rand or other, but I'm not here to publicize it, so it matters not). Tomorrow, in the hotel, if I'm hungry and I want a snack, the waiter will ask me: "Sir, which chocolate drink would you like?" Hell and damnation! The mimeme will play in me and I, the man who has trenchantly analysed the mimeme, I will be played as a child and I will say: "Give me a cup of Van . . . chocolate" or some such.

Would you like an aperitif before your meal? You are free, free as any French Citizen, absolutely free. "Men are born free and have equal rights" says the Declaration of the Rights of Man and of the Citizen . . . Here comes the waiter: "Which aperitif would you like?—Du beau, du bon, Dubonnet." Why? Precisely because one knows, without knowing, that man is a complexus of mimemes that are activated by dint of publicity and posters. Millions are spent—make no mistake, you are the one who's paying—millions are spent to *mount* in you mimemes of all the products that you will intussuscept via your throat. Not only in order to eat, but also to warm yourself, and for everything else: "We claim and proclaim that the Clamond blankets . . ." It is all there . . .

This is because it was noticed that man is constituted only of mimemes, and that mimemes replay willy-nilly. No one can afford to throw a million into marketing propaganda unless one is going to recuperate that million. That is a fact. If one wants to sell a book, it will have to be advertised, and better even, cinema and television will, so to speak, project in you the need to be like the novel's hero or heroine. That we advertise in this way indicates how well we know that Man is a complexus of mimemes . . .

If one truly had complete confidence in your essential intelligence, in your *idées-forces*, one would say: "But surely the human is intelligent enough to look for a cup of chocolate without help. If he needs an aperitif, surely he is adult enough to ask for any brand that would be *beau*, and *bon*, without it having to be *Dubonnet*."

Not at all. It is well known that none of us is sufficiently intelligent and strong-willed to resist the power of advertising: one is overwhelmed by a host of *unconsciously* intussuscepted mimemes. Which goes to show that adult Mankind is composed only of overgrown children, and that we know nothing about this mechanism embedded within us. How many things have sprouted from us, in the form of replayed intussusceptions, that were simply mounted in us by an opportune and providential glance! It was very rightly said that a life can be lost in the flash of an eye. Was it not Aristotle who said that one swallow does not make summer? This saying does not apply to anthropology. One swallow not only makes a summer, but can also cause whirlwinds and tornadoes! If you study each of the mechanisms of the child, you will notice that, often, even though the child has seen something only once, the impression is so embedded in the child that it cannot be erased by any means. It is mounted in the form of an unconscious mimeme, and the day will come when it will inevitably replay.

## The intussusception of spontaneous
## and conscious mimemes

I open my eyes. Since the beginning of this lecture, a host of things have been right in front of my eyes, yet without me having truly looked at them. However, when I concentrate my gaze and look properly, I see them as if for the first time. I am seeing those two hooks, for example. I suppose they have been there ever since I have been lecturing here, yet, this is the first time that I actually see them, or rather, that I notice them. I suppose that they were unconsciously in me because their appearance does not shock me.

That is usually the case. One looks vaguely without thinking about what one is looking at. One lets the mechanisms be mounted. One watches them play . . . I know, for instance, that there have been times when I have seen this or that person, but did not pay attention, or at least not *conscious* attention (we will later pay special attention to the power of this mechanism), but I have nonetheless been aware at some level of what was going on.

This plays an important role in pedagogy. The unconscious thing might play back in the future. What is most likely to happen is that the ocular geste, having been just normally focused on the outside geste, will replay this geste in us later. This is why we want before us children who know what it is about. They might perhaps not be very attentive, but they are there, they are not dreaming of other things. They do not replay different things, they merely *preserve* things, they merely undergo. That is something already. Our classes are ordinarily made up only of passive children who vaguely know that the teacher has spoken about something or other. They would often prefer to be elsewhere. However, at least, they are there, even though they are not paying any special attention.

### The attentive and interested intussusception of mimemes

Attention . . . Ah, there's one of those big words! Note that this is exactly the same mechanism we have already spoken of. We do not have *attention* on the one hand, and on the other *intelligence,* and then elsewhere *thought,* and still somewhere else *memory.* Not at all. *There is never anything other than mimemes.* Absolutely nothing else.

Take this sponge here. Now, I could have seen it without looking at it, looking at it without taking an interest in it and without drawing near to it; I could also use the only truly educational way of going about things, which is to become passionate about the mimeme that is being unconsciously intussuscepted, that becomes conscious of itself and that will ultimately become a child's spontaneous practice. Children need to learn about the world! What will happen if we give a child this sponge? He will do what we all do as apprentice-savants, or, more precisely, what we have *unlearned* to become *savant* . . . He will first look at it, but he will look at it not as at a sponge for which there is no use. No. He will become the sponge. He will as it were have grasped the shape of this object, he will grabble it, try to tear it apart—something I am not allowed to do here. He will do what we all do: he will want to find out what it tastes like. It is so tough . . . "Tough as a sponge" is the saying, but how do you know? Have you ever tried to bite a sponge? Your *sponge* is in the same league as a*ttention, intelligence, thought, memory, association of ideas.* If I were to ask, wickedly, that all those who have ever chewed a sponge put up their hands, there would probably not be even one! So it goes for everything we say in science, and yet, science demands experimentation.

Earlier on, I asked you: "Are you altogether sure that you have *associations of ideas?* That you have *memory?* Are you quite sure that you have *idées-forces?*" You could answer me now: "Oh, it is like a sponge, you know. I do not really care. I know that there is something in me. However, what it is . . .? I am quite happy to have been given words to express it, so I will not be looking any further." Yet, one could enrich oneself by everything that is. There are actually scientists who have spent their entire lifetime studying sponges. Moreover, there are quite a number of others who have spent their entire lifetime studying things that are worth even less than the humble sponge! This is called Superior Science! Essays galore were written about it! . . . If ever you have the time, before coming to this lecture, do as I do. I sometimes go and look at the doctoral theses in medicine. This is simply marvellous! You find books written by people who have worked for a year, two, or three years, on phenomena I did not even know existed! (Not that this proves anything)

There are people who spend their whole lives on the mounting of such mimemes, on the sponge, for instance . . . and this entails not merely an interest, but a passion. To them, everything else will pale into insignificance. Check La Bruyère's description of the man who loved tulips: "And there he is, rooted firmly before his tulips, and he becomes the tulip!" . . . That is exactly what it is: the lover of sponges becomes the sponge. And for us to share his joy, what will this man do? He will *verbalise*; he will verbalize his mimemes, he will ex-press his every replay in the form of a proposition, he will transform his inner intussuscepted gestes into a verbal mechanism so that what he knows about sponges is communicated to his listeners:

$$+{+}{+}{+}{+}{+}{+}{+} = \text{verbalization}$$

There is another system of communication too, one that I call *verbigeration*, and which merely repeats verbally what this man had previously mounted in him as propositional geste. It consists of repeating in words, without prior *intussusception* of the real, with zero intussusception:

$$\text{ooooooo} = \text{verbigeration}$$

Do not be fooled into thinking that someone who repeats what is in a book is equal to someone else who teaches from actual and real experience! Language misleads us in potentially catastrophic ways when it encourages us to believe that people using the same words mean the same things, share the same science, knowledge, and ideas. Here is the point where you will understand the non-existence of your so-called *ideas*. There are no ideas. There are only mimemes, mimemes that have perhaps been verbalised, but that, in the final analysis, must always refer back to objectively intussuscepted mimemes.

*That is the sum total of human science.* If we remain stuck in the zone of verbigeration, we have, not science, but nothingness, a kind of overweening verbosity: the kind of logomachy that characterises much of what we say.

Simply put: we should *never speak* of things that we have *not* personally *intussuscepted*. This should be the basis of education: to teach children how to learn, they must experience actual and real facts, which is to say gestes that they can then mount in themselves dynamically from real life experiences.

That is what grasping the real means. That is, after all, all we have. Do not think that you will teach me anything with words. Do not come to me with *abstract ideas*, with words like *freedom, divinity, angel* . . . These are merely words, unless of course, and we will look at this in another lecture, unless the mimemes of things visible are transposed in the world of things invisible. What you could say is: the mimemes that I will play before you—those so-called *abstract ideas*—we cannot see, they are invisible, but they will become visible and concrete if they are linked to concrete things. There is no difference between expressing things *concrete* and expressing things *abstract*: the mechanism is the same—all words need to refer to the real, all words should be verbalised mimemes.

Such words should however not be taught early in the child's education because, on the pretext of educating the child in abstract ideas, we merely train him in *verbigeration*. Such a child talks of things of which he can have no understanding whatsoever, seeing that we ourselves have no more than empty sounds coming from our lips. If I had more time, I would show you handbooks for children in which are dished up the very vacuous inanities that choke us. Under the pretence of teaching *abstract science,* we give them a void. How indeed can a thing be grasped intelligently by human consciousness without it becoming immediately abstract, this is to say *intelligent.*

What is being mounted in us in the shape of mimemes is not mounted in us as *sliced-up* mimemes: it is not the sponge cut off from everything else. From the moment the sponge arrives in my *anthropological mechanisms*, it makes a geste: the sponge moistens my hand; the sponge refreshes my fingers; the sponge weighs in my hand. Never, it is never the sponge detached from the real. This is why we must mount in us *propositional mimemes*, just as the things proposition themselves in us, as propositional—interactional—gestes.

This critically important law is largely *ignored in education*. For the *word*, as you understand it, does not exist. You have no right to teach the word *sponge*, you have no right to teach the word *moisten*, you have no right to teach the word *hand*. The child should know from experience that the *hand* or the *sponge* are always busy doing something or enduring something. This is why there are so shockingly few scientists! The fact is that most people do not bother in the least to discover the interaction of beings one upon the other. They merely repeat words. The great savants however, the greatest discoverers of all time, are those who have tried to discover the *interactions* between elements—that and that only.

Before Copernicus, everyone knew what the sun was, everyone knew what the earth was, and everyone knew what the geste was of turning around; but no one, except for a few intuitive brains in ancient Greece, no one had grasped the reality of the interactional geste of the earth turning around the sun. Now this man—even if he had discovered nothing else—is forever immortalised. Because he discovered this interaction, his name will never be forgotten. And an entire formidable theological machinery collapsed. Why? Because this man allowed a propositional geste to play in him. An honest, straightforward pedagogy would show us that all discoverers pose problems in this form. It is by giving children simple examples such as *the sponge moistens my hand*, that you give them the capacity to go and explore, with that same redoubtable hand, the depth of the skies, and transform that depth into a simple propositional geste.

People like de Broglie, like Pasteur, have all been great simplifiers because they have put the real in such simple forms. Algebra will follow of course, and endeavour to articulate the interactional complexity of each phenomenon, but the fact remains that all the great discoverers will always be capable of proposing their discovery in a simple interactional form:

*agent—action—agi*

acting-one—acting-on—acted-upon

My own discovery I propose in the following simple interactional proposition:

In the beginning was the rhythmo-mimismic geste.

Any proper grasping of the real is a grasping of an interaction. Unfortunately, the child is not trained in the study of interactions. Nowhere have I seen teachers encouraging children to express themselves only in propositional form, where there is *an acting one—acting upon—an acted-upon*, which transforms verbally into *a subject, a verb, and a complement*.

Children need to be accustomed to very simple interactional gestes, such as: *the water moistens the jar.* Then, "What does it mean, to moisten?" This geste of moistening is most interesting. There are indeed things that cannot be moistened. If I cover the table with a thin layer of oil and then pour water over it, the water will not moisten the table. That is highly significant. What can be learned from such an instance? The glass jug contains water. Yes. However, if I have a jug made of *porous* matter, the next day I will not find any water left in my jug.

The whole daily round of concrete worldly reality should be presented to the child in such interactional forms. I deliberately choose childish examples. Geniuses have always expressed themselves with childish examples, examples a child can grasp. Great discoveries, dismissed by smirking old and decrepit men, were at once understood by young people barely out of school. Your own children in the playground have no problem putting the sun at the center and having the planets circle around it, something the old astronomers of the time of Copernicus and Galileo found impossible to acknowledge. It is on such childlike receptivity that we need to build the Science of Science. Past a certain age, we no longer *discover*. The truly great discoveries—as Mr Bergson admirably put it—happen at age twenty. A man is wholly in his first book, and the rest of his life's work is but a further commentary on that first discovery.

It is indeed the child in this state of receptivity who discovers propositional gestes.


## The conservation of mimemes

Once the real is mounted in us, we are faced with a phenomenon that many have studied, but again, with words: the *unconscious*—a word that struck it rich as that has been a buzzword now for forty years.


### *Unconscious replay of mimemes*

This *unconscious* derives naturally from our mimismic mechanism. We have only unconscious mimemes in us. We have millions of them. We should be thankful for this unconsciousness because were we fully conscious, we would be right away thrown into a total panic by the mad swirl of these mechanisms. The ability to channel all these mimemes when they threaten to burst forth incoherently is the mark of the *great thinkers*. Anyone who is truly the master of his speech must be able to choose, in this flood of mimemes, one propositional geste at a time. Like a lion tamer in the lions' den, he guides the cohort of wild animals, with a flash of his eye or a gesture of his hand. Speech is, perhaps, the most fearsome thing of all. For when you speak, millions and millions of possible gestes present themselves. Only one will be expressed, the one chosen by the master.

So let us not talk any longer of the *unconscious* because there truly is in us only *unconsciousness*; let's talk rather of mimemes that replay and thus enable us to express ourselves.

In this *replay of mimemes* in us, there is, as we saw in my previous lecture, dream and daydream. From the moment we intussuscepted something, the mechanism plays, no one knows when nor how. As Descartes very rightly says: "Man thinks continuously"—"I think therefore I am." In my terminology, I prefer to put it as: "Man feels continuously, or is at any time able to feel, his *mimemes replaying in himself.*" This is what we call "daydreaming."

As soon as you allow yourself to think, the mimismic mechanism automatically and spontaneously comes into play, even when you would rather not think. This leads at times to truly horrific things happening, such as people killing themselves in order to escape this mechanism that plays beyond their control: "I will at least be able to get rid of this obsession" . . . so much are we lead, so much are we played by our intussuscepted mimemes . . . Remorse is just this. Others, not driven to suicide maybe, get intoxicated in an attempt to obliterate in them the mimeme of the loved one who, though absent, keeps on reappearing . . . This is the tragic power of these poor human mechanics that I dissect here for you.

This is what we are: replay! *Memory, association of ideas, idées-forces,* these are all replay and replay is the hallmark of the human. No animal that lost its mother, no lion that lost his lioness, will suffer this frightful experience of the replay of intussuscepted things, of intussuscepted faces, of all the gestes that are mounted in us, humans. Replay is what constitutes the human being, and it is quite possible for us to carry such unconscious, spontaneous and continuous replay in us for forty, fifty, sixty, even a hundred years. Even the slightest unexpected reference suffices for something that we thought was completely dead, to rise all alive into consciousness.

Memory is nothing but a word. We have in us only mimemes that have been mounted in us by the experience of the real that surrounds us and impacts on us.

### Conscious replay of mimemes

How can these mimemes replay in a way that defines us as human beings? How is it possible for us to adopt, and adapt to the reality of the world in which we live? My master Pierre Janet held that the power of the psyche lies in its ability to adapt to the real.

I know people who are an inexhaustible fund of information, people who know everything. Ask them for any current share listings, and they will supply them on the turn. Ask them for the list of the kings of France, of the presidents of the Republic, of the Pharaohs of Egypt, of the Mongol Emperors . . . They give it to you . . . their formidable mechanism turns and turns . . . as if it were nothing more than a list of fruits: apple, pear, apricot, cabbage, carrot, and on and on and on! Madness, madness!

There are indeed crazy people who perform stupefying feats. They know the number of bars in the fence of the Jardin du Luxembourg . . . because they went to count them! They know how many pieces of granite there are along the gutter of this or that street. You have no idea, and you are none the worse for it!

That, alas, is the kind of memory that we mount in our classrooms . . . What can the order of the Kings of France matter currently? Of what significance is the order of the presidents of the Republic to me? How can the order of the great Pharaohs—for whom I have a life-long admiration, mind you—be important to me? When needed, I can find such information in any dictionary; dictionaries are the depositories of all that we care to put in our ever so many and so precious words. That's the use of dictionaries: to allow one to *not* have to remember all this useless stuff.

If you really want to go and count the number of stones of the court-yard, or the number of pieces of chalk that are here in this box, feel free, but this is not your average person's job! What our memory should really enable us to do is to help us adapt to the real.

### Replay of remounted mimemes

One does not learn just for the sake of learning. Get all the professors of the School of Anthropology here in turn and asked them to talk on any random topic: not one of them would, because what they know is their very own topic. The professor who will follow me here today will speak about family, the next one will speak of all kinds of scholarly things that I would be quite incapable of discussing with you, yet another will talk to you about the nasal index, something he has now been studying for twenty years, turning it into an enthralling science. He is truly focused, this one.

Obviously, whoever comes here to focus rather on that awe-inspiring mechanism, the child, will have little interest in the nasal index, be it Cleopatra's. They could not care less . . . However, they will be passionate about the great mechanism of the child, something in which others again will show no interest, secure in the knowledge that they already know all there is to know about it. This is why all of us, professors, have different audiences. To each his mimeme: the possibility to focus on a particular angle of the real.

## Controlled replay of the mimemes

I give you a brief sketch of three aspects of this focus for you to work on by your selves: the guided replay of mimemes develops speedily, accurately, and with justness and suppleness.

### *Speedily*

Real life demands ultra-quick responses. On the battlefield, time to meditate is short. You need to have all your mechanisms prepared. Those who, like me, have had the honour to command a battery against the enemy know how *immediately* an operational problem has to be addressed and resolved because those mechanisms do not wait . . .

Similarly, when you need to put an issue before an audience, you need many years of training to enable you to verbalize all those mimemes mounted in you that make up the anthropology of language, so that you can verbalize them *at once*, without you having to search for words. You know how difficult it is, sometimes, to find the right word *quickly* . . . There is nothing worse than watching a great mind, and one you know to be great, who, with all the relevant mimemes mounted in him, struggles to transfer these mimemes from the inner real of his experience into their external verbal form. That does not mean that he is not fully informed from the point of view of mimemes, but it does mean that the training in the capacity to transfer the real into the algebrized verbal form is lacking. The actual speed of these internal mechanisms of transfer need to be exercised and disciplined. When you have to speak, your mimemes should be neatly clamped together, so that your account of them flows coherently. If you use these laws . . . . . . it means that they connect in this way . . .

If you use this other law . . .

then they will connect in this other way. Now, it is only by tuning in finely on the facts, that the mechanisms at first seemingly erratic will converge. It is within you that the converging takes place.

### *Accurately*

Accuracy in the replay is necessary because we are singularly apt at deforming our gestes. The study of the lie falls within this ambit. The things in us built up, and beak down: the process is the same. However, the one mechanism has the potential to fall in with a deviant mechanism that can be mistaken for the original one. One mimeme is confused with another:

### *Flexibly*

It is in this way that deviations happen. People who are not used to speak are always at risk of using words analogously, their language lacking in precision. It is the life of the geste we deal with here, not the life of the image. Images do not exist. Precisely because we are not heartless, metal machines, all is played in an extraordinarily supple fashion. Because of all the interactional factors that would need to be taken into account, not even thousands of years would suffice to take stock of all that so fluidly has played in me in the past hour.

It is this suppleness that makes it possible for the human to simultaneously play the real without, and replay the real within him. It is with these mechanisms that human thought can, simultaneously, replay the past and create the present anew.

## Conclusion: a pedagogy of things, not of words

You see then that you should refrain from using any of those words that I at the beginning of my talk marked with a red hot branding iron, so to speak; nor should you introduce them to the child. No, there is no *memory*, there is no *association of ideas*, there is only one thing, and that is the real in the form of interactional gestes that play in us in an intelligized form.

This phenomenon is inexplicable because it is *anthropological.* You would be the greatest genius of all time if you could explain the depth of human thought. We are not there yet . . . We do know however, the difference between a thing intelligized by us, and a thing received by an animal: in us, a *propositional* geste is formed that is not formed in the animal.

Now, education is no more than that. Memory is, basically, only *intelligized* propositional mimism. And faced with the child, your role is wholly and solely to allow him to mount the real in him and so to become, with the assistance of our knowledge and experience, a great scientist through his passionate intussusception of the real.

# The Sociology of Mimism

## *Algebrosis: The Death Knell of a Civilization*

### Outline

Introduction: Life is a mechanism that evacuates death

### Birth of the metaphor

The round
The lullaby
The ballad

### Death of the metaphor

Linguistic evolution
Disappeared geste
*Idle words*
*Pennitive word*
Military conquest
*Imposed phonemes*
*Unfelt phrases*
*Aristocratic algebra*
Religious conquest
*Meshihâ*

*Christos*

*Anointed*

## Resurrection of metaphor through:

The anthropology of geste

*Soul*

*Spirit*

*Idea*

The study of the geste of the ethnic milieu

*The Speaking one: Abbâ*

*The Word: Berâ*

*The Breath: Rouhâ*

The pedagogy of geste

*The yoke*

*The burden*

*The heifer*

## Conclusion

Mothers

Pre-primary teachers

Teachers and the mastery of the metaphor

**Note**: in this lecture on the mechanisms of metaphor, the 1940 debacle that saw its army defeated and France occupied for the next five years, becomes Jousse's metaphor for the rise and fall of civilizations. It is an allegorical tale, with emblematic names of characters and places: at the turn of the first century, the Gauls resisting the Roman invader; their leader Vercingetorix; the victory of Gergovia and the tragic defeat of Alesia; the collaborating indigenous gallo-roman bourgeoisie—all prefiguring the French resistance against the German invader; Henry de Montherlant's defeatist essay *The June solstice*; Charles Maurras's renouncement of his Christian faith and his right-wing anti-Semitic nationalist movement; Riom, the city in Central France where the 1942 trial was held by the collaborationist Vichy regime trying to put the blame of the defeat on its political enemies. In sum, a civilization dies for having abandoned traditional values based on the real for vacuous verbigeration, abandoned geste for text, abandoned mimism for algebrosis. Metaphor reduced to a stylistic device is ink, mimismic metaphor, blood. This lecture is about the regeneration of metaphor, and thus civilization. It is also useful to remember that this is a public lecture given in occupied Paris.

## Lecture

## Human mimism and the mechanism of metaphor

Le mimisme humain et le mécanisme de la métaphore
*EA 24/02/42*

## Introduction: life is a mechanism that evacuates death

I have said before, and will continue to stress: life is a mechanism that eats, and in order to eat, kills. This I see as the *positive* side of life. But there is another side which we are going to consider more closely here today, one we could call the *negative* mechanism: life is a mechanism that ages, and in order not to die, endeavors to evacuate old age and thus, by implication, death.

The general schema of life thus has two parts: a mechanism that intussuscepts, and a mechanism that ejects. The mechanism of intussusception rests as much on physical as on gestual nutrients. The living being must eat and gather its mimemes from the ambient milieu, especially when this living being is the miming being par excellence, the human being—the anthropos. The anthropos must also, as must any living being, evacuate not only physical matter, but also, and of all necessity, gestual matter. This has been studied very little until now. Until now, anthropology has been, above all else, a study of the dead human being, of the skeleton. I was one of the first to institute dynamic anthropology as the study of the *living* human being.

Therefore, today, I would like to show you how important it is to study this system of *evacuation* of the aging gestes, that would fast become mortifying gestes, if they were not eliminated. I showed you last time the schema, which is, in a manner of speaking, the study plan of my anthropological work. Some of you found me very demanding. I am not demanding: I am objective. I cannot renege on the science that I have undertaken. When I told you that I wanted to resuscitate two primordial beings, Vercingetorix and Ieshua, the very fact of wanting to resuscitate them carries with it the absolute necessity to evacuate the parasitic elements that were inserted in the Gallo-Galilean mechanism.

In Gaul, the mimo-dramatic civilization of Montignac merged with the Gallic rhythmo-catechistic civilization. The latter was in full bloom when it was broken up at the battle of Alesia. It did however live on with all the characteristics of traditional paysanism. Anyone research in paysan questions needs to take this intertwining of two great primordial rhythmo-catechistic paysan mechanisms into account. When the Galilean mechanism was added, there was no deviation, on the contrary, because both are of the same nature: both use greatly analogous and often identical gestual systems. What did however muddle the Gallic tradition was the fact that the aristocratic Gallic milieu immediately rallied under the invader. And this is why the study of the Roman influence on, and contribution to, the original Gallic tradition, needs to carefully discern what belongs to whom in this cultural amalgam.

We have before us a history that ended in 1940, but 1789 gave us a foretaste of what awaited us. Seventeen eighty-nine marked the normal outcome of the Gallo-Romans' denial of their Gallic roots. Read Taine, and you will see what this particular tradition embraced. The 1789 petty bourgeois usurped the people's revolution and took up the Gallo-Roman legacy of collaboration with the enemy. Our 1940 petty bourgeois took over this legacy and carried it to its normal and logical conclusion. So, do not be surprised that the anthropologist who is speaking to you here is single-minded in the execution of only one task, and one task only: to discard the distorting Gallo-Roman tradition so as to safeguard the *pure* Gallo-Galilean tradition.

What has the Gallo-Roman tradition bequeathed us? Its bequest has been what I have called the *pennitive-oratory-preachy* tradition. So let us discard, with the greatest scientific detachment, these three conjoint traditions: that of the pen-pushers, that of the orators and that of the preachers.

At our last lecture, one of you said to me: "But what have the orators and the preachers done to you that you should carry on against them?" To me personally? Nothing. To me as anthropologist? Everything. Essentially, they have destroyed my tradition. This is why I will never accept and allow that the formation and upbringing of a child should begin with pennitive writing and verbose oratory, and I would even add, with preachy religion. On the contrary, I would send my child to be formed initially by rhythmo-catechism, and once formed, all the other mechanisms could be added without *fundamentally* distorting the child. The rhetoric that is taking place presently at Riom stinks to high heaven. When I read the reports of what is currently happening there, I am filled with disgust: have we really regressed to this level of overweening verbosity that we thought was gone for good? What I seek is total renewal. This is why the young understand me best: they have felt, not the call of race, but the call of tradition, the call of the Gallo-Galilean paysan.

Beware! We are no longer at a point in history that you find described in a book entitled *The June Solstice*. Read this and you will see why we need anthropologists who will address these burning issues objectively. The author of that book has done all his studies under priests. What knowledge of the Gospel has he received in his formation and training? None. His reactions are generally simply identical to those this other man, Maurras. Maurras has walked the perfect straight and narrow Greco-Roman path, because he had not been taught the great Gallo-Galilean anthropology, which is based on the objective study of facts. Read, even cursorily, my recent essay *Human bilateralism and the anthropology of language*. In it you will see how far removed from the Gallo-Galilean tradition are our biblical manuals and the lessons that our young clergy are being taught.

My position is not that of a polemist: I want to reconstruct, to rebuild. To build solidly, bases are needed. One does not build in the air. One hears from all sides, moaning and crying: "Our poor prisoners, our poor prisoners!" Bewailing our lot in ineffective words serves no real purpose: there is work to be done! We have to rebuild structures that will operate, not in the religious field, but in the field of tradition, on the traditional terrain, on the anthropological terrain. That is an altogether a different thing.

What we thus have to do is simply to "evacuate"—to use the term of Ieshua *In cessorum mititu*—to the cesspit all that that has killed our deepest traditions. Once we have rid ourselves of this slime, it will be possible to study ourselves objectively. For this can be done. What cannot be studied objectively are people who produce nothing more than empty words, because there is nothing there but hot air. They, they will remain the target of my attack. Therefore, don't be surprised by my vehemence, and if it offends or troubles you, abstain from coming to listen to me, because I am determined to clear my terrain systematically of the entire muddle that should be seen as a frightening disease. In the process of our study, a kind of awakening, a kind of resurrection has to take place, because, purposely or not, the French paysan has not been afforded his rightful place, or been given, up until the present, an audience, as have been the aristocrats or the petty bourgeois.

Now, I am paysan, and I can tell you that your suffering is not going to be short-lived. You can only be freed from your distress by us, the objective paysans who have an understanding of things as they really are.

In the future, you can expect to see paysans come forward everywhere. Even so, we, paysans, cannot restore the situation for a number of years to come, perhaps even for centuries to come. Recall how long the Roman Empire lasted in Gaul, and start counting . . . One does not construct and deconstruct empires glibly as Bossuet in his *Discourse on Universal History*. Civilizations do not come about that easily and rapidly.

We have to reject the verbiage, and study the objective anthropological geste.

Up until now, the geste was considered irrelevant in anthropology. Now let us ask: where is the geste's place in anthropology? Everywhere. What does it want? To be recognized for what it is, which is something to be reckoned with. We will then search for the geste wherever geste needs to be resuscitated. In this place, this year, I will resuscitate it in the working tools of the teacher, in the mechanism of investigation and of explication. This is why I have chosen as a topic this year: *The gestual comparison in the child and in the primitive*, and I remind you that to me, *the primitive* has none of the meaning that Lévy-Bruhl gives it, but means, precisely, the *paysan*, the man of his *pays*, his land, and that last word resonates most significantly in my mouth!

Heretofore, the studies on the *primitives* were made without any real knowledge of the primitive. Lévy-Bruhl had his first intuition of the possible implications of what *the primitive* could be whilst studying the Chinese! I am, I believe, taking the opposite position to Lévy-Bruhl. I have shown how language can be studied from the perspective, and through the perceptions of a Chinese person from China. I took on a Jesuit, a young Chinese man who was already so contaminated by the Latin mechanism that he thought it quite normal to come and see me and to ask me how to *romanize* Chinese writing (you see how effectively the pennitive-oratory-preachy mechanism had begun to colonize him!)

So I then told this student what I am telling you now: that the Gallo-Roman influence that claimed to have *civilized* us all, was over . . . Once he understood this, he got to work, and wrote a doctorate that a number of you have had in your hands, and which you must all read: *Chinese writing and the human geste*. This meant that he had become aware of what the true primitive is—*the living Man*. To talk of 'savages,' to talk of *prelogical* and *inferior* mentality shows that one has understood nothing of the fundamental human mechanics—of the basic workings of the human being.

Have we not all heard often enough that peasants are clumsy and coarse? Our so-called clumsiness and coarseness are actually the objectivity with which we handle things, instead of producing only glib, empty words, or fickle, journalistic columns. We are grave and weighty beings that contend with reality, and whose labours enable others to live. We produce your food. You are aware of this presently, are you not? For too long we have believed that we were only truly worth something, only truly cultivated, only truly knowledgeable, once we had reneged all that formed the very basis of those you called *primitive*.

All our current studies are distorted at the *base*, at the *foundation*, and I do mean *all* of them. I therefore cannot take them into account, neither to redress them, nor to destroy them. There is no point busying myself with their destruction: because of their flawed foundations, they will collapse of their own accord.

Etymology teaches us that *savages* are simply "people who live in forests." They were savages, our druids, living as they did in *the learned Gallic forests*. The great authority on Gaul, Camille Jullian, tells us that the oral teaching of the druids was infinitely greater than what the Romans brought us, that it was something analogous to the geneses and the apocalypses that came from the Galilean milieu. All this needs to be studied in depth and at length.

The great masters who have preceded me have laid the basis of our redress. As a teacher intent at effectively reconstructing life, I need to raise an observed fact with every single sentence. If each of my oral interactions is not underpinned by an objective interaction, then I am an orator, I am a pennitive, I nearly said (God forbid!) a preacher! That is the last thing I want to be. This is why I began to show you last year how the most powerful tool a teacher has is the power to show, to point, to indicate. What you do not know is that the very word *dire* [= to say], *il dit* [he says] . . . implies this. If you were into Indo-European and you tried to make your audience *feel* the phrasing, it would immediately become clear to you how to go about it: *dixit* is *dix-it*—meaning *says-he* where the action, *dix-* (*says*), comes first, and the person who does the action—*it* (*he*), comes after. In-*dic*-ating is the geste that he makes of *pointing with his finger*. In Greek, this Latin *dic-* is *dec-*, whence *dac*tylos and its Latin equivalent *dig*itus: the finger that points out. It is the *show*-er, the *point*-er, the in*dic*ator, the *member that shows*, that in-*dec*'s.

We human beings are formed to *show*, not *dire* in the usual sense of *to say*, but in its etymological sense of *to point with finger and hand*—*to indicate*. We are *handlers*. It is precisely this handling that I would like restored in all the stages and aspects of pedagogics. We should use nothing other than demonstration as a teaching tool. Now, the very best tool of demonstration is the object itself, or its reflection by mimism, or its transfer by analogy. This process goes by the name of metaphor, using a Greek term: *metaphora*, meaning to transport of one object onto another.

Until now, the metaphor was perceived as a tool of literature, which is a travesty, because the totality of human expression is then immediately diverted to the purpose of syllogisms or pure verse, and not at all to handle what is real.

We need to go back to conscious and organized *showing*—de-*mon-strat*-ing—even from the earliest stage, from the mother's womb. The fact of the matter is that we are, in our civilization, deformed from childhood, warped by educators who are themselves warped. What we actually need is a profound disinfection from the present pre-primary schoolteachers all the way up to the professors of the most elevated chairs, because none of these men and women was ever properly initiated in teaching.

It is an exhausting task, teaching without poisoning someone in the process. What I am suggesting today could be a kind of synthesis of how teaching needs to be restored. Any person who undertakes to teach others needs to be fully equipped to do so.

In the past, from 1914 to 1918, when a leader was promoted to a command position, he had to have formidable training. Read Marshall Foch's two beautiful introductory books: *Principles of War*, and *How a Battle Should Be Conducted*. Reality deceived Foch, however, as it invariably does. He believed that the war would be over in a very short time, but it lasted four years. This time round, we might well have to add a few years more. . . . Read Foch's preface in the book, *On the Conduct of War*: "Above the façade of this Staff College, you will read the words *School* and *War*: *École de Guerre*. Is this not a contradiction? When one says *school*, one is referring to quiet, calm, thoughtfulness and sensibility. *War*, on the other hand, is about violence, sudden bursts of energy, and bolts of vicious lightning!" Foch sums this up brilliantly and succinctly when he adds that "the greatness of a brilliant leader is synthesized in the calm sensibility of the school and the violent force of gunpowder."[1]

In 1940, it is the Bavarian peasant [Hitler] who exposed us to this synthesis of the calm sensibility of the school and the violent force of gunpowder: "I will surge from the night like lightning," he said. People burst out laughing at this pretentiousness. The petty pennitives at a dime a dozen, laughed at him and said that he was mentally ill. If he has a mental illness, then what is it that we are suffering from? What did our leaders suffer from? Yes, he has a mental illness: genius. That does not happen to everyone. Those that have been affected by it were called Alexander, and Caesar—to our greatest misfortune. And then, too, they were called Napoleon.

It is this synthesis of the lightning and the school that I try to point out to you. Not, alas, in myself, but in one of you who could at any time be

1. *De la conduite de la guerre: la manœuvre pour la bataille* (Paris: Berger-Levrault, 1904) 1.

waking up and who is unknown to us at the present moment . . . because I work "so that someone greater than I may come after me" said Iôhânân the Immersor . . . and someone greater certainly did follow him.

We need to tell our young preprimary schoolteachers: "You are touching the virginal being of a child with hands sullied by microbes: go and wash your hands anthropologically." . . . To the primary schoolteachers, we will say the same. To the high schoolteachers we will say: "Start by studying the great mechanisms that shaped human expression before drowning us in Latin and Greek grammars!" To the professorial chairs and men like Milman Parry, and others whom you will find in the bibliographical references, I have nothing to say because they immediately understood me.

What I bring is simply *the awareness* of our tool of lightning. In school, we were shown a rather Olympian Jupiter who brandished some sort of instrument of lightning. As an anthropologist, I do not handle metaphoric lightning, but I do handle the gestual lightning that I have in me. I also know how terribly destructive lightning can be when it is not properly directed.

This is why, all those brave little soldiers notwithstanding, who could have given so much, we have ended up only with an immense debacle. Just read what the arch pen pushers dish up for us day after day. The Riom court case where heaven knows how many hundreds of speechifiers will parade before us . . . At Riom, a world is dying. In this lecture room, a world is being resuscitated in as far as you will understand me, and perpetuate my words in your personal reactions. Because here, let me make this very clear, we do not speechify, we do not follow the catechism doggedly merely for its own sake. Here we do dynamic anthropology.

Sometimes I have before me brave souls of Kindergarten teachers who, at the sight of my soutane say: "How differently he speaks from Father So-and-So or Father So-and-So!" Well, of course I do! When I am here, I am not Father So-and-So. You will never see the title of Father anywhere on my programs or on the posters advertising these lectures. Here I am the professor of the anthropology of mimism. You will never find in me a preacher who tries to impress you with pious slipperiness, and please, do not cultivate in yourselves a dogged obedience to accepted doctrine. In the same vein, the Jesuit Father present here is not going to faint when I say publicly that his—and my—confrere Père Riquet is nothing but a Père Roquet, a *perroquet*—a sacred parrot who preaches Ieshua in total ignorance of his subject. The Father here present knows this as well as I do. That is precisely why he comes here to listen to me, because he, for one, does not want to be someone who teaches Ieshua without knowing Him!

You may think that this is rather harsh, but rest assured that I have demonstrated the true nature of Rabbi Ieshua of Nazareth at the Vatican in

Rome, and my position was ratified. I am well equipped to attack and I am sure not to be vanquished. So, I am asking you in turn to make the same effort and, if there is a sentence or two which startles you, please do not think that your whole world is going to crumble simply because the pretty little notions that you have held so dear since childhood, are being uprooted. I am telling you: everything that needs to be uprooted I will uproot, with scientific means. That is my straightforward and honest aim.

All the meaningless towers of verbosity that you were taught to uphold, have to come down. It is the great Gallo-Galilean tradition of Vercingetorix and Ieshua that needs to be revisited all over again, and understood, and anthropologically followed at the deepest level. This will be achieved with the tool that is called metaphor, which is to say, language which *shows*, *demonstrates*, *points*.

Let me now summarize for you what I said last time, because what is important today is above all else the question of words. You were never taught a proper work method. All you ever did was dabble in lectures, going to the lectures of Professor So-and-So, then of Professor Such-and-Such, each contradicting the other, and you trying to synthesize what you heard. A little bit of everything, and a little extra bit added on the side, that is not a proper training. It is only with a real tool, the true living tool that you can go forward. This living tool, let us outline it again and let us see together:

- Birth of the metaphor,
- Death of the metaphor,
- Resurrection of the metaphor.

## The birth of the metaphor

Today's lecture could be entitled: *Human mimism and the mechanism of the metaphor*. Let us then see the metaphor being born.

The metaphor will be born from a geste. I will give you three very simple pedagogical examples:

- in the *round,*
- in the *berceuse* or lullaby,
- in the *ballad.*

### The round

Let us say that you go somewhere in our French countryside. In the market place, you see little girls, holding hands, walking, and skipping in rounds, as they recite things that I used to sing when I was very young and still dressed in a smock, before being dressed in another altogether more austere cassock. This is what these little girls recite :

À *la ronde des petites filles blondes*

*Qui font danser la guenille*

*Pie la roupille*

This can be repeated as many times as you wish. Insignificant? Not at all. It can demonstrate, quite simply, how one can sometimes rectify the biblical mistranslations of preachers, as the good Father Bainvel used to say. Ask these little children: "What is it that you are doing here?" and one little girl will answer you: "I sing a round."

This little girl has given you there, unknowingly of course, a metaphor. It is true that she is playing, that she has *corporalized* the round, which refers to the round circles that the little girls create as they recite the text. Now this text, by transposition, by transport, by metaphor, has taken the name of the dance, of the *round*. There you have the very simple mechanics of the operation, and it will always be like that. If you want to understand what a metaphor is, find the underlying geste.

### The berceuse

Here is another of the same kind: you have a Sarthois mother or grandmother who cradles her little *quéniau,* her little child. This is extremely interesting. As an aside, I have to say that I have grasped the deepest things—those that have turned, for me, the question of language and pedagogy upside down—from the simplest things, just as Newton discovered universal gravity by seeing an apple fall.

One has to be very intelligent to see the profound implications of simple things. It is so easy to think that the more complicated one is, the more knowing one is. However, this is not so. When you watch a mother nursing her child, do not become sentimental. Instead, watch her gestes. Observe and analyze all the movements of her cradling. Watch as she sings words in a melody, the rhythms of which coincide with her movements, as she balances from front to back and from left to right. By metaphor, this is to say by transport of gestes, she is *metaphorizing* the geste of the cradling in the recitation, and so you say: "She is singing a *berceuse*, a cradling, a cradle song."

## *The ballad*

There is a third example, one I will come back to later again. It was outlined by a professor of the Sorbonne, who did however not see it as a paysan would. It is the mechanism of the ballad. This is what professor Baud-Bovy has also studied among the reciters of the Greek Dodecanese islands: the way in which the paysans there recite their recitations.

They balance. They *ballent*, as is said in Old French, meaning they *dance*. By *ballant*, by *dancing*, is meant that they operate the normal mechanisms of the human body. So 'they are dancing,' you would say? This is where the error creeps in. *Dancing* is a word that should be reserved for your frivolous social hops that bear no resemblance to the gestual mechanisms used for the ballad. In the ballad, we have the same operation as that of memorization, which is performed normally by oscillation of the whole body, sometimes accompanied by the tapping of the foot to mark the beat even more clearly. If you ask the name of these texts, the name of these sometimes improvised compositions, you will be told: "It is a ballad." The operation of the ballad lies in *baller*, in balancing while tapping the rhythm. Here again, the geste onto which the sound has been transposed has given the recitation its name. Again then, a metaphor. Our literature manuals refer to the *Ballads of the ladies of yesteryear*. This again has become *textual* and the *gestual* paysan mechanism has disappeared. That is what we need to re-integrate in *paysanism*, and therefore in pedagogy, and therefore in your Kindergartens. The true method of memorization is what Mlle Desgrées du Loû does in the recitation of the Gospel where the balancings, the gestes and the words all coincide with the melody to aid memorization. When the Jesuit Fathers say that "Father Jousse dances the Gospel," they show their ignorance of the normal operation of human expression and memory. We need to study and perform focused pedagogy, and stop picking up bits and pieces from the Montessoris, the Decrolys and the Piagets. What has been done so far is nothing more than daydreaming without method, without laws, without terminology.

There then is how the metaphor is born. How will it die?

## The death of the metaphor

Here we will look at the processes through which necrosis of the metaphor will occur:

- either by linguistic evolution,

- or by military conquest,

- or by religious conquest.

### Through linguistic evolution

I gave you the word *ballade*. When the paysans were no longer master of their mechanisms of memorization and expression, they no longer *ballade-d*. Paysans nowadays no longer speak with the full richness of past times when their traditional mnemonic *oral style*, as I term it, blossomed.

When the *ballade* geste disappeared, its signifying verb and its meaning remained suspended in the air. What is a *ballade*? Recitation is no longer performed with the whole body, therefore the texts of the *ballades* are no longer sounded to be heard, and can now be found only in writing in anthologies. So, quite simply, the word *ballade* has no meaning any longer. It is finished. It is dead. I believe that, currently, there would be very few matriculation candidates who could *baller* for you in the way normal peasants would have *balleed*.

Well, it is precisely with these laws of the normal gestual operation that we will analyze the texts of the paysan Ieshua. The sacred Père Riquet *perroquet*-parrot types naturally never noticed any of this. Lost in writing as they were, they could not have noticed. At the Vatican in Rome, however, all of this was perfectly understood, and it is for this reason that Pope Pius XI said: "This is a revolution in the making." A necessary revolution and one bound to happen.

### Through military conquest

Linguistic evolution can be brutally hastened by another violent phenomenon: military conquest, as happened at Alesia. How does this happen? Quite simply, the conqueror inflicts brutally, by dint of sanctions, the foreign language. This could very well happen to us again right now. It is altogether possible that in a short while, we will have to ask for our metro tickets in the language that you see alongside French on a number of posters, those terrible posters that recall the geste of Uxellodunum.

Military conquest inflict foreign phonemes. How could one possibly understand the internal workings of such imposed language when one is, so to speak deafened by the sudden total impact of the change. This in contrast to a language acquired by tradition, the complexities of which one can follow and analyze, phase by phase, through phonetic evolution.

Since the events at Alesia, this is no longer possible among us, and this is extremely significant. Those who introduce language to the schools being mostly rhetors, it follows that we will be confronted by the kind of snobbery that refuses to recognize concretism. What sets in is a kind of hypnosis, a kind of obsession with what are known as *abstract terms*. This is precisely what you can hear happening in any number of speeches, and even in the sermons preached at Notre Dame cathedral: they are nothing but streams of voiced algebrosemes! Meaning what? There is no meaning, and that is why they sound so nice.

## *Through religious conquest*

Religious conquest sometimes happens under the cover of military conquest, and after one thousand years, or even two thousand years, collapses along with it. We have to accept that the little Galilean paysan was brought to us through the Greco-Latin civilization, and now that the Greco-Latin civilization has collapsed, will all else also collapse as in *The June Solstice*? Come on!

*The June Solstice* was able to topple Greco-Latinism. Palestinian, Galilean, Aramaean Ieshuaism, however, is brand new! Read the essay that I have devoted to the revelation of Ieshua emerging in all his true Aramaic spontaneity. I was the first to say: "The mechanisms of Ieshua must be replayed *in Aramaic*."

There are three ways in which we this religious conquest can take place.

First, the autochthonous Aramaic term *Meshihâ* alludes to the Targum that I researched for years and years, and that was simply transferred in Hebrew. The Messiah is the Meshihâ. In our milieu, however, there is nothing that resonates with this. Nothing. There is not even a single recorded study of it yet, seeing that I am the only one to have studied the Targum. I told you that Joseph Bonsirven thought that the Targum were composed only very late, because he confused *composition*-in-writing with oral composition *put-in-writing*. Only Mgr. Gry said: "Jousse has given us the method," and then applied the method himself in his two enormous volumes of the Apocalypse of Esdras.

The context allows us to transfer the word Meshihâ into "he who is oiled," I venture "he who is consecrated by oil" or, in Greek, *Christos*, which in Latin became *Christus*. You can hear preachers clamor: "Christ! Ah, Christ!" This while they have no idea of the background of this term and of what the complex network the term sets off in the Targum. How could they, seeing that they never even bothered to open a Targum. What then is this name they are clamoring—that very same geste of old when we used to oil our hands, and by doing so, call up an immense complex of invisible powers.

Merely clamoring "Christ" does not help to understand anything of this formidable question or of the greatness of Ieshua the Galilean. That, however, is what was done until now: merely uttering the name Christ and harping on this ceaselessly during catechism.

Ethnically and anthropologically, the religious conquest was formidably equipped. Let us start then by studying the matter anthropologically and ethnically. Had those that wrote *The June Solstice* been taught properly, in line with these fundamental methodological principles, this book might well never have been written.

That is how metaphor dies.


## The resurrection of the metaphor

How can the metaphor be resuscitated?

- through the anthropology of geste,

- through the study of the geste of the ethnic milieus,

- through the pedagogy of the geste.


### Through the anthropology of geste

First, we must try to understand the exact nature of the geste, and its operation in this whole formidable human machinery that had never been studied before I arrived. There is glib talk about the soul, the spirit, the idea! These are all just words! What is this thing called the soul? What is this thing called the spirit? Where did you fish these words from? What does each of them contain as geste? Ideas, images? These words are not self-evident. Try as you may, metaphysics does not resolve the problems. *Images simply do not exist*. The whole psychiatric school of Pierre Marie refuses to use this terminology because it is so distorting.

## Through the study of the geste of the ethnic milieus

There are laws that you can bring into play, and operate according to specific ethnic milieus. So, for example, if you want to explain the function and meaning of the teacher in the Galilean ethnic milieu, you will come upon *The Speaking One, the Word and the Breath, unified* and operating as one.

The teacher will be *a speaking one*, called ABBA, which should not be translated as Father in our affective sense.

He who repeats the ABBA will be his echo, and so will be his word, and he will be called BERA, which should not be translated as Son, because those two terms do not share the same meaning.

Then, there is the breath that proceeds from the one and from the other, from the Speaking one and from the Word, called ROUHA in Aramaic. From the moment you translate this as *spiritus*, you will no longer understand, and when you say: "The Father, the Son, and the Holy Spirit," you break the logic of the metaphor, and you make your children make the sign of the cross without having even a basic understanding of the great geste that you make them perform. This is no longer scientifically acceptable. In the name of the most intelligent of Men to have appeared among Men, and who was more than a man, it is your duty to work, to labor, and so to deserve and be allowed to teach the little children for whom He has given his Blood, his Life and all his Gestes.

## Through the pedagogy of the geste

The pedagogy of the geste will help us to understand that one does not translate the metaphors of one ethnic milieu into those of another ethnic milieu, without a great deal of work.

Thus, when one balances, as in the recitations of the Palestinian milieu, with the balancing from right and from left, this balancing will be analogous to a YOKE. This word no longer has this meaning among us. The lifting from front to back is the recitation that is performed while balancing from front to back, as when one lifts a BURDEN. In France, this word has no recitational meaning.

Consequently, by translating "My yoke is easy and my burden is light," you reduce the great pedagogical mechanisms of Palestine to the level of the saccharine stories you dish up to obedient little girls in your obligatory catechism classes. It is very sweet and completely misses the point.

We must, therefore, simply take up again the great mechanics of the expressive geste, and understand that the metaphoric geste of transporting needs to be studied anthropologically. The mothers, the Kindergarten teachers, the primary schoolteachers and all the other teachers at every level, will have to work at these questions scientifically.

For indeed, the future lies in an awareness of the tool. We will all be workers, and our working tools will be up to the task and efficient insofar as they will have been drawn from *life*.

# The Worldview of Mimism 1

## Mimism and Metaphor: The Humanizing Geste

### Outline

Introduction: off words, into things

Receptivity of the child

Metaphor in children

Why metaphor

Comparison and metaphor

Bergson and metaphor

Metaphor and the style of the child

Receptivity of mimismic peoples

Grasping the invisible world through metaphor

Receptivity of people who remained childlike

The experimental savant

The dramatic artist

The pedagogue

Conclusion: the secret of all human intercommunication

**Lecture**

**Mimismic geste and the creation of metaphor**

Le geste mimique et la création de la métaphore. *S 14/01/32*

## Introduction

*Off words . . .*

Those of you who have for two years now attended my lectures, each Thursday, have no doubt become aware that I try, week after week, to free them from the circle of iron in which society locks them through its vocabulary. I want them to become childlike again and playful before the real.

*. . . into things?*

The fact is that most people are no longer capable of placing themselves new and afresh before things. As we say in a commonplace metaphor: their eye got used to it. This is why we find some otherwise very intelligent people who, when confronted with new ideas, are as absolutely sincere as wholly incapable of understanding them. It is not within their circle of iron. They are no longer flexible enough to adapt to the unexpected novelty of a real that is new. It seems to me then that I can justifiably broach the topic on today's program: *The mimismic geste and the creation of metaphor*. It is about new metaphor.

Children, as we saw last time, are a kind of extremely receptive and supple small amoeba. It is in this vein then that we will study, in our accustomed tri-phase fashion:

-The receptivity of the child

-The receptivity of mimismic peoples, who remained young and who are improperly called primitive

-The receptivity of those among us who preserved this adaptive suppleness

## Receptivity of the child

Children are wholly fixated on the real, insert the real in their entire musculature, in their whole active, feeling and knowing small being, and express themselves by expressing things as they are. To talk to children about metaphor is perfectly pointless because children express themselves instinctively through metaphor. A few days ago in the rythmo-pedagogical laboratory, I had a small Parisian child draw a crescent and whilst drawing the crescent, this child told me: "Ah, but the crescent, I know what it is, it is like a banana."

### Children and metaphor

Clearly this metaphor would not have come to the geste of anyone of us here. Young children from Paris have not seen a great deal of the gestes of nature, and they therefore exercise their intussusception on the things they see. Immediately, the metaphor jumps out at their muscles: "The crescent is like a banana." It is altogether pretty and, as we will see, great poets say quite similar things, with another metaphor:

> What god, cropping the timeless summer yield,
> Had dropped so carelessly as he departed
> That golden sickle in the starry field.

The process is much the same. It is no longer the banana, but the golden sickle . . .

The crescent crops up in another metaphor of Victor Hugo. The soldiers had lost their captain. As you know, at that time, army officers sported a metal neckpiece in the shape of a crescent called gorget, and Victor Hugo shows us how, at night, some soldiers, strolling about, thought they saw the captain's gorget in the sky . . .

There you have explained, in all its grace, the metaphor of my young child. It is an important problem I put to you here, and I would like to see it solved by one of you.

### Why metaphor?

Why does a child feel the need to compare everything with everything? It is a most curious phenomenon and one that we will encounter everywhere. We play the real and we could play it in itself, but no, we take the real, and we throw it immediately in an adjoining form.

In the lecture he gave today, professor Janet returned to his idea of play. To him, the human geste is play, and indeed, we do feel that human beings first play with their gestual expressions. Why would that be? The answer, I think, can only be found in the human's need to compare a known thing to something less known, or conversely. A beautiful study waits on this topic for philosophers and scientists.

You know of Plato's great metaphors. Plato creates a myth not only in the story itself, but in his vocabulary too. Aristotle equally, but all these concrete expressions are algebrized in our translations.

If, however, making a quick leap over the centuries, we come face to face with Newton, the savant who had the greatest influence on modern science, we see how he seizes the real as an immense dance. We know that the Gauls mimed the dance of the stars. Well, Newton seizes this dance of the stars, places the sun at the center and has the planets gravitating, dancing around this central star according to a law. Then he says, no, not: "Bodies attract," but "bodies do *as if* . . . they attracted."

### Comparison and metaphor

What we have here is the difference between comparison and metaphor. You have studied rhetorical treatises for long enough for me not to dwell on this difference between the two. When one says: "Achilles is a lion," we have a metaphor. When one says: "Achilles is like a lion," we have a comparison. It is a little subtle and purely a matter of grammar. A comparison is a shy metaphor. Which is why creators of vocabulary use expressions such as: "If you allow me—If I may say . . . If one is allowed to put is like this." Then rises a well struck metaphor, and the audience is satisfied. Otherwise, people would say: "But this is too daring an expression. One does not say that."

### Bergson and metaphor

When Bergson attempted to grasp the real, he expressed it with fresh metaphors and this is how his élan vital came about. A most interesting study could be done on new metaphors in Bergson's style. Bergson owns his success in society—dare I add in feminine society?—to these admirable metaphors. I am not saying he is easily understood, but his style seems to play easily in the fibres of our muscles.

What we see happening then is life *inserting itself*; life *insinuating itself*; matter *wasting*; intuition *penetrating*. An entire great mimodrama of creative evolution is being played out. Bergson's style is mimodrama in the making. When Bergson came on the scene, artists looked at each other and they knew something fresh and youthful was arising: new metaphors.

I have tried to lead you into this realm of supple receptivity, and we should now be able to understand children, first their outlook on the real, then their understanding of the real, and finally the style of their expression of the real.

## The child's outlook

I told you last time how children are interested in everything, how they let themselves be informed by everything, and how then, with the real having given them their form, they replay it at once with startling and obvious diligence and finesse.

Ask a child what grass is. As a young fellow told me yesterday morning: "Grass? Grass is what grows!" and he made for me the firm gesture of shoots of grass growing.

Curiously enough, this young Parisian child I asked questions from reproduced unwittingly the gesture of the Indians miming the growth of grass. Grass is . . . *the growing one*. Just as the crescent is the thing that increases, *crescere* in Latin. The cutting one is the thing that *cuts*.

Without knowing, the child reproduces, and replays, the primordial human expression.

He replays with his gesture first. The child has first made the gesture, and from beneath the geste, the word arises.

## Gestures and eloquence

This is why in classes where eloquence is taught, the speakers are told: "Gesture always precedes speech." This is then very conscientiously applied: on paper first, by dint of many a deletion, a beautiful speech is prepared; which is then learned by heart; after which one learns how to make the gestures. For gestures one will need to make, not too many, but in just the right dose.

## In medio virtus: the happy medium.

Passages are underlined in red, but gestures need to precede diction. It is such a headache and I never managed to achieve this. However, there is no need to make gestures! The gestures that accompany your text resemble the colours of those cheap pictures that always spill over the drawing because they were added on later. The gestures we make are no different. They are conventional add-ons to a dead text. One senses, through some vague instinct, that the gesture is meant to underscore the meaning of certain verbs, and so one takes the coarsest, as I showed you before, the likes of: "And he descended . . . ," ". . . and he went up . . ." Of course! Now, if it were left to a child rather than to a teacher of eloquence, this child would play all this out with all his muscles, and he would tell you afterwards, with his mouth, what he has first mimed. If the rules of eloquence advise you that the gesture must precede the word, it is because this is the spontaneous and fundamental psycho-physiological process of the child.

## The gesture must precede the word

What has helped me to, shall I say, to mould my thought? What will allow me to make my thought fluid or rigid? It is my gesture; my gesture guides me. It is not my word that guides me, it is my gesture. Which is why, and I had been unaware of it, some of my listeners tell me: "Yes, we know your thought. Before you expressed it, you had played it out."

This is why the child embraces the real with his whole body, replays it, and transposes this intussuscepted real orally, and in doing so, invariably through comparison. This compelling need to compare I have yet been unable to explain. I am myself amazed at having arrived at the definition that: "Man is an animal that makes comparisons." It is indeed so that children, before an object, will invariably mime it, and that, invariably too, and right away, a comparison will come into play. Children render the gesture they have seen as closely as possible, and it is precisely in this closeness that lays one of the joys of their expression.

## The child's style

When a child sees leaves falling, it is not the *leaves* that strike him, it is the *falling*. Before this scattering of small leaves, having seen a hen shaking herself and her feathers fall, he replays that scattering of small feathers and says: "Mom, look the feathers of the tree are falling." Here we have a beautiful example of a child's gestual expression.

Herein perhaps lays our answer: the leaves and the feathers are making the same gesture. There is something altogether very subtle, something airily gliding, whirling, twirling, swirling, and coming to rest. The child has captured and linked up the mimismic nature of the two objects, and so flowed what we are wont to call: poetry.

I need again here rectify what seems to me inadequate terminology, for we say that children are by nature poetic. No, children are by nature *concrete*, let us not confuse things. The child expresses what he sees. We, we express through formulas, through clichés what we never saw. A child does not bother if something is said or is not said. But the teacher checks the child's homework and remarks: "One does not say this in French."

One day, Victor Hugo stood up: "One does not say this? No, but I, I am going to say it." But he was Victor Hugo. Later on, teachers will give it the nod: "How admirable! Victor Hugo said it." What if we went to find our Victor Hugo's among our children? Someone should produce the doctoral thesis I have dreamt of for so long: *Children's metaphors*. The child is greater than Victor Hugo, greater than any of our stylists! We are in raptures before one of Victor Hugo's expressions: "Ah, that, how observant!" Children see and observe things all the time, uncontaminated by the ready-made and conventional formulas bought at some dictionary bazaar. Children are qualitative, having not yet thrown themselves in the social quantitative. They are there, before things, before the real, themselves. No one has said this, no, but the child, the child says it.

If all these remarks by children were collected, they would throw a completely new and unexpected light on our psychology of language and expression.

The child's beautiful style is his spontaneous style; it is not the style imposed on him in school.

There are manuals on children's *composition*. True children's writing is not done in front of paper and inkwell, it happens in break time, when they play with their little friends. That is where a style comes into being, unplanned, made of short little sentences, but full of the real and full of play. As children play with gestures, so they play with metaphors, for geste is metaphor.

We dwelt on three striking metaphors: the crescent, which is not something that grows, but something that is curved and yellow, it is the geste of his banana. The grass, it is the grass that sprouts. From this metaphor, many more will derive, and then, we have those fine and fluttering things, the feathers of the tree.

I have given you a quick sketch of an immense theme, that of children's style and their creation of metaphor through their mimismic geste. The development of this geste in the child should be encouraged, not smothered, as is presently the case. Note that all great stylists are creators of new metaphors. Many authors in fact only survived because they had a fresh style, full of *images*, as we call them, full of metaphors, full of gestes.

I have shown that children have their own marvellously configured style, a style we kill off because we do not know it and because we are unwilling to know it. We impose on the children our written style and our trite metaphors.

## Receptivity of mimismic peoples

Those peoples that remained young and spontaneous replicate the very same phenomenon, but with the added richness of many centuries of observation and experience. Children create their vocabulary alone, and when they create their style, they are truly and wholly themselves. They have only the words heard in their environment to go by, and these they use as they please. A child heard the word feather, the word tree, and, at once, puts together "the feathers of the tree."

In those milieus, however, of people younger than we are, two facts need to be kept in mind. The first is the phenomenon of uninterrupted spontaneity, for, as their intussusception is richer, so is their expression. Those among you who have been at the mimodramas of the Indian chief OS KO MON recently know how richly he expresses himself in all his gestes. One cannot but feel how he truly creates specific expressions with a disconcerting suppleness and richness.

Thus is fashioned an extraordinary rich gestual, mimismic language.

Look what comes out of the hands of a sculptor after he has let his fingers shape a lump of clay. His workshop is strewn with mock-ups, a muscular arm here, and an athlete's torso there—in an instant a face has appeared! His hand sufficed for something new to be created.

This license of the artist is, in a spontaneous, mimismic, so-called "primitive" milieu, the daily bread of the *creator of gestes*. Year after year, century after century, a social treasure chest is established from all those individual intussusceptions. So much so that after a number of generations, a formidable extensive and organized set of mimismic expressions confronts us. It is from this treasure chest that I have tried to unearth the etymology of our desiccated terms. Here, a whole new science lies in wait.

The work is similar to that we should undertake for the ethnic gestes. Move into all the spontaneous ethnic milieus with recording apparatus, film the mimismic creations, ask those people about the real they intussuscept and express, ask them about the static etymology they embody: "What is this?—That? The cloud.—And that? The sun with its roundness.—That? It is the crescent with its curvature." This way we could record the as yet unsuspected richness of spontaneous human expression, not word-for-word, but *sentence-for-sentence*.

Nothing of the sort has yet been done. It is altogether painful for me to watch a documentary film. These documentaries are nothing but randomly and carelessly rolled up meters of film, no one having bothered to put some logical order in the pile, some method and comprehension, some thought of what is at stake. The problem is that the underlying law is not understood.

You have surely seen some of those dances, some of those perfect gestes that are the envy of our own sculptors and rhythmo-mimers! We have some unique treasures there and yet, all this will come to pass, and will be left to gather dust in a corner.

I appeal to you who work from a secondary real, copying master pieces in museums, sculpting and modelling clay while standing before a Michelangelo or some or other admirably executed sculpture. Do you understand that these films present you with a formidable documentation for you to experience and work with? I do not know who will do the responsible thing, but it needs to be done, urgently.

We should select and collect all that is truly documentary in these films. It is easy to see that at a given moment the filmmaker adds a little love story to please his own ethnic audience, and for the film to be financially viable, for a documentary in itself might seem a bit heavy going.

I saw a film recently about the Indians of North America. Left to its ethnic spontaneity, the film is a marvel! No tricks. Pure true mimism. At the time of filming, the director, Paul Coze, told the cast: "Do as if there were a battle between Indians, and I will film you. You are free, do as you please." They did. Two warriors attacked each other, dragged each other from their horses, fought on foot, man to man. At last, one of them fell. At once, all the warriors of the victorious tribe surrounded the defeated enemy to dance the famous dance of the scalp, which is to us altogether new and spellbinding.

Here is what Paul Coze told me: "I let them do . . . it flowed from their muscles!" For the film to stand up commercially, however, some fake romance was added in the guise of a young Indian girl awaiting her sweetheart. We are left with a beautiful film spoiled by an untimely intrusion. Why not cut out this abominably artificial scene and preserve that what is truly genuine, truly concrete in this whole film.

What I propose is for you to collect, directly or indirectly, this kind of great mimismic expression. Could you obtain such films? A number among you are writing theses—and I congratulate several among you on this—theses on the science of the psychology of the cinema. There is here a most interesting subject matter waiting to be exploited, and your documents are here, at the ready. You will no doubt come and ask me for printed documents on cinema, and I will let you have whatever I collect—but is there anything I could give you comparable to all these *live* films which are of true social importance?

Our present-day cinema is puerile compared to all those great traditional and age-old gestes. Just as one cannot stitch together a living language by assembling a few linguistic features. Cinema alone will no doubt soon afford a few men some glory. In fact, one such made his appearance here who is famous already for having created a cinematographic style. Others will follow with different techniques. Where will they get their training and inspiration from, if not from the age-old input of people who confronted and expressed the real. They did so either directly or through the play and interplay of metaphors, as I have just shown you.

### Grasping the invisible world through metaphor

Here arises, inevitably, a problem that is greater even than that concerning children. Although children no doubt already posed this question: that of the *invisible world*. Send a young child alone into the night. He sees astonishing things, he hominifies, he metaphorizes: "O, that thing there, it is a big man looking at me." It is only a tree trunk, but the child has seen, and metaphor arose. Paul Valéry says that metaphor comes from a quick glance at a thing. That is very correctly observed. A white curtain? It turns at once into a kind of phantom where the child will distinguish a long dress from which arms emerge and a scary head. We might say that the child throws his whole mimism into the things he glimpsed. He will always tend to feel around him a host of things that stir, things unseen: the fear of the invisible.

All religion set aside, when those young peoples face nature, they are seized by a kind of sacred thrill. They know that all the things we see are nothing compared to what we do not see. How to express these things, how to play out these invisible beings? Precisely through metaphors. This thing will be the *powerful* thing; this will be the *biting* or the *grimacing* thing. Whence all those curious expressions you see in the statues of the divinities of various peoples.

All the concretely expressed qualities of the invisible are found in the child's comparison of the leaf with the feather. Take the falcon that dominates and whose look pierces the horizon, it is the *All Seeing One*; this is why, in order to symbolize him as the one who sees all, a particular god is given a falcon's head. For the thing that is timid, that equivocates, and that is at the same time prudent, a deer is chosen, and the head of this animal is, directly or directly, fitted on the rhytmo-mimer's head. This is why the sacred dances of the gods are done with masks that reproduce the concrete gestes and the characteristic geste of all those animals that we come across, without us understanding clearly their full meaning.

There is research to be done on all those these figures of the invisible world that are reproduced, dare I say, metaphorized, by things visible.

We are often taken aback by what we see as apparently gross symbols for such very pure things, but the apparently gross things are metaphorical realisations of a transcendent quality. Can you truly expect human beings for whom the concrete exists, to cloud their expressions? Take the word GOD = THEOS, it is the bright one. Take = LUNA, it is the illuminating one [the notion of MOON is linked to measuring time]. All the words you presently use are fundamentally gestual.

If you entered inside these animalizations of the gods, you might well find that characteristic geste that signifies their greatness. We do indeed still have comparisons like:

Be humble like the dove.

Be prudent like the serpent.

Do we think of animalizing our expressions? Not at all. All these concrete gestes, all these metaphors that we have adopted from the Semitic milieu, are to us expressions of gestes: "I saw her speed off like a little mouse."

Free up your gestes and see how those, dare I say expressions of animal symbols, will come to you spontaneously. Take our terminology, we say: "He is a donkey." What has the "donkey" done to us for us to inflict on him the indignity of being compared to one of us. Conversely, "O, he! He is an eagle": lucky eagle to be compared to such men! It does not ever occur to us to animalize anyone. We hominize rather, we throw all the animal's qualities into the qualities of the human.

So far then the mechanism of metaphor in the spontaneous ethnic milieus.


## Receptivity of people who remained childlike

A few among us are still capable of regaining the suppleness of those peoples that retained their spontaneity: our artists and our scientists.


### *The experimental savant*

Since my last lecture, not a few people came to see me, some were artists, others scientists. The scientists told me: "You cannot possibly compare artists to savants, it's over the top!" I answered: "I don't think so, because I am presently studying *the adaptation to the real*. That is what an artist does."

That is precisely where my interest lies, in the intussusception of this real in the human compound of the artist. The savant on the other hand, confronted with the real, will attempt to give an approximate formula, which is a pure algorithm: "It is a perhaps well-organized cage, but I see how the real seeps out from all parts."

### The dramatic artist

On the other hand, some artists came to pay me a visit. They told me: "Thank you. You have restored the artists' reputation which is often misunderstood, and sometimes simply bad." I am very pleased with this approval. I do indeed think that we need to return to the true artist his full worth.

### The pedagogue

Let us take the dramatic artist, for example, the actor. Or our pedagogy. Is our pedagogy today what it should be? It should be a perpetual drama: make see, make feel, make touch. What is a chemistry experiment if not a drama? What is the observation of the stars by a knowledgeable teacher if not an admirable drama in which we see the round dance of the stars? I could watch such a spectacle for hours.

That is the point towards which pedagogy should converge, while remaining scientific. A fair balance needs to be found here and maintained.

In truth, every teacher should be an actor and a playwright. What does he need to get across? Not ideas, one does not grab ideas from one's head to put them in that of someone else; one does not give ideas as one administers pills. What needs to happen is that my auditor also becomes my spectator, and that whatever geste I make, reverberates in him.

Sound will no doubt, through some sort of convention, bring pre-established mechanisms into play again, but are they as pre-established as all that? When the teacher's whole being expresses itself, the spectator's whole being will necessarily open itself too. A frightful wrestling match takes place between audience and teacher. Faced for the first time with an audience, you can feel some real reluctance. It is terrible. Who will eat and who will be eaten? Those people before you are all *themselves*. They have now to give rhythm to your rhythm, and to mime your mimism.

It is, truly, Daniel in the lions' den.

A pedagogue, an instructor, or, in that beautiful sense of the word, a builder, who knows his trade, will take on one only of these reluctant people before him—people who are "themselves" and who are justifiably "themselves"—and concentrate on one of those faces that can unmistakably be read. He needs to smoothly insert himself in all these reluctant mechanisms; make people smile, but not too much, for he needs to look serious, scientific. That is all-important! Be incomprehensible for a quarter of an hour, and you are a great man . . .

After ten minutes, having managed all this, it may be after half an hour, at times, with two minutes left, you carry the day and . . . the hostility. The game is yours.

It is the most fearful drama imaginable in human organization.

You need to be "me" and I need to be "you," or the great drama, or tragedy, of human intercommunication.

## Conclusion: the secret of all human intercommunication

This is what the artist is so good at. He ejects and projects his work, a work that is in essence *he*, and so he creates the beauty of enthusiasm. It is with his whole being that he grasps the real and renders it. That is the secret of masterpiece.

Victor Hugo shows the kind of dialogue that exists between him and the real, and the things. Hugo is understood to be a visual being, but he is I fact above all a global gestualizer:

> *Le lis que tu comprends, en toi s'épanouit* (The lilies that you
> grasp blossom within you).[1]

Is that not the most beautiful rythmo-mimismic metaphor? *The lilies that you grasp blossom within you.* You see this great corolla, proffered.

Such comparisons abound in Victor Hugo. What he feels before nature is what every artist feels: "Nature imbues all and lives in various degrees in the savage beast as it does in the beast of burden: forever in dialogue with the human spirit, it calls on him to decipher the animals bound up in a profound and sombre wondrous alphabet, with words like bird, worm, insect, nature speaks two languages. The one admirable in its precision, the other an unintelligible stammer. The heavy-footed elephant, the lion with the mighty forehead—the eagle, the bear, the bull, the horse, the tiger and

---

1. Victor Hugo, *Les Comtemplations*, in *The Essential Victor Hugo* (Oxford: Oxford University Press, 2004) 255.

his superb leap are a haughty, splendid language: the Verb . . . And the bat, the toad, the polecat, the crab, the owl, the pig: the patois."

This is the poet speaking to us. Just as I asked you to take up Bergson again, I ask you to return to Victor Hugo, or any of the great authors who brought something new.

The secret of all human expression, you will see, is always to take the whole world, to get it to pass through our whole being, and to passed it on, rejuvenated and quivering with life, to other beings that become "you."

# The Worldview of Mimism 2

## *Mimism and Comparison: An Interconnected Universe*

### Outline

Introduction: comparison is *cum*—parison: assembling similar gestes

*Globalism*

*Generalization*

### Mechanism of comparison

Gestual substitution

Characteristic gestes

Transitory gestes

### The operation of comparison

gestes of the invisible world

gestes of the mineral realm                    gestes of the human realm

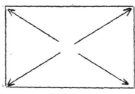

gestes of the vegetal realm                    gestes of the animal realm

167

The expression of comparison

Juxtaposing

Highlighting

Implying

## Conclusion: comparison and pedagogy

## Lecture

## Comparison in the child

La comparaison chez l'enfant. *Labo 30/01/35*

## Introduction

### *Globalism*

The latest research of modern physics has shown that the entire universe is nothing but energy. What this energy truly is, we are not too sure. Let us say that we use the word "energy" as a cover-up for our ignorance. What we may assert, however, is that energy is something impalpable and invisible that we can know through indirect procedures. Simply put, this energy formed clusters of atoms, and these atoms in turn shaped themselves in a variety of bodies, bundles of energy that constitute the world as we know it.

Although this clustered energy appears to us as a multiplicity of masses, it is not, in itself, partitioned. It is rather like an immense ocean wherein ice cubes float, but it is in no way clear to us where one thing begins and another ends. Bergson did express this very well, but he veered too much in the direction of metaphysics. Let us keep it physical, and let us try to understand, for example, the boundaries of our body.

If I move my cold hand close to your face, I will experience something that emanates from you, a kind of tepid warmth coming from the heath of your blood. Where then do you end and do I begin? As it is, you are not in me (which is fortunate because you would be far inferior to what you are now), and yet, I affect you as I constantly jolt your ears. My influence on you is not limited to this sheath of skin that constricts my so-called body.

Our science, the human science of us anthropologists, is vast and gross compared to the science of the physicists. We, anthropologists, we go global and look at the world as and how it foists itself on us in the form of global gestes. This happens whenever I come face to face with the world. For example, when facing an endless stretch of sand, I sense myself stretching out endlessly, as does the desert. Try as I might, I have become nothing but a global mass. The tree I come across is neither larger nor smaller than a mountain. We cannot possibly define the *absolute* dimension of anything. There may be no doubt that a fir tree is smaller than a mountain, but that tree remains a small *mass*. Physicists who hear me qualify a fir tree as a *small* mass will mock me: "If you had done any research at all in the microscopic world of the atom, you would know that that fir tree is a huge mass."

It would take a prodigious genius to know in detail all the ins and outs of just one fir tree. This is why we, humans, are per force globalists. As it is, in this lecture room, I see before me only bundles, small fidgety packs called young women. All my perceptions are global: these small bundles of young women, just as this small basket here next to me. In the same vein, this small wristwatch here: it is a *global* mass. If I were to do now what I used to do as a child, I would open it up, take out all its small mechanical parts, and later reassemble them again, somehow. I would be obvious that this watch is an assembly, a global ensemble. So is this desk lamp here. Again a small global ensemble in which there are millions and billions of things.

This is how a human confronts the world: as a globalist. He cannot do otherwise. He grasps the things by their totality. It seems odd that we should have discovered this in our time only, because we never looked at things properly. Now that we are starting to do experimental science, we realize that it is simple common sense.

Our pre-primary teachers need constant reminding to look at the child in its living globality. Everything applied from outside, on and above this globality, is distorted and distorting trifle. There will always be attempts at paralyzing and ossifying the real in order to size down the child to fit our ignorance. It is one thing to teach penny whistling, as is the fashion now, but quite another to study how a child functions. To proof: children have, on all accounts, be around for a fair number of millions of years, yet, we have only just begun to suspect that the question needs to be dealt with anew and in its *totality*.

We are confronted with global gesticulations, and so we need to disentangle things, to discriminate between things. How? Well, they do so by themselves: they impose on us what I have called their discrete *characteristic geste*. These global energy packs appear to us as forms.

This mountain inflicts itself on us as a whole:

This fir tree inflicts itself on us as a whole that makes a gesture:

We perceive each thing through the characteristic geste it imposes on us, and which is its name. There is no need to go in search of a name for the things; these things impose their name on us. Children give names to whatever they have seen, and these are not dead social names! French, Chinese or Arabic, children could not care less about our denominations. Their play is all they care about. Children play out the characteristics of the things, meaning: the names of things. A child will even dress up in the name of the things—they will fashion an elephant's trunk *because it is an animal that has a trunk* (geste). A child fetches his mother's bedside rug to rap himself in it *for it is a lion's fur*. He has its name, but he wants his body to become lion.

I need here to give thanks to Mademoiselle Perron for a splendid and as always spontaneous experience.

Children, when confronted with us, adults, are reticent. The little fellow who was here last time told Mlle Perron: "The man—and it was me he was talking about—when he asks me questions, he talks too fast." He is right; one should talk very slowly to a child. In truth, my pedagogical laboratory here is parody. It takes a year to ask a child a question; in fact, the question should not even be asked, one should go out in search of the question. That child was perfectly right to chide me.

Unfortunately, I dispose of only a handful of lectures, when we should be spending a life-time together working on this. "This man talks too fast?" Yes, indeed, because this man here has too many things to tell you and, knowing that you know nothing, he is in a hurry. So, instead of being taught proper things properly, you are being whistled to and taught penny-whistling. That is what I have to warn you against: "Beware of the penny-whistling course to your right, of the course in rhythmic gymnastics to your left, of the stock drawings of stereotyped storks course in front of you—you know those storks that stand to life-long attention. Beware of anything and everything you are told. It's all chicken feed. There exists one thing, and one only, the child. The child as he appears before you, spontaneous, fresh, wholesome."

From his answers, you all gathered that this young chap dreams every night of what he has seen. He verifies this great living law: we are the things that we dream, we are the things that we know, and we become, through our whole body, the thing we dreamt of, the known thing. There are moments, even, when we no longer know if we are ourselves (which does not mean much), or if we are the thing that we mime (which means a lot). We are mimers, successive mimers; we *are* successively the thing of which we speak.

Mlle Perron tells me that this child dreams of animals all the time, and, perhaps of some or other particular animal characteristic. He lives, then, in his sleeping dream at night, and he dreams in his awake dream during the day. He dreams, he plays I might say, the animal all the time. Whence the question he asked his mother: "When will I become an animal, mom?"

This question poses nothing less than the formidable problem of knowledge. We become the known object, *adequatio mentis et rei*, as the scholastics have it—the assimilation of the known thing by the knowing object. It is fantastic that this child senses this in himself: he is the known thing: "Mom, when will I become the lion? . . . the wolf? . . . the goat?" That is what we are all the time, and it is that, the characteristic of the human being. A young anthropoid never asks such a question. No young anthropoid will ever ask his keeper, or the observer-anthropologist: "When will I become a beast the way you are?" That is not a question he asks, but that we ask. We ask to become a thing and to intelligize that thing, ask to become a wolf and to intelligize that what we have become . . .

A whole world is locked in that word *to intelligize*, to become all things—to intelligize, to become all those small bundles of globalizing energy in order to know them, to comprehend them, in the etymological sense of the word, to prehend them, to take them in me and to know that that is what I am. "I am all things and every single thing," but all and everything as knowing and comprehending itself. It is a formidable problem, and it is the problem this child puts to you.

This matter is a whole lot more interesting than all the penny whistles of the world! The whistle is dead. Look at both sides of this story: on the one side, emptiness, on the other—what an experience: whatever way you look, what is the story? On the one side you have falsehoods, on the other . . . how I thank Mlle Perron for the gift of this experience! It may well be the most beautiful thing I have heard in my life. So entirely is this child taken in by the real that he wants, that he awaits his metamorphosis.

A most compelling study could be done on the question of metamorphoses. Metamorphoses . . . and all things becoming anything . . . What this child is showing you is that for the so-called *primitive*, metamorphosis is the norm.

You will come across some very curious facts of metamorphoses in Father Trilles's book. Here we find the reasons for those rhythmo-mimics around the lion, as we encounter them in the film that is presently on show: "Africa speaks to you!" For the lion becomes, the lion is something nearly akin to me, when I am in the dance of the lion, or, more exactly, because I rhythmo-mime the lion, and I know, I know very well, that when I rhythm the lion, I am in an extraordinary royal frame of mind. The requests for pardon after having killed the lion of the savannah stem from this. Such are the kind of things I become in an extraordinary mysterious fashion, and it is those gestes that are the names. If you have understood this, you have understood everything: that is what pedagogy is all about.

There should be as many names, *nominal gestes*, as there are energy bundles. Indeed, here is one energy bundle with this particular geste, and next to it another bundle with its own geste too—and the latter is not the same as the former. There are in nature no two identical gestes, and I should thus have a special nominal geste for this mountain here, and another nominal geste for another, different mountain. There would be then at bottom only proper names for each and every thing. True science per se should be such and consist in knowing all things *individually*. There is no geste signifying *mountain* in general, there is the geste op this mountain doing this or that. We would have to have gestes by the myriad of myriads if we were to truly intussuscept the real. It would be altogether crushing for us. Yet, theology tells us that "God knows each thing by its name." We need not go into the question of theology and metaphysics, but we do need to admit that our science is a very limited science indeed, a sluggard's science, because of our fear, and perhaps of the impossibility, of such a labor.

Fortunately, we do have in our gesticulatory system something that will assist us in this reception and knowledge of things: it is that one characteristic geste can be singularly *analogous* to another. What we then do is to execute the geste of the mountain *vaguely enough* for it to mime in a sufficiently recognizable form a *skeleton* geste, and the name will be applicable then to whatever is analogous.

Here is a fir tree—I make this geste—it is this particular tree here before me. Then, next to it, I have this other fir tree, which resembles it. It resembles it only superficially, if I look close enough, and indeed, the painter in his painting will paint both very differently. He will avoid stereotyping them, for he wants his painting to conform to what he sees. There are in nature no identical gestes. We ourselves never have two identical gestes, and proof comes easily enough: if I enlarge each of the o's and a's of your handwriting, not one is the same. We never recite the same verse-line; we never pronounce the same sentence. Frightening, but that is how it is.

What then do we do? We *generalize*, we do *as if* it were the same . . .

*Generalization*

A formidable power, generalization! We schematize the geste. I have here before me this unique thing—a young woman. What does this mean? Nothing: I could give this small bundle of energy any kind of name, but I chose to call it by the conventional social term *young woman*. Turning left, there is another *young woman*, turning right, wow, another *young woman*? Well, yes. This it is that allows me *to classify* things by their characteristic geste. The young woman is, put correctly and fashion aside, the *long maned one*, the one with the long mane. I chose this characteristic of her, which is the one the Indians and ancient Egyptians choose: a woman is characterized by her long hair.

Well, you are all *long maned* ones, however much your hairstyles may differ. This is how we characterize and categorize in science. This is what we teach our children from their very first months! This strange man who leans over him every morning and, again, when he returns in the evening, this large dark form with, or maybe without, a moustache, the child calls that form *daddy*. That is the name he was dealt to point out this particular grouping of gesticulations, one so different from that other grouping called *mommy*. That then is daddy. Arrives a man from deepest Africa where he has lived for the last ten years. He comes up to the child and the child sees a large dark form *analogous* to the form he is used to, and he says *daddy*. Mother is quick to tell him: "No, poor child, this is not your daddy!" To the child, this is his dad, because the characteristic geste is roughly the same.

This is what allows for quick classification, and this is how we classify objects, crudely, as children do. We made a world in the form of *maned ones*, of *dads* and *moms*, in whatever form, ignoring the untold numbers of individual differences we end up not even noticing anymore. We have become accustomed to generalization.

I come now to that particular gross pedagogical error we commit when we talk of *the child*. It is a fundamental error! There is no Child with a capital C, there is no Dad with capital D: there are as many small differentiated individual bundles as there are individuals.

It is on this point that Henri Bergson made a serious metaphysical error. The fact is that each of us is *his own person*. I am not here to do philosophy. Yet, what does this mean: *his own person*? *Person* means *mask*: persona. In Hebrew, it is called *the face*. Well, each person has his own face, his own mask, and one need only to have a proper look at the mask, at the persona, to realize that the one I have here before me is not the same as the next . . .

The equivalent of this iron mask, in our pedagogy, is the name, the *common name*, you understand: *the dreadful common name*. Such an iron mask is fitted on children when still very small, still very supple, and pressed on them for there is only one mask, one cloned a millions times, and placed on their faces—and screwed on so that when I look, I see exactly the same face everywhere.

Thankfully, this has not yet been achieved, that point not yet been reached. Life stood up for itself. Not, though, for wont of trying to bring about what is the very negation of anthropology. This is the origin of collective pedagogies, pedagogies copied from our own iron mask. Do you realize the need to seize every single child, to seize him, and to see what his small young individual system is made of? You are not dealing with The Child in general, it is *this* child you have before you.

When I felt in me a most curious mechanism of gestes and of energetic explosion, I felt it in an individual way. So individual in fact, that many have not yet succeeded in grasping in themselves this thing that is in me, although they have it in them *analogically*. Language is a gestual thing. Many thought it was something heard. Language was understood as a vibration of sound, and not at all as a global gesticulation.

How is it that I personally discovered this? It is because I came to realize that to truly create a science, one needs to see the things, and to see what they are made of. This is why I cannot but repeat to you: "Look at the child, take note of each of its gesticulations in accordance with your topic of research. Of course, it takes time, and of course you have only a few months for such an assignment. I understand and I pity you, but there is no other way. This is what is needed for you to fully understand."

One of you is doing a most interesting study on music of and among children, and she does this the right way, which is by observing children. What struck her is that children spontaneously melodize and psalmodize.

Now, let us imagine that instead of starting right away by observing, she had plunged into books. She would have taken a music dictionary with the various beats—one does not conceive of music without beating time. She would as soon have stuck on some or other beat, and the child would have marched to this beat . . . The big question would have been: "Will the child opt for a two-time or three-time beat?" Children don't give a hoot about your two or three time beat. In the whole history of humanity, not a single truly spontaneous person bothered about two or three-time beats. It is our bookishness, our tendency to rely on the immobile letter, and thus on death, which prevented us from beholding life.

Such is our fear of life and its movement that we flee from it at all cost.

When studies began, some ten years ago, on how children melodized, a good soul appeared on the scene who invented a number of gimmicks for your average pedagogue to have fun with, and to turn him away from properly observing how children operated. This person [Maria Montessori] confected some sort of whistle or flute to teach children music. You might, I do not know, but you might be great admirers of whistle blowing. For as far I am concerned, and I always take a purely objective standpoint, this method shows a total disregard of child psychology. Those flutes are sticks on living things, and when I was asked a couple of days ago what I thought of her travails, I said: "It is for people who fail to observe children. What counts is the child's mouth, and the mouth is the very laryngo-buccal mechanism that you ignore. If only you took the trouble to study experimental phonetics, you would soon enough realize that this so subtle mechanism produces sound infinitely more beautiful and varied than all your flutes, whistles and whistling will ever be."

So, do not come to me with such methods: observe the child and let him become conscious of all *he* has in his global living being. Children learn rhythm through their global mechanism, not through some whistle. One does not learn melody by playing a tin whistle or a reed flute, but through one's oral mechanism . . . O, those people who dabble in pedagogics! If I am so hard on them, it is because they contaminate all of us, those people. They ply us with tools that only distract us from observing, when our focus should be on the child and the child only, the child operating with its own mechanisms.

The whistle is the iron mask imposed on the child. What use can the child possibly have for such iron mechanics, even if shows up as a reed?

## The mechanism of comparison

I am coming now to what the title of today's lecture promised: 'The comparison in the child'—and therefore in all human beings.

Man is an animal that makes comparisons. Nothing more. We are told that "Man is a reasonable animal" precisely because he makes comparisons, because he is able to group analogous things in small bunches. What I am touching on here is the great problem of the One and the Many, a problem that has haunted all thinkers.

### The one and the many

In philosophy, this problem resurfaces repeatedly. It explains why children, when you try to teach them to count one, two, three . . . invariably ask "One what? Two what?" The reason is that the child you are dealing with has not yet arrived at this difficult stage of making an empty geste, a geste that is only a number and not a real thing. This is the difficulty with algebra and with mathematical analysis and infinitesimal calculus. Such is this difficulty that when Leibniz invented, with Newton, infinitesimal calculus, the greatest mathematicians of the world went against him. This, then, is not an easy matter. Again, we need to realize this if we are to do pedagogy, for that is precisely what we are doing when, because of laziness, we start thinking in numbers and 1 child = 1 child. Comparison is in full play here. Characteristic gestes can be substituted, and are substituted.

### Substitution of characteristic gestes.

A mountain? It is what does this, vaguely. A young woman? It is what does this, vaguely. A horse? It is what walks like this, vaguely. We do such vagueisms daylong.

Why should we be altogether satisfied with the words our ethnic milieu dealt us? For example: "That there is a mountain." It is the general term, vague, without precision. Later comes a balloon, two balloons, ten balloons . . . It's ballooning all right. How odd, this geste: here I have the geste *mountain* and I have the geste *balloon*. At close look, they do not seem much alike. Yet, there are particular mountains that are not pointed as their sisters, they are rather rounded off like . . . surprise! They are rounded like balloons! Having seen a balloon as "doing this particular geste," I have this geste at the ready when I find myself facing the mountain and I say: the characteristic geste of the balloon is that it is "ballooning" and it is the same geste I come across here at this mountain. Thus, I make the same geste for that balloon and for this mountain here in Alsace. There is my *metaphor*: the geste of the rounded balloon, in me, and the geste of the round-topped mountain, before me, are similar, and I have my *Ballon d'Alsace* . . . Why is this mountain called *Ballon*? Because it does like this—it is round-topped.

All our linguistic creations are transpositions of the geste, the characteristic geste of one object onto another object, to which it does not, in itself, apply. A balloon is a very special thing. It is a very special thing, a balloon, this small global bundle of energy that constitutes a balloon is very characteristic, it is entirely special. I return to my previous metaphor now of the *iron mask*: I put this mountain with its rounded head in the iron mask of the geste of the balloon and I say: "The Ballon d'Alsace."

Children do this instinctively, they are born givers of names, born nomenclators, who grasp the characteristic gestes, play them in themselves, and so create spontaneously and unconsciously new metaphors. Children have no regard for our social language: they play our words according to the gestes he has in himself.

## Characteristic gestes

Comparison operates according to the characteristic geste, and the characteristic geste is what imposes itself on us globally. Wouldn't it be a splendid topic for a pre-primary teacher: "The metaphor in the child?" Not that anyone will take it up: it demands observation and is not your ready-made whistle. You cannot stock up on comparisons as you would stack up dominoes, because *each* child has his own set of comparisons, according to the subtleness of his own gestual intussusceptions. Just as each author has his own comparisons, and that is what makes up one's style.

This, you understand, is the very negation of the algebraic formula and of the one-size-fits-all word. We are fully in the characteristic geste. We apply the essential gestes from one object to another object. We transpose the mountain and it is the balloon.

I see a sharp rock, and I have seen needles. A needle is sharp and it makes the geste of going up. That rock makes this very same geste and so, half consciously, half instinctively, I call this rock a peak, in French: une aiguille, a needle. Hence: "L'Aiguille du Midi," the Needle of the South, because both the needle and the mountain have the same characteristic geste. However different a needle from a rocky outcrop, they are both pointed, and it is this point that creates the designation and name, and ultimately "style."

## Transitory gestes

I told you that the small bundle of energy we call an object, has not just characteristic gestes. Any object has its own numerous transitory gestes. Let us say that I mime the fir tree as *the wide-stretching one*, because it spreads out its branches. That is not all. There will be a number of transitory gestes. For example, it has small, light and fine things fallen from its branches, it projects small pikes. We could say that the fir tree is characteristically *the spreading* one, and that one of the transitory gestes of this *spreading one* is to send out needles. Other trees too have their transitory gestes. Take this oak tree; it is a strong, powerful thing—its Latin name is robur, robust. It too has its transitory gestes. Thus, in autumn the leaves it sheds come down whirling.

A young child, crouching under an oak tree, sees leaves airily whirling down; quite an odd spectacle, those autumn leaves falling down. This child has also seen something else happening, something altogether different from this characteristic geste of the oak tree . . . a chicken, a chicken flapping its wings, and so producing some transitory gestes such as little airy things called fluffy feathers escaping and flying off. Children are observant and this child has well observed this characteristic geste of the chicken flapping its wings *and* the curious transitory geste of the feather that did this airily whirling down. The whole scene is stored in his whole body.

Then, he sees the leaves that fall of this big oak, and the geste is quite the same. "Not identical," you protest, "analogous." Yes, but your head too is analogous to that of your companions, and yet I call all those heads that are before me heads of young women. This child then was overheard to call his mother: "Mom, the feathers of the tree are falling." How did this splendid expression come to the child? An interesting point, but check all your papers, dictionaries and so on, you will not find anything on this, because no one ever analyzed children in themselves. Children spontaneously notice gestual analogies, the *superpositions* of gestes. What the essential geste that is a chicken transmitted, was similar and analogous, one could say quasi-identical, to what the big oak tree transmitted. Yet, there is no comparison between the geste of being a chicken and the geste of being an oak.

## How comparison operates

There is at present an interest developing in the use of comparison by our great authors. A recent splendid thesis on "Flaubert's comparisons" is a good example of this. Each individual has his own, characteristic way of seeing the real and of engaging with it in new ways. Only strong and spontaneous individuals manage to remain like children in their receptive and expressive mechanisms. This is why geniuses can be compared to children for, like children, they keep their gestes fresh and new.

Great writers create their own style, because the way society expresses itself does not correspond with their perception and expression of things. I asked a great many authors who all told me: "I write with my whole body." One of our youngest writers, Delteil—too pampered, he unfortunately became self-indulgent—told me: "I always felt the need to stand when writing, now I know now why this is so." At that time, his was so very eager, hungry, and so new. Too bad that fame embraced him too young and that he was stuck in his mechanisms, and failed to analyze himself critically.

It is with such richness children come to you, but you remain unaware. Why did no one ever study *children's metaphors*? You who pretend to educate children, who want to be pedagogues—pedagogues, meaning modelers of children's gestes—you do not even know the basics of how children express themselves. Dead or alive, you are catastrophes, and I take fright when I see the unconscious arrogance with which you inflict yourselves on those young children.

The pedagogy of spontaneity is a brilliant pedagogy, but hard to master. In fact, pedagogy does not exist, there are only pedagogues. A single method, in different hands, will yield opposite results. So, for as far as Father Jousse is concerned, you can take his pedagogy with you . . . I know that just as many of you will fail me, as will be successful. You are not me. We are of different type, our characters are not the same, I have behind me 30 or 40 years of experience, experience you lack—how then could you possibly understand and apply my pedagogy? It needs a subtle, organic approach, not your slapdash, crude, mechanical application from without. My pedagogy is not about gesticulating—"Come, make me some gestes . . ."—but about being, understanding, generating your very own comparisons.

I have given you an outline of how children's instinctive comparison works, in its various phases, as characteristic gestes and as transitory gestes. I also showed you how comparison works among our greatest poets, who are invariably those who retained this childlike capacity. Poetry is said to be the childhood of literature. Not so: in the cradle of all literatures, there are living creatures who create from the real. Later arrive parrots who coarsely imitate what others did create; parrots who do stuff "in the manner of."

This is why Men of genius impose their expressive ways on their milieu. Our present day language of psychology, for example, is entirely made up of Bergson's enri Bergson's formulas. All you read and hear, everywhere, is how one *settles* in the real, how one *slides* into, how life *inserts* itself, how one *intuits* something—all language created anew by Bergson in his childlike brilliance. Others only settled in the real following him, not with their own bodies, but in Bergson's ready-made formulas. Pied pipers all.

## The expression of comparison

How will this take shape in a child's expression? You realize now what it meant when this child called out to its mother: "Look, mom, the feathers of the tree." It is a comparison, a transposition of gestes. Between what we know as two discrete gestes, this child played out a new, identical or analogous geste, and by doing this, he did what science does: generalizing a set of phenomena and so creating a *system*.

### Juxtaposition

Remember Newton, the most formidable man of the last few centuries. For years, he was in search of the law governing those large balls called stars, those large packs of bundled energy. He was in ceaseless pursuit of that law: "It was always on my mind." Stars by the millions, stars everywhere. What then was the law of these stars? What was their characteristic geste? or their main transitory geste? He sits down, he who watched long nights, full of spheres, under this very simple thing that we who are from the Sarthe know so well—an apple tree. It has many branches, an apple tree! . . . And these branches carry large numbers of small things called apples.

There you have Newton sitting under that tree, with *it* on his mind, always . . . and then, how very curious! Some of these small, or, of these large apples, from time to time, make this particular geste: they fall and they go boom!

Newton then . . . well, on hearing this very curious sound of the apple falling, Newton says to himself: "But why do they fall and why is it that they don't fly off in the air? How strange! Why are they heavy? It looks *as if* they were caught . . . sniffed at, attracted . . . It is like a large hand catching the apples and drawing them, drawing them towards the center of the earth. So that this apple falls, attracted by a central force that is here . . . How odd, this. There is the moon roaming around the earth, but why does this moon not roam around elsewhere, all over the sky? If this apple is attracted, then it is because perhaps this moon, which could well speed off in that other direction, continues along this curve because at any moment, she falls on the earth from that angle there. My apple here makes the same gesture as the moon. The moon is a big apple."

At this point, my child reappears: what a most formidable discovery! Then all these so-called planets (surely your Greek is good enough for you to know that *planet* means wandering, they had a problem handling them because they wandered all over the place), the planets are big apples that fall on, on what, indeed? Then you see the whole mechanics of the apples and the stars that fall with the same word: it *attracts* . . . Do you see the geste, it *attracts*. This *universal attraction* is the great discovery of the modern times and it is the same law as the naming of the leaves of the oak.

There you have the law, and this law will effectively find its expression in the sensation of something analogous and not identical.

Read Newton's books. He is not saying as some handbooks of astronomy have it: "Any two bodies in the universe attract each other with a force that is directly proportional to the product of their masses and inversely proportional to the square of the distance between them."

No! What he says is: "Any two bodies in the universe do as if they attracted each other . . ." That is the crux of the matter! He is not fooled by his own game: "It is *as if* they attracted each other," ". . . *as if they* were caught so as to get closer" . . . yes: *as if.*

## Putting into relief

This is genius, this "*as if.*" It is what children say: "It does *as if* it is smoking." Why? A child saw a big heap of fermenting grass giving off vapors: "It does *as if* it were smoking."

When one has the good fortune of going through a winter as severe as the one we are presently going through, one can understand another great discovery. It is that each of us is like a small chimney, "as if we were smoking," not here, inside, but outside. You see, children like playing locomotive in winter because in winter, *one smokes.* Children have played at this since there were winters that allowed one to visibly smoke, and it becomes obvious that breathing is something akin to what makes smoke.

Breathing as you know led to great discoveries, breathing being a type of combustion. Who discovered this? Lavoisier. Combustion and respiration both free up carbon, and both need oxygen. Conclusion: do not remain locked up in rooms, have your classrooms aired—we are engines that burn and give off smoke. Again, a comparison: it does *as if.*

That is how children express themselves: "There, look, watch the rabbit. It does *as if* it were a large cigar." Poets like Victor Hugo are full of such expressions: "It seemed . . . it looked like . . . it did as . . . it appeared . . ." I could have brought here to bear so many more exquisite examples of style from the great among our writers.

## Implied comparison

How do comparison and metaphor differ? From the gestual point of view, not at all. They only differ in verbal expression: "Achilles is like, is comparable to, looks like a lion" is, we are told, a comparison, because the word pointing to a comparison is pointedly present. "Achilles is a lion" is a metaphor. Such finesse is no doubt useful for finishing school grammar, but the gestual mechanism is exactly the same. Grammar, like penny-whistling, was created to keep busy four to fifteen year-olds, and some older people, even, if they happen to teach grammar.

Grammar versus the real: that sums it up, somehow . . .

# The Worldview of Mimism 3

## Mimism and the Invisible: Ethnic Liturgies

### Outline

### Introduction

Man, a complexus of energetic and rhythmo-mimismic gestes

### Liturgies

A religious phenomenon; all liturgies have as their point of departure the great primordial gestes

- From the visible to the invisible world

- How to understand traditional rhythmo-mimics. Father Trilles: *Among the pygmies.*

- The rhythmo-mimismic geste: Man's first *language*

- Concretism in liturgies

 *in China*

 *in Plato's World of* ideas

 *in the Palestinian milieu: the traditional geste of the Consecration*

### Conclusion

An appeal for fraternal collaboration

# Lecture

## Mimism and the liturgies

*Le mimisme et les liturgies EA 30/01/33*

## Introduction: Man, a complexus of energetic and rhythmo-mimismic gestes.

A researcher is greatly comforted in his science when, after long years of labor in his specialized field, he sees his conclusions confirmed by other researchers who dealt with the same facts from a different working hypothesis.

When I came here before you last November, I presented what seemed at first sight to be an altogether daring synthesis. My synthesis, however, proves by the day to be nothing but mere common sense. Man was, until now, studied mainly from a *static* point of view. From a psychological viewpoint, what I was confronted by was but the grand and redoubtable system called the psychology of images. I said then, deliberately: "One needs to go further. Man is not just a stable complexus of bones interlinked by muscles, he is also, *above all*, an ensemble of gestes." I set about analyzing the characteristics of those gestes.

Because of the human body's wonderful suppleness, these gestes are *infinite* in number; propelled by an explosion of nervous energy that sets off at biologically equivalent intervals, they are *energetic* and *rhythmic*, and they have the most curious human-specific characteristic of being are *mimismic*. By crosschecking all these characteristics of the human being, I have been able to explain the essential traits of the human's behavior, when this human confronts things real, confronts the reality of things.

The study of the child and the study of spontaneous Man, made it clear to me that the anthropos is subject to the law of mimism, and that mimism should be our very first consideration in the study of the anthropos.

Last time, I briefly mentioned the title and author of a book that has just come out: *The Pygmies of the equatorial* forest, by the reverend Trilles. This man has been in personal, in family contact, even, with the Pygmies, long thought to be the most depraved or the most inferior, if I may risk this superlative, of Men. A vast network of research developed around these Pygmies, most of it embroidered and imagined. There was an attempt at a few serious studies, but nobody gave us a study of such rigorous objectivity and of such immediate and close contact. How great then my joy to see confirmed, at every page of this book, and with the greatest amount of precision, the broad research outline I proposed to you at the beginning of the year.

Here we have a people that, according to the most knowledgeable ethnologists, belong to the oldest remnants of humanity. Yet, this people prove to be stunningly complex. Be it in their *social life*, in their *language*, in their *mimism*, I am confronted with something I never even dared to dream of. My joy stems precisely from the fact that for some twenty, thirty years, I have endeavored to search for, to grasp, I would say element by element, everything that is truly mimismically gestual in human behavior.

No people could be found that has been shielded more from each and every of our algebrized civilizations. They are a people, hidden and isolated, because of their life style, living all by themselves in the middle of inaccessible forests. If ever we are to encounter mimism and gestualism in their purest manifestation, it should be here. Furthermore, if such a people had, in addition to its communication procedures, kept an utmost traditional liturgy alive, then I would find enacted by them what I had suspected earlier in the Amerindian tribes I met, and whose liturgical practices had not been shielded from outside influences.

Liturgies, I discovered, confer upon gestual and human characteristics something altogether striking. This book confirms this, furnishing me with tangible, wholly unexpected proof from someone who in no way intended to write a study on mimism. On the contrary, I could cite pages that clearly go counter my working hypothesis, which is, I believe, as far as can be ascertained, biological fact.

I am the more at ease then to assert that all the facts recorded in this study prove as convincingly as possible the role of mimism in the development of human language. I will touch later on the examples given by Father Trilles of counting done first by the fingers, then by the hands and all the parts of the body, findings that confirm my observations of the Amerindians.

## Liturgies are a religious phenomenon and all liturgies have the great primordial gestes at base.

Before coming to this point, we need to ask if liturgies preserved anything that can enlighten us about human mimism.

Given the complexity of the topic, I cannot do more give you an outline of the role social constraint plays in mimism. Our civilization throws us in a pool of social stereotypes that limit our actions to what *the proprieties* allow: certain movements are forbidden, forbidden too to be too emotional, forbidden to make too many hand gestures, forbidden . . . so much is forbidden

that children and socialized Men turn into rigid beings who are very eco-
nomic indeed with their expressive gestes. This inhibiting social constraint
notwithstanding, the great fundamental law of mimism manifests itself over
and over. Human mimism is not to be chased away from our civilization,
and in some serious cases, mimism returns to the fore, forcefully, violently
and explicitly. One of my most distinguished listeners confirmed this after
my last lecture when he told me how he himself had been compelled to rely
on mimism in order to discover how exactly a crime he investigated had
been committed. That is how little trust we put in writing, which we make
use of all the time, and in our language, which is purportedly the very apex
of social intercommunication.

If language, if writing were so perfect, there would be no need for us to
reconstruct a crime scene, to replay, to remime some of our most worrying
social behaviors. If mimism were as savage, as rudimentary, as gross a thing
as some would have it, there would be no need for us to have recourse to the
finesse and subtlety of mimismic expression in order to make a diagnosis
that might decide a human being's death.

Against the social inhibiting constraint that restricts, diminishes, and
at times even annihilates mimismic expression, we have another, contrary
social form, which is liturgy.

### From the visible world to the invisible world

Liturgy is characteristically a religious phenomenon. It is, at the dawn of all
civilizations, quite difficult to distinguish what is and what is not religious,
so very much does the religious, the invisible penetrate the visible.

This is where I feel my revered master Lévy-Bruhl stumbled when he
spoke of prelogical mentalities, for he measured, with our algebraic distinctions, peoples who totally ignore such dissociated algebrism. We place ourselves on the algebraic plane, and cleanly cleave the invisible from the visible
world; these civilizations, on the contrary, conceive of zones of influence
and interfluence:

In our civilization, we remain systematically in our objective world,
we only believe what our recording machines record. A scientist enters his
laboratory, does phonetics, and forces all the laryngo-buccal muscles to

inscribe themselves on his recording apparatus. If it is mimism he wants to study, he will put all his energy on the capture of all the gestes of the subject of his research and he will study nothing but those gestes. A chemist will operate in the same vein, and so will the physicist. This is the ideal, perfect procedure for us to reach our aim. Anthropologists, psychologists, ethnologists, we all do so- called experimental science, and thus we try to always remain in the domain of the visible, recorded or recordable. This is what I have always done here, and you can testify to this: I have only dealt with recordable things, things that can be measured, that can be counted, and that can be observed. I need to know of no other ways to proceed: as anthropologist of geste, my technique is to deal with the visible only.

However, when I deal with different ethnic milieus, I am not entitled, *scientifically*, to assert: "This particular group of people will categorically divide the visible from the invisible world. Nothing that is not recordable can produce an effect." The great and fundamental error of some of the masters of the sociological school has been to ignore that there are ethnic milieus for whom the invisible world exists and acts, and will even be seen to operate in human behaviors and in their reactions to these behaviors. Assuming then that the invisible intervenes constantly in those people's actions, and that they explain their actions by powers supposedly "not seen," how will these powers manifest themselves? By visible gestes.

These peoples are not "primitive," they are concrete and spontaneous. We will never be able to understand them, if we ignore their ways of integrating the visible and the invisible, if we have not observed their gestes and molded ourselves into their behaviors. This is what the great ethnologist and savant Cushing did: he adopted the ways and teachings of the Zunis, in order to integrate their gestes and mental attitudes, what he called their *manual concepts*. For one to truly understand and enact these manual concepts might take up to ten years, ten years of adjusting one's personal formulas to another real, and to understand not just each and every of the gestes played, but their interplay too, for logic implies interlacing and seamless transition of one attitude into another.

A simple example: let us assume that you have never seen "winner crowned with laurels." How will you, coming from another civilization, establish the connection we establish between laurel and victor? At every turn behaviors will manifest that will seem to us wholly devoid of logic. Anyone who believes not just in a symbolic but in a real, active invisible world, will see an invisible power at work behind any action done under the influence of this invisible world. Yet, he will see the very next action as falling within the ambit of the visible. You, as outsider, you will try to connect the former geste powered by an invisible power, with the latter powered by a visible power. You will see a hiatus here, and the workings of a pre-logical mindset.

If, however, in contrast, you accept, *scientifically* accept, that certain ethnic milieus believe as strongly, or even more strongly, in an invisible than in a visible world, you will be able to grasp the *logic* of their gestual expression. This is a fundamental matter for anyone handling anthropological questions! Human behavior is *not of one kind* and may prove to be quite disconcerting to some.

Bar a few privileged individuals, I doubt many French people understand any of Einstein's logic. From the moment an invention is made, from the moment a new way of thinking enters a social milieu, it will immediately be branded verbose, nonsensical, outrageous, absurd, an impossibility—simply because people have not made enough of an effort to reconcile conceptually with the innovation. They find a scientific theory absurd and illogical because their own, often narrow, logic has been too rigid to adjust to the new thinking. All creative minds struggle to get admission in their social milieu. They meet with the inane sniggers of people who seem intelligent but who, as Lévy-Bruhl might say, are a-logical and prelogical when faced with thought that plumbs depths too deep for their superficial mindsets. Any specialized field, be it mathematics, de Broglie's physics, psychological or artistic theory, invariably hits a wall of uncomprehending people. Yet, if yesterday's mass remains uncomprehending, tomorrow's mass will understand. Why? Because the young are infinitely suppler, not having been subjected to the algebraic cutting up that forces people to follow predetermined groves. They know that the real is countless and that scientific positions of fifty years ago no longer pertain today. Today's true scientists no longer dare to affirm anything for they know, and so do we, that truth is like water running through our fingers.

So then, if we are incapable of understanding our very own creative and innovative thinkers, imagine how difficult it will be, anthropologically speaking, for us to replay with any ease and suppleness other peoples' idiosyncratic intellectual and gestual practices. They are logical, those peoples, but logical in accordance with the gestes they make. We who did not make those gestes, how will we understand them? More specifically, how can we understand the gestes concerning the "invisible world," for it is those gestes we should intussuscept if we are to see, to feel and, I would add, to act out their attitudes. This is why it is so infinitely interesting to see how a number of facts from among the Pygmies, as related by Father Trilles, verifies my thesis. We sense, both how much these peoples disconcert us, and how they gratify us as we delve deeper in their gestual psychology.

## How to understand traditional rhythmo-mimism

Rythmo-mimism is to us an appetizer, an extra, something we stubbornly call *dance,* but rhythmo-mimics are for those peoples their soul's daily bread.

I open chapter 2, which, naturally, has the title *Dance.* This word inevitably throws us into confusion, so let us quash it and look at the facts beyond our distorting vocabulary, in line with what I have taught you since last November and which is here abundantly corroborated: "Someone wrote rightly that when the moon appears, all Africa dances. He could have added: when the moon does not appear, Africa dances just as well, unless it rains. For the African and the Pygmy, everything is reason to dance."[1]

Indeed, because everything is reason to mime, because everything is reason to enter in intercommunication with everything. Does it seem odd to speak when the sun shines? Rain or shine, the French talk. Of course! Why wonder, as it is their way to communicate. Come rain or shine, the African dances, as it is his normal global expression. I am surprised at the author's surprise. In the presence of a people that has preserved so much of its tradition, a people that is famed as one of the most ancient of the *untainted* peoples, we should, if I have reasoned correctly, find confirmation of everything I have told you since November.

So let us listen: our criterion is perfect, being a book that seems clearly at odds with my mimism of language. Of course, we are unable to know original mimism, but we know what mimism is at present. At present, it is a traditional power we need to take into account in all our research in human behavior related to language.

"For the African and the Pygmy, everything is occasion to dance: religious or magic ceremonies, social and domestic ceremonies such as birth, marriage, hunting and fishing, the arrival of a white man, everything is reason enough to dance" (ibid.).

As I told you: "In the beginning, poetry, music—vocal or instrumental—and dance are closely linked." Here you have living confirmation of what I said. I know for sure, because it is the language of Man himself, Man's very own language . . .

"The three 'arts'—let us say the three manifestations of thought—have a common link: the rhythm that rules words as well as sound, the steps and the gestures. We encounter this triple execution still today in the dances of the primitives, of the Pygmies, for example. As I have done previously for the chants, I rank the pygmy dances too in three distinct chapters" (ibid.).

---

1. R. P. Trilles, *Les Pygmées de la forêt équatoriale* (Paris: Blaud et Gay, 1932) 356.

Now, here comes what the author tells us about the *dances* of the *primitives*—which are neither *dances* nor *primitives*, but let us move on: "There can be no doubt whatsoever: they are all *mimetic*. (I explained elsewhere why the word 'mimetic' should not be used. They are 'mimismic'). They try ('try'?), they try to reproduce the nature and habits of the animals, so that, to the tribes in their savage state ('savage'?), the mimetic dances are a kind of drawing in action, an etching or a sculpture with life and movement added" (ibid.).

We came across this same point last week in Georges Hardy, who said that Africans are living statues, infinitely more expressive than our statuary: "Their purpose is to confer on the dancers ('on the human beings' rather) a magic power on the game whose movements they imitate ('whose movements they mime'). It is some kind of homeopathic magic creating an imaginary power over an object by replicating this object" (ibid., 357).

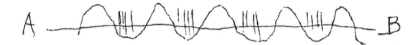

This by means of a series of conditioned reflexes that will alternatively lean on the invisible. Measured against our algebraic thought, this procedure is puzzling, but if an invisible force is brought into the equation, it becomes obvious that a visible geste will immediately impact on an invisible geste, and that this invisible geste in turn will impact on a visible geste, and so on. The progression from A to B becomes the most anthropo-logical of all logic.

This is the domain of dynamic anthropology because we are dealing here with extraordinarily complex beings, whose complexity eludes us who are less complex. We were told in the past that the languages of these *savages* were childishly simple. How bewildering then the richness of their vocabulary and the richness of their syntax and the richness of their means of expression, once we got to study these so-called savages. They have languages of a perplexing precision, these *savages*, as anyone who studied Amerindian languages will confirm.

Gestes are thought of as vague and inexpressive, which is true of *our* gestes, but once we took the trouble to film those "savage" peoples, there rose before our eyes splendid, living statuary, one our poor and puny dancers of the Opéra were no match for. We had discovered something alive and meaningful, against which our poor residue of sensations was found wanting.

We touch here the very heart of our subject: for thousands of years, liturgy has preserved its mimismic formulas untouched. Imagine then my scientific delight at being able to report to you these findings from the Pygmy milieu! It is my greatest reward for twenty-five years of study, for I know now that from now on, anyone willing to do research on spontaneous peoples will share in the very same intensity of life.

My working hypothesis might or might not seem plausible to others, to me it is an absolute *certainty*. I am not looking for approval when, as is the case here, thousands of objectively recorded facts that square perfectly with what I have postulated, and that square much better with my propositions, than with any presumed 'prelogism.'

My observation here about dance does however need further refinement, because the Pygmy *dances* are addressed to *particular types* of invisibles, and are admirably differentiated. In an altogether very new chapter, Trilles writes as follows of these mimetic (mimismic) dances:

"The mimetic dances replicate the appearance and habits of the animals. Their purpose, as we have seen, is liturgical. They either precede or follow the great hunting expeditions. Originally reserved for the heads of family only and their officers (*see how contamination creeps in!*) they are today, one could say, in the public domain, but it used not to be like that. Although the dances still accompany the sacrifices, as I noted before, there are a few renowned Pygmy dancers who do not hesitate to copy them freely, for the greatest joy of their friends or of the villages where they perform" (ibid.).

What occurs, inevitably, is the kind of creeping vulgarizing irradiation that is the death-knell of anything tradition in a milieu as closed as that of the Pygmies. Here is a description of one such rhythmo-mimismic liturgical enactment: "Mba Shole (*the Pygmy dancer's name*) having mimed for us during the day a few animal hunts, we ask him to act the dance out again according to the rules (*thus, according to all the traditional methods*). The dance becomes simply inimitable" (ibid.).

Notice how poor these words come across. What we need is the cinematographic recording of what words cannot convey.

First comes the elephant, and before us unfolds the whole hunting drama: the departure for the hunt, the march through the forest, the beast's appearance, moving slowly. One arm of the dancer makes the elephant's trump, raising the fruit to its mouth; the hunter's cautious approach, how he slides under the animal, and, once there, a foot solidly planted behind (these are all the characteristics we find in mimology), "the quick release of the energy with which he slashes the animal's belly with his terrible lance; the noise of the race, and finally, the heavy thud of the colossus. He is then quartered, has its tusks removed; the children rejoicing around the corpse" (ibid., 358).

But this extraordinary mimicry is not a scene on its own . . .

"Now we are to witness the dance of the gorilla (*chase and death of the gorilla well portrayed*) rolling voluptuously on his back in the grass and stretching his long arms to catch some fruit within his reach. Suddenly he sits up, alarmed, looks around and departing heavily, on all four hands, the first phalanges bent, he sets off, and the Pygmy draws his bow and shoots his small poisoned arrow. A muffled roar, a pause, then a furious rush and suddenly the mass collapses, the hunter rushes forward, plunges his knife in the heart, the gorilla passes out, his arm stretches, shudders, licking his blood, he agonizes before our eyes" (ibid.).

### *The rhythmo-mimismic geste: the human's first language*

These extracts perfectly typify geste. Whoever masters such a fine and subtle mimismic expression, will use it to tell a tale, to recall the past, to project the future, which is what language is about. For what is related on this page (and I have quoted from only one of the numerous pages of this book that deal with human expression) is expression without any intervention of laryngo-buccal language. The laryngo-buccal muscles will intervene later, but oral expression never attains the precision, the fine concrete detail that geste conveys. Sound does not paint, sound does not mime, and sound does not play the action back to us. Everywhere in this Pygmy milieu, *the great traditional geste of the human* has been preserved. It is mimismic replay, it is, as we are constantly reminded, rhythmic replay. For anyone working in the anthropology of mimismic geste, this book is a marvel, and I could quote from it for hours.

Written by someone wholly unconnected with my work, it simply gives facts, facts that, as you see, offer convincing proof. Anyone among you with an interest in mimismic gestual expression, should read this book very closely. The author of the preface remarks rightly that it is one of the great events in anthropology. We have here a body of proof that answers any possible objection to my work.

## Concretism in the liturgies

Now that we have *concretism* by the handful, and substantiated by other researchers, let us have a look at what other ethnic milieus have yielded in the matter of *mimism in liturgy*.

### In China

Just now, we were in the middle of the equatorial forest. Now we move to China, and, always mindful that "In the beginning was the rhythmo-mimismic geste," we take all the things that comprise the universe. We find them, so to speak, understood through direct or through reflected mimism.

In the book of d'Ardenne de Tizac, *Classical Chinese art*, you will find, on page 32, the following about the Chinese conception of the world: "The primitive conception of the world in China finds its origin in the contemplation of the heavens. Earth thus appears only afterwards as an image, as a reflection of heaven (*I would say: as a mimeme of heaven*). On this earth, which is subordinate to the immense system of the universe, the human appears in his proper place and rank in life's hierarchy of physical, moral and social values. In a surprise reversal, however, in this inferior world and the modest place he was assigned, the human, not as a personal entity, but under the guise of the Sovereign who looks over the relation between heaven and earth, acquires a cosmic and regulating value. Such a conception is almost unique in the history of belief systems (*not so, the Chinese conception is obviously a mimismic hypertrophy, but one finds this elsewhere too*). The primitive Chinese has created neither a mythology nor a religion; from the beginning, his thought has taken the form of a philosophy and of a natural philosophy (*I would venture, mimismic philosophy*). This philosophy has an astronomic origin. Above, in the sky, the entire pole, at the immobile center . . . The four . . . separate a kind of projection that one conceives. The terrestrial center, this is to say, the civilized core surrounded by barbarians who live in the four cardinal regions. Just as the lodestar rules the sky (*the lodestar in the sky, the sovereign on the earth*),

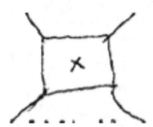

"Just as the lodestar rules Heaven, the emperor, son of Heaven, rules the earth, surrounded by the barbarians, who live in the four cardinal regions; the son of Heaven ruling the earth acts by delegation."

These concrete peoples, everywhere, invariably try to mime this whole immense cosmic machine through their mimismic conceptions. It would be interesting to discover how they conceive of the relation between the world of Up-high, as it reverberates on the world Below. I suggested this topic to a young researcher who is presently working on it.

### Plato's world of ideas

We come across something not identical—nothing is ever identical from one ethnic milieu to another—not identical, but analogous in Plato's ideas. I was much struck when examining the various worldviews of Egypt, China or this or other ethnic milieu, to find that the Platonic system that we called the world of *ideas* came remarkably close to these views.

What does Plato say? I treat here in rough outline only a matter that would demand ample detail. Plato says: "There is a world of . . . ,' and we translate of *ideas*, which should be more precisely of *types*, of *archetypes*, on which all objects hereunder depend, not only by mimism but by participation."

I read recently a study on this difference between mimism and participation in Plato. Everyone says: "It is unclear . . ." But there is a fact, and that fact is that for Plato each of the objects mimes an archetypal object, or participates in an archetypal object, of the world of *ideas*. What we have then is (*Jousse points to the familiar jug on the desk*) the *archetype*-jug, of which this one is only the *mime*. The desk here is a mime of that other *archetype*, and so on . . . and so all the objects of the universe are *miming* and *participating* in this "archetypal" *world of forms, world of types*.

There is great study to be written on this topic that, as you know, is invariably crops up when Plato is mentioned among the Ancients. The whole matter of mimism arises at every page, a point highlighted by Valéry in his essay *The soul and the dance*. I greatly admire Valéry: deeply nourished by the great classics, he sensed that if he was to successfully promote *The soul and the dance*, he needed to demonstrate how mimism invaded the rhythmo-mimers, the *dancers*, as we have it.

A proper study of mimism, so it seems to me, would greatly clarify this *Platonian world of ideas*. The way this subject was taught to us in the past not only killed it but made sure it would remain incomprehensible. What indeed is The *world of ideas* indeed? What is an idea? If an *idea* does not correspond with ". . . ," what then does it correspond with? We are again dealing with an algebrization. What is truly meant by *idea* is the thing seen, the thing as a model, the thing mimed before us. They are, these *ideas*, models that project themselves upon the things that are being imitated.

Our milieu will inevitably be overrun by the cinematograph, so we should more than ever show the child that some sort of cinema from this world of archetypal forms is projecting itself on the things of our world. You all know the famous myth of the cave in which humans are, so to speak, entranced while facing the back of the cave. They are forbidden to look backwards. Now if that is not a presentiment of the cinematograph, then what is? The forms are shown before us . . . when behind, there are the archetypes. More mimism one could not dream of in an anthropological study.

## On some criticism of my research

Most recently, I read a critique of my work in a rather sympathetic book. Unfortunately, one senses that the author has never spent five minutes on questions concerning anthropology, psychology and rhythmics. Let me make it clear: my work is not an open house for anyone to wander in and loiter about. Counting on your fingers and putting on a cocked hat does not entitle you to enter our École Polytechnique Some measure of scientific loyalty surely shouldn't go amiss, such as the simple precaution of not barging into anyone subject unprepared, or to muster sufficient basic humility not to assume one can treat a subject before having studied it properly. Mimism is a world in itself, and you here sense how I buckle under its weight. Me, so small for a subject so vast, I rely, per force, on authorities who, admittedly, do at times furnish me with defective documents.

It would be unanthropological to confine myself to the Chinese or Greek ethnic milieus, yet, I cannot know everything . . . One needs to make a profession of humility, which is altogether rare, but that I did come across in the listeners who come to see me, in a brotherly fashion, heart to heart, eye to eye, and who tell me: "I do not understand this point, perhaps you did not explain it very well." This I freely admit, because if I did not explain it well, then my argument becomes less plausible. What I do not accept however, is for people to come here, and then, after a single lecture, or even five minutes of a lecture, pose as antagonists. I know my science has its limitations, and I can say, without any false humility: "I do not know everything." We can only approach and grasp the real piecemeal.

To operate a 75 cannon, a number of people were needed. One could fire on the order of the captain, simply, but one would fire more efficiently on the objective. All manner of things operated in this division of labor! If for a 75 so many organisms with metallic and vibrant flexibility are needed, how many more then for a phenomenon as formidable as human mimism: thousands upon thousands individuals taking position, not with pieces of heavy machinery, but with unequalled souplesse. Even then, an in-depth understanding would escape us, because there will always be one science missing, the science of synthesis. What I have tried to do, and you are well aware of this, is just such a kind of synthesis. I am not so naïve to think that the synthesis is achieved, I am rather like those signposts that tell you: "So many kilometers left . . ." What I am saying is: "The kilometers are long and they are many." Still, there are, I believe, in the question that concerns us, a sufficient number of facts for us to declare the question to be serious and worthy of examination. Other people besides me as the creator of the anthropology of gestes, other people are now involved who said: "The phenomenon of mimism is undoubtedly of great interest and it goes to the very core of the anthropological enterprise."

So then, let us get down to work. The particular criticism of my work I am referring to here, although amicable—which is in sharp contrast to some other acerbic and ignorant reviews—leaves me somewhat puzzled. I know this man is of good intention, yet he is also totally incapable to get what I am about. So he goes full steam into verbosity. We can go on like this for a very long time, adverse towards each other, harmful and even hurtful, because there is nothing worse than to see people flinging obnoxious monstrosities at you in otherwise excellent books. Never forget though that research such as I expose to you here needs much sympathy if it is to make progress.

## The Palestinian milieu

There is an ethnic milieu that justifiably interests us these days, and that requires proper study: the Palestinian milieu, not from a religious standpoint, but from the ethnic point of view. It is a milieu I have intensely studied, because it is the only one to have preserved great richness of human expression, both in the matter of the psychology of mimism—liturgical and demonstrative mimism—and in the matter of oral style, about which later. There is truly a whole world for us to explore here, and one of intimate concern to us.

We are indeed indebted to two ethnic milieus: the Greco-Roman milieu with its two constituents, and the Palestinian milieu which provides us with an immense traditional civilization in which liturgy has played a crucial role.

The first question we should ask ourselves is: "Will we not, in this Palestinian milieu, come across something comparable, something analogous to what we found among the Pygmy?" I am not saying identical; I am not so simple-minded that I would compare a Rabbi of Israel with a Pygmy rhythmer. There are some very major differences between these two civilizations, I know. What I am concerned with here is not with *ethnic*, but with *anthropological* references? Let me make the following comparison: if I ask, "Do all languages have vowels and consonants?" the answer will be: "Yes, they do." I then conclude that the phenomenon depends on the very constitution of the organism. So, when I ask: "Do we find that all civilizations have preserved, in their liturgies the significative and demonstrative mimismic expression we are concerned with here?" I check and find that we are able to align such expressions by the hundred in the Pygmy milieu. Will the Palestinian milieu yield as much? We have their books—that some of us consider them being sacred but is not relevant here. What is relevant is that we have documents at our disposal, documents to scrutinize.

One such book is the Acts of the Apostles. It came down to us written in Greek, but it relates facts from this milieu of Palestinian traditions:

"We had been for a few days in this town, in Caesarea, when there arrived from Judea a prophet by the name of Habacuc. Having come to us (*he came from Judea, thus from the Palestinian milieu*), he took Paul's waistband and tied up his feet and hands with it . . ." (Acts 22:10–11).

Have you seen anything like it in our civilization? Try to find our present president Monsieur Lebrun, take his hash and tie him up with it . . . Might that not be a problem? It is a problem one might chose to ignore, but one that an anthropologist has the right, and indeed the duty, to raise, and many other problems that were ignored until now and that need to be posed.

"[A]nd he said: 'This the Holy Spirit proclaims . . . the man this waistband belongs to, will be tied up in this way by the Jews in Jerusalem, and handed over to the Gentiles" (Acts 22:11).

It certainly does not look like any common procedure in our civilization. That is the point: we are dealing with a liturgically traditional civilization. The Palestinian milieu has for thousands of years preserved its tradition, and studies done these past years allow us to get an understanding of the formidable power of mimism.

I have mentioned a few times de Buzy's book: *The symbols of the Old testament*, which should rather be called *Mimism in the Palestinian ethnic milieu.*[2] At every page, you will find proof of mimismic expression as a means of expression and of intercommunication. There are words too of course, because we are in a relatively recent milieu here, but in the more traditional Pygmy milieu, speech does not always play a part. As for the Palestinian milieu, we need to appreciate how much gestual expression underlies speech, appreciate that speech has, fortunately, failed to shed its layers of gestual traditions.

2. *Les symboles de l'Ancien Testament* (Paris: Gabalda, 1923).

Let us see for example what has been called *the symbol of the yoke* and what I would rather call *the cogent mimism of the yoke*: "And it happened, in the fourth year of Sedecias, son of Josias, king of Juda, that the following words were addressed to Jeremiah from Yahweh. Yahweh spoke as follows: 'Make you for yourself a rope and a yoke (*and not simply as a metaphor, as you will see . . .*) and put them around your neck. And you shall send a message to the king of Moab, to the king of Bene-Ammon, to the king of Tyre, and to the king of Sidon, through the messengers that came to Jerusalem near Sedecias, king of Juda, and you will give them the following message for their master: The nation that will put its yoke in the yoke of the king of Babylon and that will serve him, I will leave in peace in her land, she will cultivate it and live in it. Oracle of Yahweh'" (Jer 27:1–8).

Another example is that of the prophet who makes a yoke for himself and who, in order to prove that the people will be put under the yoke, shows them how he himself is under the yoke.

Another, last example, for I hope that you will read this book that is the most convincing proof of mimism in this Palestinian milieu. The language is stereotyped, formulaic and traditional and thus easy to remember:

> Yahweh spoke to me in the following words: "Go and buy a potter's jug and bring here elders of the people and elders of the priests. Then you shall go out to the valley of Ben-Himmon that is at the entrance of the pottery's door and there you shall make public the words I am going to say to you. This is what you will say to them: 'Listen to the words of Yahweh, king of Juda and citizens of Jerusalem.'" Thus Yahweh spoke, God of the armies, God of Israel: "I bring upon you in this place a misfortune such that the ears will ring of anyone who will hear it, for they have filled this place with the blood of innocents, they have built the high altars to Baal in order to burn their children in the fire. The days are near when this place will no longer be called Tohec and the valley of Ben-Himmon, but this valley will be called *the valley of carnage*. Then you will smash the jug under the eyes of the people that came with you and you will say to them: 'So has spoken Yahweh of the armies: This is how I will smash the people and this town, as one smashes the potter's vase so that it cannot be repaired.'" (Jer 19:1–11)

There you have a tangible form of gestual language, and you do get a sense of how unexpressive our present-day puny gestes have become, when compared to these formidable mimodramatics of the Nabi in Israel who says: "You will be smashed, and the proof, here it is . . ." Of course, you are entitled to counter that we have other ways of expression ourselves, but admit that such traditional expression is so much more powerful than our algebraic phrasing. We who built fantastic technological systems, we still flock to movie theatres to see films that do exactly what I have just read out to you: to watch some or other famous film star who exhibits that very gestual richness that we ourselves have lost. It is through the cinema that the power of the mimismic geste will make its re-entry, and it is through the cinema that we will regain the understanding of the true expressive character of these languages of geste that we lost. My hour has come, and I can see cinema restoring human expression.

### The traditional gestes of the Consecration

However, we need to look deeper than that, we need to gain an understanding of the traditional power of liturgy that is still operating even today in our algebrized religions.

In our catholic religion, for example, we still have such gestures. I drew your attention to this here, if I am not mistaken: when the catholic priest arrives at the most traditional passage of the sacrifice of the mass, he does not simply make the stereotype geste that consists of reading from a book: he takes the bread that is there, he makes the traditional gestes that have been transmitted from priest to priest. Priests, you should know, do not learn to say mass from books, but by miming the gestes of an Elder and, from time to time, we have, should I say *inspectors of mimism*, who come to observe a priest saying mass, unbeknown to him. If the priest does not make the traditional gestes as they should be performed, it will be pointed out to him. That is how much the conservation of mimism is valued, even in a religion as algebrized as ours, in which geste has hardly any part to play anymore, and in which there are hardly any significative gestes left. Hardly any, but comes that moment of high drama: "Then, he took bread and he lifted his eyes . . ." How marvelous then that we should have managed to keep this moment!

There are, in fact, other instances too of the survival of great liturgical dramas. Baptism is such an instance, and communion, confirmation, extreme unction. There we have not only the word, but the geste in all its extraordinary concretism. At baptism, the priest breaths over the child's head, but he breaths not only by saying a sentence, but by miming the breath, when saying: 'Leave this one, impure breath.'"

We have then, despite all, conserved in our liturgy the most concrete, if *insufficiently understood* mimisms. Herein lays the great difficulty with our liturgical acts: that *we no longer understand* them because we are an algebrized people. How odd that we should still partake in ceremonies where gestes are made, because from the moment we have a book, everything has to be in the book, and yet, great liturgies are liturgies played, not read. The Consecration is one such.

We have here then, in our catholic religion, and unwittingly, an exceptional contact with the very core of human nature. An immense task awaits us, in not only our catholic liturgy, but everywhere, to make us apprehend anew life that we no longer understand.

## Conclusion: an appeal for fraternal collaboration

The distant past cannot be recorded all over again, unfortunately, but film allows us to bring distant lands close to us. This is what makes the recordings of present-day ethnology so interesting. My invariable leitmotiv is for us to establish here at the School of Anthropology, a dynamic anthropology, rather than a static anthropology learnedly assembling skulls and skeletons; a dynamic anthropology collecting kilometres and myriameters of recordings of human gestes, so that my successors in two hundred, five hundred, or a thousand years—when I myself will have become quite static, no doubt— may say: "A few centuries ago someone here said: 'There is more than static anthropology, there is dynamic anthropology, there is life to observe and to preserve.' For you here to have understood this, I thank you."

I was quite anxious when I started this series of lectures at this school. I am of course very much taken by my discipline, but that is not enough to create an interest. What I did wish for then, was to find out if there were, around me, other living beings wanting to understand life, if there were others younger than I am who thought: there is one primordial question, and that is the study of life. How do we go about this?

If I cannot show you how a perfect method can be set up, I can outline an alphabet to this aim. Before an audience such as this one, in an auditorium filled to the rafters, this poor researcher is overwhelmed with emotion, for I know that I will not die completely: I am surrounded by other researchers, who will take over the baton, and push ahead.

On the static anthropology done here in the past by some brilliant people, a host of collaborators need to build a dynamic anthropology. The task is vast, and a single man of genius will not suffice, what is needed is a brotherhood of researchers.

# PART 3

# Marcel Jousse

*Five Essays on Mimism*

# Introduction

## *Oral Lectures and Written Essays:*
## *Fluidism and Formulism*

DURING A TEACHING CAREER spanning twenty-five years—from December 1931 to March 1957—Jousse published twelve short essays. They were, with his book-length 1925 *The oral style*, his only anthumous publications, a scarcity that lead him to self-mockingly refer to his "graphic abstinence." The twenty-thousand-odd pages of recordings of his oral lectures are his main intellectual legacy. The essays are a precipitation, a condensation of some key-points of his teaching. Jousse referred to them as the *solomonization* of his *heraclitism*, which was more than a simple sally: the title of the lecture in which this remark appears is *The formulism of rhythmo-catechism*, and its subtitle specifies: *Heraclitism and solomonism. Fluidism and formulism.* Fluidly or formulaically? How we humans deal with the real is at the core of Jousse's anthropology of mimism.

> The child, we saw, is a mirror, and, the more spontaneous the child, the purer a mirror. Some children will forever remain very pure mirrors and the purest of them will be those whom people call "thinkers." A child who became a thinker at play, or more exactly, a thinker who remained child-like in his approach to the real at play, adopts one of two attitudes in his handling of the real. These two approaches I heraclitism and solomonism.
>
> There is no need for me to explain what the great Greek thinker Heraclites contributed. Having remained in deep-seated "mirror" mode, he felt that the gestes of the things reverberating in him were never the same. He is usually represented on a bank, watching the river flow, uttering this phrase that set thinking so many other thinkers: "One never bathes twice in the same water."

This is so true, for never are two phenomena identical, nor does any phenomenon ever repeat itself. As all great thinkers, Heraclites had the gift of compressing his thought like a diamond, and he said: "Panta rei"—all flows. "The sun rises," we say, but the sun does not rise as it did yesterday, myriads and myriads of elements are not the same and the phenomenon is not an exact replica.

Against this heraclitism, there is another attitude, one that I call solomonism. You would have come across solomonism in Qohelet, a work that you should know by heart, but were never made to learn. Qohelet is a philosophical collection in Hebrew, and Qohelet means "he who teaches in the assembly," it is the catechist of the assembly, of the Qehilla. Transferred in Greek as the Ecclesiast, "he who speaks in the meeting" the Greek title is meaningless as this function did not exist in the Greek context. You should know this book by heart because it is even more powerful than what Heraclites left us. Unfortunately, we never made it a scientific point of honor for us to know the science and wisdom of Palestine. I do recommend that you study this book in depth.

I identified the author of this work as Solomon, which, through oral tradition, is not impossible. I have of course been savagely attacked for saying that the Ecclesiast could very easily go back to Solomon through oral tradition. It is a view I still hold, along with many fathers of the Church, a view that the modernist Loisy and his bedfellows continue to negate. This book deals with a profoundly Palestinian, a profoundly oriental train of thought, namely that there is nothing new under the sun. The sun rises, the sun sets and the day after tomorrow, the sun rises and the sun sets. What this mechanism brings about is the most formidable ennui imaginable any human mechanism could generate.

Some people are unable to view the new and cannot enter in the novel workings of Heraclitian discoverers. It is Heraclitians then who make new discoveries, but true power lies with he who is both Heraclitian and Solomonian, because he will seize the multiply new and fluid, and embed it in a new law that will allow him to probe it further.

This is what we need to prepare the child for. We need to let the child remain Heraclitian and point him towards Solomonism. He needs to retain his interest and curiosity of all things, yet he also needs to become aware of the possibility of finding a rule in which the phenomenon will replay time and again—without it ever being be the same phenomenon. That is the play artists are engaged in. *Labo 18/01/39*

Of the twelve essays, six deal specifically with traditional Palestinian matters: "The gestual tools of memory in the Palestinian ethnic milieu: the Aramaic formulism of the evangelical narratives" (1935), "Judahen, Judean, Judaïst in the Palestinian Ethnic Milieu" (1946), "Father, Son, and Paraclete in the Palestinian ethnic milieu" (1948), "The Targumic Formulas of the Our Father in the Palestinian Ethnic Milieu" (1949), "The Manducation of the Lesson in the Palestinian Ethnic Milieu" (1950), "Rythmo-Melodism and Rythmo-Typographism for the Palestinian Oral Style" (1952).

The other six essays deal with mimism and aspects of the expressive mimismic process. One essay, "Human Mimism and the Psychology of Reading" (1935) was omitted as its multiple references demand a sustained familiarity with French literature. The essays here reproduced in translation are ordered from the general to the specific.

Essay 1, "Human Mimism and Manual Style" ("Mimisme humain et style manuel," 1936) is foundational as it sets out mimage as the primordial universal human means of expression.

Essays 2 and 3 describe the development of human expression, or mimage,

- from manual to oral: "Human Mmimism and the Anthropology of Language" ("Le mimisme humain et l'anthropologie du langage," 1936)

- from manualage to langage: "From Mimism to Music in the Child" ("Du mimisme à la musique chez l'enfant," 1935)

Essays 4 and 5 are about the formation of the proposition and of an oral text:

- the formation of the proposition: "The Psycho-Physiological Laws of Living Oral Style and Their Use in Philology" ("Les lois psycho-physiologiques du style oral vivant et leur utilisation philologique," 1931)

- the construction of an oral text: "Human Bilateralism and the Anthropology of Language" ("Le bilatéralisme humain et l'anthropologie du langage," 1940).

# Human Mimism and Manual Style

## The Primordial Universal Human Expression Is Mimage

### Outline

Introduction: ethnic and pedagogic psychology

Human gesticulation is universal

Human mimism and the utilization of mimemes

Corporeal-manual style and the propositional geste

The visible world and objective gesticulation

The invisible world and symbolic gesticulation

Conclusion: balancing of propositional gestes—parallelism

### Human mimism and manual style

### Introduction: ethnic and pedagogic psychology

WHENEVER MAN, BY DINT of ingenuity, and even genius, appears to have subdued and overtaken nature, nature seems to seek furtive, underhanded revenge.

The discovery of the printing press was a noteworthy victory over space and time. Because of print, the thinker's faint voice transferred to the eye and, spread over millions of pages, disseminated to the four corners of the earth. The fleeting echo of the voice no longer fell into memories easily deformed and forgetful. Metal type rendered the ephemeral, immutable, and almost eternal. Man, however, has begun to notice the psychological damage caused by premature and immoderate use of the book.

A child, scarcely able to babble his first melodic sentences, is condemned to the hard labour of reading. His eyes, so curious to inspect living, moving things and beings, are mercilessly turned away from them, to be riveted on the algebraic signs of the alphabet. His hands, so avid to grasp everything, are no longer permitted to handle anything but the dull, monotonous pages of manuals. His fingers, made to feel, to take apart, and to put together again all manner of things, are clenched solely about a pen, destined to shape graphics whose orthography often does not even correspond to the sonorous articulations that play on his lips. His entire body, that fluid and spontaneous mimer of all the gestes and all the actions of the surrounding universe, is immediately forced to sit rigidly on the school bench, in the hieratic pose of a young pharaoh, hands on knees, facing his "eternal home." To us here, to be good is to be immobile, and our prize for best behaviour is incompatible with the exuberance of life.

Thus is interposed, between the living child and the universe in motion, a strange Platonic world of ideas, a world frozen in black, inert, and often meaningless characters. What is learned no longer has contact with, or relevance to, what is experienced: the opaque density of a sheet of paper separates them. Our social ideal demands that the child be made a scholar as soon as possible, a "card index" who knows of the real world only what he is told by the countless books he read. To such schooling, to know the world is to know where and how books speak about the world. How many people in our midst, people bookishly mummified and buried in sarcophagi of printed-paper, were unable later—or unwilling even—to burst free from the mortifying bandages that suffocated them from the very beginning.

Threatened with such atrophy of their living beings, the most intelligent of our educators became concerned. Such justifiable disquiet coincided moreover with what some psychologists had come to feel when confronted with the factitious results obtained from laboratory tests in experimental psychology. In those tests, the psychological faculties of the "bookish intellectual," white, adult, and civilized according to *our* Greco-Latin scholastic culture, had become the accepted norm of human nature. The rest of humanity found itself endowed with some degree of "primitive and prelogical mentality." Such artificial categories are singularly dangerous to any healthy psychology, and are fortunately fast falling apart everywhere. The focus henceforth is on Man, Man grasped, wherever possible, in his gushing spontaneity: the *anthropos*.

Present-day truly objective psychological research turns therefore to the child and to individuals of the least "dissociated" ethnic milieus. This explains the large, at times outstanding, number of studies on child psychology, and on the psychology of more spontaneous peoples, peoples all the richer in active life for being less bookish than we are. This new ethnic psychology, especially, and the psychology of education, should henceforth lend each other mutual enlightening support.

Humankind does not date from today. It has not refrained from thinking and searching beyond and outside us and in our, per force restricted, formulas. The library of our so-called classical authors in no ways contains the sum total of humanity's age-old experiences, experiences forever enriched with new psychological discoveries drawn from life. There can be no doubt that a broader based study of the whole of human thought, and of all its existing means of expression, will steer us towards more life.

I believe that pedagogical psychology, thus conceived, could become something more than a passive codification of a few routine procedures. And to think that such codification was sometimes drawn up by people who knew a child's life from books only, when only keen awareness of other people's underlying psychological potential and resourcefulness through personal experience enables one to guide the development of another human being as a whole, without deforming him or reducing him to one's own image and likeness. Education is not something one receives from without. The word itself (*ex ducere*) implies that education has to arise from within. An educator worthy of the name will and should be able to let blossom forth a psychologically and morally infinitely richer nature than his own.

Now, human nature has psychological resources that often lay outside the scope of our customary categories, and we need to increase our knowledge on this point by broadening our field of vision to encompass the immense "ethnic laboratory." Spontaneous psychological manifestations that one ethnic milieu for some or other reason compresses or even suppresses may very well continue to flourish freely and richly in another ethnic milieu. It is in this spirit of broad human experimentation that I will pursue my study of the psychology of geste, essay by essay. In the present essay and in the next two, I will limit myself to an outline of the fundamental laws of this psychology of geste, more particularly of the manual geste, the oral geste and of the geste graphically fixed in writing. I will subsequently apply these laws of gesticulation to the psychology of education.

In order to facilitate access to this rather complex matter I have published a "general methodology" giving a broad outline and a provisional synthesis of the varied anthropological studies I have undertaken. I refer the reader to these preliminary *Studies in linguistic psychology*. I need perhaps make the point again that by "linguistic psychology" I understand the whole spectrum of logical human expression, whatever form this intelligent and propositional expression may take, be it manual, laryngo-buccal or graphic. The anthropos, that mysterious compound of flesh and spirit, is indeed essentially intelligent and endeavours ceaselessly to render intelligent even the most material of his potentialities. Intellectualisation however is not mummification. Is not intelligence the most divine gift life bestowed on life?

## Human gesticulation is universal

Viewed from the outside, man is a complexus of gestes. I call gestes all the movements executed in the human compound. Visible or invisible, macroscopic or microscopic, elaborate or in mere outline, conscious or unconscious, voluntary or involuntary, these gestes nonetheless manifest the same essentially motor nature.

The limitations of the average human vision cannot be the gauge of an objective study of the psychophysiology of human gesticulation. The human visual capacity varies constantly, depending on the construction of our optical lenses and on the varying ingenious capabilities of our visual recording and amplifying equipment. Some gestes, receiving greater attention, may move from one category to another and progress imperceptibly from absolute unconsciousness to full consciousness, from purely automatic reflex action to totally voluntary activity.

Such coming to consciousness, such "conscientization" of a geste, naturally contains the "functional characteristic" of the varied organs that emit that geste. Thus, different "functional characteristics" will emerge depending on whether the gestes are corporeal, manual, ocular, auricular, laryngo-buccal, papillary, pituitary, etc. For example, an ocular geste makes us *see*, an auricular geste makes us *hear*, a papillary geste makes us *taste*, etc.

In naming the "conscious re-play" of these different gestes, I have always carefully avoided using the word *image*. Weighed down by so many transitory and contradictory theories, this aged term has created great confusion in the analysis of human gesticulation. One need only recall the case of the strange "motor images": Is not everything in Man *first and foremost* "motor response"? I agree with Dr. Pierre Marie, the eminent neurologist of the *Salpétrière* and his followers, when he claims: "Images do not exist. The term should be struck from our vocabulary." Man has nothing but gestes, gestes played and re-played. Even if this process of interchangeable gestual play and re-play of all sorts is mostly unconscious, it is nonetheless forever ongoing.

The human being is capable both of emitting gestes physiologically and of psychologically intellectualizing and "propositioning" these gestes, which allows him to give expression to even the most intangible of his mental attitudes. Faced with this, I asked myself this question: "How does the human compound, situated at the very core of the universe's perpetual motion, react to this activity and manage to hold it in his memory?"

Jean-Pierre Rousselot, my master and the founder of experimental phonetics, used to say that "careful observation of nature always yields more than we expect." Knowing this, I had only one fear: that I might imagine rather than observe. This is why I relied as far as I possibly could, on all the modern scientific techniques which have already, fragmentarily but experientially, touched upon the complex problem of human gestual expression. Physiology, neurology, rhythmology, anthropology, psychology, psychiatry, phonetics, linguistics, ethnology, etc. all need to collaborate with their respective methods and more or less perfected tools (movie film, phonograph records, recorders of every kind). To an impartial observer, these disciplines will provide *facts* that are rigorously void of any subjective bias.

I have tried to borrow from the objective terminology of these different techniques an exact vocabulary, one that fits the facts that, until now, had often been insufficiently analysed or scientifically isolated. Consider how poor geometry would be if we spoke only of "straight lines" and "circles." Now, in the science of Man, we are all too often still pegged at the level of "straight lines" and "circles." Just think, for example, to what different realities, contradictory realities even, authors apply the word *rhythm*. The immediate adoption of some of my terms by a number of other researchers proved to me the urgency felt by those dealing with the psychology of human expression in any of its forms for a richer and clearer terminology. Science begins with precise language.

## Human mimism and the utilization of mimemes

Of paramount importance to the scientific observation of gesticulation, is the understanding of Man still operating in a state of maximum spontaneity.

What immediately strikes one when observing a human being in such an optimal state of spontaneity, is his instinctive tendency to re-play gesturally, or, to be more exact, to *mime* all the actions of the living beings and all the traits of the inanimate objects that surround him. Aristotle alerted us to this deep-seated anthropological tendency that he identified as an almost human-specific capacity: "For miming is congenital to the young anthropos, who differs from other animals in that he is the greatest mimer of all and that he acquires his first knowledge through mimism" (*Poetics* IV.2).

One obviously cannot study seriously the original richness of mimism in our present social milieu, characterised as it is by conventions of civility and propriety. Such spontaneous tendency was the first to meet with the rigours of our social intercourse. It seems that our ideal has been to kill off all instinctive movements and to become straight-laced, rigid, and slightly disdainful. Yet, all our rules of civility notwithstanding, *difficile est naturam exuere*—it is difficult to cast off nature:

> *What is bred in the bone comes out in the flesh.*

Even in the most distinguished circles, speakers find themselves expressing physically what they are talking about, either with their whole body or with their hands. The old story of someone explaining a spiral staircase illustrates this perfectly: "A spiral staircase is a staircase . . . which goes like this!" (Has not your hand, dear impulsive reader, already spontaneously begun to mime in space the "action" of the said staircase?)

A mischievous observer needs no more than five minutes of objective viewing, or better still, of clandestine filming of the attitudes and gestures of those who talk around him, to establish the continuing vitality of the secret and mysterious anthropological tendency of mimism. This mimismic gesticulation comes even more to the fore when a speaker is searching for words. We all know people who do not speak with ease and whose sentences start more often than not with words only to tail off with varyingly expressive gestures. You may call this pure habit and this is no doubt so, but it does reveal the immutable underlying psycho-physiological energies that emerge when, for some reason, the inhibition of social pressure is reduced.

The question of temperament and of internal and external temperature also impacts, of course. In Southern climes, people without gestes would be like birds without wings. Everyone is invariably someone else's "Southerner." To the English, the French are "Southerners"—we speak with our shoulders, they claim—and the French consider the Italians, geographically and gestually, to be "Southerners" *par excellence*. Mention gesticulators to the citizens of Rome and they will refer you with a knowing smile to the Neapolitans.

The phenomenon is well-known of mimismic gesticulation regaining all its anthropological spontaneity when, at the conclusion of a banquet, internal warmth prevails over cold social inhibition. Israel's Rabbis used to recite this proverb:

> *When wine makes its entry*
>
> *secrets sally forth.*

Generalizing the same psycho-physiological law, one could as justifiably claim that

*When wine makes its entry*

*the geste sallies forth.*

It is from this significant mimismic gesticulation in particular—which is a momentary return to childhood—that popular wisdom concluded that wine rejuvenates the heart of man. It is indeed far easier to observe the persistence of mimism in children before their complete subjugation by strict social constraints. Bubbling over with life and gestes, these little beings are very slow in succumbing to stiffness and constraint, even at the risk of severe reprimand.

Is not all children's "play" mimismic "re-play"? Are they not always playing out charming small *mimodramas* of everything that has happened around them? We have all had occasion to witness the malicious delight and the insolent accuracy with which children pick up the mannerisms, tics, and characteristic gait of houseguests: so perfect is the replay that the piteously mimicked victim of the child's mimodrama is readily recognizable.

However, all that is only a residue, or the revengeful return of spontaneous nature frustrated by the "social paralysis" that invariably and variously inhibits its free play. This explains why anyone wishing to observe pure anthropological reality needs to conduct his methodical principles.

To study mimism with any objectivity, one should turn to the African, Amerindian, and Australian ethnic milieus, where Man's expressive spontaneity remained for ages unconstrained, where his mimismic tendency could blossom forth freely and where it is still at its most striking. It is on these environments scientific observation should concentrate. It is in such "ethnic laboratory" that I have, for close to thirty years now, directed my research on the anthropology of mimism.

In these spontaneous ethnic milieus—they are neither *primitive* nor *savage*, as our Greco-Latin psychology maintained for so long with haughty disdain—social constraint has not atrophied cinemimism. Quite the contrary: it has for ages elaborated, developed, refined and utilized it to the maximum. There, cinemimism has turned into a marvellous instrument for *logical and grammatical* intercommunication, one of such richness and plastic expressivity that it leaves us, simplifying "algebrists," perplexed.

I have given to this "language of gestes," or to be more precise, to this logical cinemimage, the name *manualage*. The collection of its expressive procedures constitute the *manual style*. It is so that the mimer's entire body enters into the modelling play of cinemimage, but it is *especially* the particular suppleness and creativity of the hands that provide fluid detail and that perfect the sculpting of each significant expression. In the words of the poet Georges Rodenbach:

> *Les mains qui sont un peu notre âme faite chair.*

> Hands that are a little our soul made flesh.


## Corporeal-manual style and the propositional geste

A human being who remained a spontaneous *mimer* is psychologically and logically inclined to look upon and *to conceive* the beings around him according to his own image and likeness. He sees, rightly or wrongly, the universe as an immense and mysterious *mimodrama* of beings similar to himself who "act" on other beings. It is this mimodramatic hominization that some ethnologists have mistakenly called *animism*.

The mimer perceives each of these animate or inanimate beings as striking spontaneously a kind of "attitude," as performing a sort of stable characteristic "gesture." This stable gesture—or characteristic attitude—is, so to speak, *essential* to the observed being and *substitutes* for that being's essence. Essence is what all human intelligence searches for, even before it starts to analyse its own ways of being and doing.

When then the occasion arises to mime—to re-play gesturally a particular being—the various mimers almost all agree, instinctively, to choose this being's "characteristic mimeme" and to make it that being's "gestual name." Here "the name" is indeed "the essence of the thing"—its "essential action." Mimed significantly by the geste of *suckling*, a baby becomes *the suckling one*; significantly mimed by the geste of *shuffling*, the old man becomes *the shuffling one*. Each being then has its "gestual name," chosen with delicacy and intuitive finesse from among its most characteristic gestes.

So develops in the *whole human compound* of the mimer a vast mimismic terminology of corporeal style, a terminology as rich and differentiated as his need for expression demands: each of the *interesting* beings of the universe will be "expressed" within the human compound by its essential action. However, these "in-attitude beings," if we may call them such, do not confine themselves to "keep" to this or that characteristic position. They do not have one essential geste only, one only "immanent" action. They also act each one upon the other, in perpetual interaction, through multiple and ceaselessly diversified "transitory actions." Each action activates other actions, and each does so in accordance with its own specific "potentiality."

Corporeal-manual style man is a subtle observer and a supple "receptor." He faithfully reproduces within himself what is played without himself. He replays and gesticulates mimismically and logically, like a live and conscious plastic mirror, the three *phases* of all interactions: 1—the *essential* action of the subject; 2—the *transitory* action of the subject; and 3—the object on which this transitory action focuses, that object itself being mimed as an *essential* action.

A certain species of bird, for example, nominally mimed as *flying* in its characteristic fashion, will "action" in several particular ways a certain species of fish, nominally mimed as *swimming* in its characteristic fashion. Thus this *flying one* could be either "catching" or "carrying off" or "dropping" or "eating" the *swimming one*.

Such is the precision of the corporeal-manual style mimemes that they prevent the mimer from adopting a one-geste-fits-all *unique* mimismic geste, a geste that would be so vague, so general, as to be applicable to *all the ways* of "flying," or *all the ways* of "eating," or *all the ways* of "catching," or *all the ways* of "carrying off," or *all the ways* of "dropping off," etc. For an observer as keen as the corporeal-manual style mimer, there are, properly speaking, no synonymous gestes: not all species of birds "fly" *in the same way* nor do all species of fish "swim" *in the same way*; a person who "eats" does not perform the same geste as a bird—of any particular species—that "eats."

This *penchant* of manual style for the concrete lead a number of *our* Greco-Latin psychologists to conclude that the mimer cannot "abstract" and "generalize." Their overly narrow "algebrized" terminology misled them: when he truly feels *the need*—all expression being indeed utilitarian—manual-style man knows very well how to "generalize" one of his "particularized" mimemes. In this respect, he acts according to the universal laws of human and intelligent semantics. *Abstraction* should not be confused with *algebrization*. Too many vague and therefore too broadly applicable mimemes would weaken a system of expression that has as its ideal the plastic reproduction and translation of every geste of the surrounding universe, however subtle.

How does this living *concrete abstraction* succeed in "expressing" a transitory action executed by an essential action on another essential action? To express, for example "the bird is eating the fish," manual-style man needs to play out a complex geste which is intuitively mimismic, consisting of three "phases" or mimismic gestes that are intimately and muscularly prolonged one by the other, without any real break in continuity, without any "cutting up":

*(the) flying one—eating—(the) swimming one*

I have called *propositional geste* this complex, intuitively mimismo-logic and intellectually logical geste, which very finely expresses the "intus-suscepted" reality through the *entire* acting, feeling and knowing *human compound.*

My exposé here is very technical because I am dealing with things new and highly precise that demand a vocabulary that is clearly discriminating and that at the same time interlinks a number of critically important psychological facts so that we can arrive at an empirical solution to the so-called *problem of human knowledge.*

Only through the continuous enhancement and deepening of its terminology can science progress. All experts are aware of the work that remains to be done for us to handle the facts of human psychology with tools appropriate to the formidable complexity of the real as we know it. We also know that however adequate our vocabulary, we will never fully grasp the refinement and the highly expressive power of this intuitive, logical, mimismic gesticulation and that such density of life cannot possibly "be expressed" statically on paper. What a proper lesson in cinemimage would demand is the presence and collaboration of a person of pure manual style or, at the very least, a cinematographic recording of his mimismic expression.

The movie film indeed—*running* as it does *without interruption*—constitutes the only "continuous, moving book" capable of receiving and rendering, *in its full duration*, the movement and indivisible continuity of the logical, living, propositional geste. The "static book" introduces an unduly and dangerous graphic "fragmenting" *in space*. It distorts the immediate data of the dynamic psychology of intelligent, human expression, making us run the risk of confusing *sequence* and *fragmentation.*

I will deal elsewhere and in more detail with the artificial conventions of the dead and fragmented "graphism" that seem to have been not altogether foreign to the regrettable antinomy Henri Bergson claims to have discovered in *living Man* between sinuous and invasive *intuition*, and divisive *discourse* hewing the real in implacably geometrical chunks.

With his supple hands full of intuitive and logical propositional gestes, the living and intelligent manual-style mimer draws together with ease the two sides of this so-called unbridgeable abyss between *intelligence* and *life* and he fashioned the human propositional geste. The propositional geste is the result of a half-instinctive and half-voluntary muscularly continuous and logically "tri-phase" conjoint process. It is, in the history of human evolution, a uniquely important development for the *objective* expression of the real and for the *living* preservation of human thought.

## The visible world and objective gesticulation

Once in possession of the intelligent, fluid mechanism of propositional gesticulation, manual-style man is psycho-physiologically and logically ready to *objectively* intussuscept, conceive—in the full meaning of the word— know and express all the 'gestes' that spring forth from the nature of the things that make up the visible.

*Science* is henceforth possible. For indeed *to know* an object in some depth, the 'human compound' must first receive within itself, and thus become capable of re-playing *consciously* and *intelligently*, a number of this object's transitory actions upon some other object. These objects themselves were previously defined and known by the gestural name drawn from their essential action. In a number of instances, etymological analysis enables us to retrieve and revive this gestural name in spite of our desiccated and algebrozed terms.

For example: "the fire *burns* the tree"; "the fire *liquifies* the wax," "the fire *hardens* the clay," "the fire *reddens* the iron" and so on . . . or, "the eye *sees* the man"; "the eye *sees* the fire"; "the eye does *not see* the breath" (or the spirit); "the eye *casts* a spell" . . . This for *each* essential action of the universe and until is exhausted the mysterious sum of transitory actions with which the universe is, one might say, "pregnant."

The subtle ethnic "logic of pregnancy" we see at work here still awaits proper scholarly attention. What we do know is that, grounded in its past, but subject to revision, each ethnic milieu *rightly or otherwise* attributes *a* number of transitory actions to an object. Anyone who experienced life in a variety of ethnic milieus knows that they each attribute different and even contradictory effects to the action objects inflict on other objects, and particularly on the human. Such attribution of power to an action of an object, whether true or *imagined*, obviously influences the human's reactions, comportment and gestes toward these objects. The propositional geste that I deliberately cited above, "the eye *casts* a spell" is a well-known and excellent illustration of this process.

Having embedded the countless actions and interactions of the universe in *his entire* acting, sensing and knowing *being*, corporeal-manual style Man is able to replay them at will, either for himself or for others. For others he lets his corporeal and manual mimemes irradiate macroscopically with all the amplitude needed to make them easily recognizable and understood; for himself a summarised microscopic outline gesticulation suffices as long as it allows him to grasp with full consciousness and to trace with clarity each of the phases of his propositional gestes.

This is the point where my *psychology of geste* and Pierre Janet's powerful *behavioural psychology* meet and, given some indispensable adaptation and fine-tuning, can integrate.

In his lecture of April 15, 1926, Pierre Janet asked: "What, basically, is the brain? In no way is it the organ of action. Action does not depend on the brain; it is not performed by it. We used to be told that the brain secreted thought much as the liver secretes bile. That is childish. A brain separated from a living being is incapable of thought or action. The brain is one of the elements of the extremely complex circuit that we call action; when the brain is separated from the muscle, there is no longer action. Action is dependent on both brain and muscle. In reality, man thinks with his whole body; he thinks with his hands, his feet, his ears, as well as with his brain. It is ridiculous to claim that his thought depends on a part of himself: it is tantamount to saying that our manual ability depends on our fingernails. Psychological activity is global, not local. The brain is a set of switches . . . The brain does not determine psychological activity; it only regulates this activity."

To the *integral* mimer then, the universe presents itself as a formidable interlacing of unconscious, unavoidable interactional gestes that he can and will re-play consciously and voluntarily. As a kind of microcosm, Man *receives* and *renders* as propositional gestes through his whole corporeal and spiritual being, the countless actions of the macrocosm.

Here then, in the visible expression itself, the knower somehow *becomes* the object known. Through his entire acting, sensing and knowing being, the expressive mimer metamorphoses successively, without being fragmented, into the various phases of the propositional gestes that he is expressing: he first briefly *becomes* the being that is known and mimed; he then *becomes the* action that flows from this being; he finally *incarnates* the being on which this action is performed.

The mimer, as Paul Valéry might put it, "is devoured by countless forms." As a *human compound,* he "is activated in all its parts, co-ordinates everything within itself and takes on shape after shape, as he continuously steps outside of himself . . . The *one* wants to play at being *everything* . . . He wants to enhance his identity through the range of his actions," of his intellectualized gestes.

Thanks to the technical wizardry of the movie screen, we at times get to witness this fluid passage from one being into another, this gradual, imperceptible fusion of Man into an object, of which he performs the characteristic actions and particular gestes. This kind of magnification of the vital act of human intellectual knowledge acquisition is a great help in the study of the psychological laws with which modern cinematographic style has inevitably to comply. Indeed, the multitude of difficult problems faced by the technicians of "silent" cinema are no different from the problems faced and resolved long ago by the spontaneous cinemimage of corporeal-manual style ethnic milieus. If we are to penetrate *more deeply* the living mechanism of human logical expression, it is in those still spontaneous milieus that we need to conduct our anthropological research.

It is also clear why every *expression* that is truly spontaneous and objective *is necessarily concrete*. Contrary to the French sociological school's ambiguous and catastrophic usage of vocabulary that warped proper observation, I differentiate not between *concrete* and *abstract*, but between *concrete* and *algebrized*. I do so because no human can "think," which means to "consciously proposition any of his mimemes," without having recourse to abstraction—which is why corporeal-manual style Man is perfectly capable of instantly propositionning and of expressing his mimemes (which are at once concrete and abstract) without having to algebrize them as we, present-day Greco-Latins, are wont to do by transposing them in so-called uniquely "abstract expressions."

Their name notwithstanding (*ex pressio*), these so-called abstract "expressions" no longer flow from within miming man under the "sealing" pressure of the gestes of the real. They are more likely social and superficial "impositions" from without, in the manner of purely conventional labels: *voces significant ad arbitrium*—sounds are of arbitrary significance.

These socially imposed expressions too were no doubt once mimemes fashioned objectively from real things. However, having over thousands of years slowly lost contact with the objects themselves, they became deformed, disfigured, "algebrized." They became pure social "algebremes" that we call "abstract" out of ignorance, setting them against "concrete" mimismic gestes, which would then not be "abstract." That is why you deem your *primitive*, who uses only concrete expressions, incapable of abstraction!

For better or for worse, our knowledge or ignorance of Greco-Latin etymologies—which are in origin always mimismically concrete and always intellectually abstract—is irrelevant where the fundamental anthropological mechanisms of man's intellectual and expressive gesticulation are concerned: the anthropos is a mimismically and abstractively propositioning animal.

Moreover, the more plastic a "transfer" it is of the object to express, the more fully modelled it is by the contemplation of the object to express, the more mimismically concrete and intellectually an abstract expression will be.

It would be a profound mistake then to assume that manual-style Man is reduced to some rough outline whenever he wants to express subtle and delicate actions in refined detail. Quite the contrary: it is through concrete intuition that one reaches precision. Manual-style man is constantly in direct contact with the things and gestes of *ambient* nature. He is able then to grasp in each being that he observes over time, countless actions—to us unimportant or unknown—which he mimes with finely differentiated gestes. As I said earlier, there are no synonymous gestes.

Notwithstanding the richness of manual style in differentiated mimemes, through *transport* of gestes or *metaphor*, and because of some subtle gestual relationship and fine resemblance between them, a great number of actions by one set of people will be mimed through actions that habitually characterize another set of people. In essence an intelligent being capable of grasping and expressing mimismically and logically these gestual relationships between the actions of the *visible* world, Man is an animal that plays with metaphors and learns through comparisons.

## The invisible world and symbolic gesticulation

Everything I have said so far has to do exclusively with the actions and interactions of the *visible* world. Man however is a far too profoundly "spiritual" being to waste away, imprisoned in the cinemimage of this visible world. Man too *ad majora natus est*: he is born for greater things.

A *compound* of flesh and spirit, Man can no more ignore his body when he expresses the real (for Man is not an angel), than he can ignore his soul when he wants to express the *whole* real (because he is a being "for whom the *invisible* world exists").

Even when Man's gestes are abstractively intellectualized, they remain mimismic and objective transfers of the visible world (*gestus mimici non significant ad arbitrium*: mimismic gestes are not arbitrary), they remain in essence material and concrete and it is through their concrete and material mediation that Man will try to mime the actions and interactions of the invisible world.

Moreover, Man senses that this must be how the beings of the invisible world proceed when they, in turn, try to reveal themselves to him. It is logical indeed that they can only do this by making the normal, ordinary "actions" of the visible world "act" in an unusual and astonishing fashion. It is not illogical at all to believe that invisible beings can stage such acts seeing that they are more "powerful" than visible beings. The concrete, visible world is here sublimated and this "sublimation"—not "algebrization"—of the concrete is a veritable drama: what we are witnessing is the supremely poignant and magnificent struggle of two substantially mutually dependent components of the mysterious human compound.

It is the struggle, continual and ever-present, oscillating tragically between spirit and flesh and flesh and spirit. Victory, however partial, belongs no doubt to the spirit over the flesh and the spirit's triumphal song is the invention of analogy. From this moment on, Man is able to grasp each of his mimismic gestes and *to sublimate* their meaning. The greatness of Man as the creator of symbol cannot be overstated. Through symbol, manual-style Man makes a breath-taking leap into the infinite.

These "sublimated expressions," however concrete they remain, do invariably refer to the invisible world, as the Catholic Church chants with such psychological exactness in the preface to the mass on Christmas day: *Ut dum visibiliter . . . cognoscimus . . . in invisibilium amorem rapiamur*—"So that the knowledge of things visible may bring us to the love of things invisible."

Herein lies the origin of the glorious Greek religious dances (or better, rhythmo-mimisms) which Lucian analysed so pertinently long ago. As did all manual-style peoples, the Palestinian Nabis performed these deeply meaningful mimo-pedagogical liturgies: they allowed their performers to reach that state of mind where they could integrate and incarnate in themselves something of the invisible real.

Whenever the need arises for us, "algebrists," to incorporate in us *something* of such incorporeal real, we are wont to disparage concrete gestual expression. Concrete expressions of incorporeal realities we call crude and materialistic, proof of the dismal failure of our bookish psychology to understand the nature of symbol. We do indeed fail to understand the subtle logic of propositional gestes that mime through concrete actions that are alternatively objective and symbolic.

I mentioned earlier how not all ethnic milieus necessarily attribute the same actions, the same "gestes" to the same objects. It is quite possible for one ethnic milieu to perceive the connection established between a visible and an invisible object in another ethnic milieu as shocking, or even illogical and contradictory, only to then refer to such reaction as the expression of "prelogical mentality."

Only by placing ourselves *within the cinemimic system* of an ethnic milieu whose understanding of the interactions between objects differs from ours will we able to see what logic is at play there. The so-called "prelogical mentality" is nothing more than a pronounced instance of the well-known psychological phenomenon: *traduttore, traditore*—"translator, traitor." "Pre-logical mentality" vanishes as soon as we acquire for ourselves sufficient expressive sensitivity to retrieve all subtle, seemingly incoherent gestes, and rediscover their delicate interlinkages.

## Conclusion: balancing of propositional gestes—parallelism

Like multiform Proteus, who might after all be no more than his traditional and mysterious symbol, manual-style man

> . . . transformed himself in all sorts of wondrous shapes,
>
> A fire, a dreadful wild beast, and a flowing river.

> *Ommia transformat sese in miracula rerum,*
>
> *Ignemque, horribilemque feram, fluviumque liquentem.*

Thanks to the multifold fluid, mimismically objective or subtly symbolic propositional gestes he devises, preserves, and replays in his whole being, the gesticulator has henceforth taken intellectual and logical possession of the invisible and of the visible world.

This is the point where the curious psycho-physiological law comes to bear that I have analysed elsewhere: the law of parallelism.

Manual-style Man no doubt incessantly trained himself to mime and to re-play, corporeally and especially manually, all the actions and interactions of the universe in his concrete, modelling, logical propositional gestes, to the point of rendering them automatic. It is from the depths of his *bilaterally structured* organism and almost in spite of himself, that he feels himself impelled to replay each propositional geste once played and to re-play this propositional geste in a form that is identical, analogous or antithetical.

A single propositional geste will thus trigger one or two others that physiologically balance with the first. These two or three physiological and semantic *balancings* form a living, dancing, logical unit, a kind of manual binary or ternary *rhythmic schema*, the influence of which will be apparent universally, manifesting even in our current literary and pedagogical discussions.

Here, for example, a gestual binary and ternary, balance as follows, propositional geste by propositional geste:

Binary:

> *(the) shuffling one—hitting—(the) suckling one,*
>
> *(the) suckling one—stroking—(the) shuffling one.*

Ternary:

> (*the*) *flying one—eating—*(*the*) *blowing one,*
>
> (*the*) *swimming one—drinking—*(*the*) *flowing one,*
>
> (*the*) *crawling one—fleeing—*(*the*) *burning one.*

Translated into our algebrized modern style, this becomes:

> *The old man hits the infant,*
> *The infant strokes the old Man.*

> *The bird eats the wind,*
> *The fish drinks the water*
> *The snake flees the fire.*

Sadly, the latter leaves us at a far remove from the concrete manual, danced and balanced mimodramas.

I conclude on this all too brief outline of the major law of *parallelism*, a psycho-physiological and logical law with which I will again engage in the future: as soon as human thought seeks to express itself *immediately* by letting its bilateral and instinctive mechanisms come into play, it recovers the spontaneous balancings of the manual-style propositional gestes. M. Le Du's beautiful discoveries concerning the binaries and ternaries of Victor Hugo illustrate this for us.

We find ourselves here at the very root of the creation of style. At this depth, style is really the *whole* Man, invaded and intuitively modelled by the real; it is the *whole* Man triumphantly propositioning and balancing his proteiform invader according to the living and logical laws of the human compound, made of flesh and of spirit.

# Human Mimism and the Anthropology of Language

## The Development of Human Expression — 1 — Mimage, from Manual to Oral

### Outline

Introduction: static anthropology and dynamic anthropology

Human mimism

Cinemimism and *manualage*

Phonomimism and *langage*

Conclusion: human expression, from *manualage* to *langage*

### Human mimism and the anthropology of language

#### Introduction: Static anthropology and dynamic anthropology

FOR MANY YEARS NOW, static anthropology has compared the anthropoid and the anthropos anatomically in a range of both widely diverse and narrowly specific aspects, resulting in a host of well-known outstanding studies.

Dynamic anthropology has in its turn begun to compare the gestual behaviour of anthropoid and anthropos, applying equally rigorous methods and analyses that augur well for future outcomes. The number and quality of the works published thus far testify to the sustained attention of a large number of elite observers and experimenters in the comparative study of such gestual behaviours. I mention in particular the names of Köhler, Yerkès, and Kellog, whose authority was immediately recognized.

Such parallel research on the anthropoid and anthropos can only benefit that most sensitive branch of anthropology, the *anthropology of language* or *science of significant gesticulation*—incidentally, not to be confused with *linguistics* or *science of languages*, the grammatico-philological domain so expertly handled by scholars like Meillet, Vendryès, and others. Some anthropologists of language may have unwittingly contributed to the frequent confusion of these two scientific disciplines that are simultaneously interdependent and distinctive. Until recently, the anthropology of language, by limiting itself to incursions into the grammatical phenomena of particular tongues, i.e., in linguistics, seemed intent on ignoring all too often the unexplored wealth of its own terrain. Yet, we must not be too hard on the mostly eminent professors who every year and for so many years had to come up with a new set of lectures for their faithful audience. A purely anthropological approach must have felt too restricted for such an annual renewal in view of the then prevailing concept of language: language was indeed rarely seen as anything but an ensemble of sounds normally and easily transcribed by the letters of the alphabet.

Faced with such unacceptable impoverishment of an extraordinarily complex matter, the anthropology of language felt compelled to react and it did so appropriately and successfully. This can be gauged from a comparison of two studies, which appeared ten years apart: the 1923 article by Dr. L. Barat entitled "Language,"[1] and the 1933 article by Dr. André Ombredane, "Language, Significant, Mimic, and Conventional Gesticulation."[2] Scientific loyalty compels me to add that as far back as 1928—three years only after the publication of my first study on geste as the basis of language—Dr. Morlaâs published a *Contribution to the Study of Apraxy* (*Contribution à l'étude de l'apraxie*)[3] in which he adopts my point of view on the matter. In "From Mimage to Language" ("Du mimage au langage"), a 1935 article in the journal *L'Encéphale*,[4] the same author drew attention to the convergence of my observations on aphasia with those of Dr. Pierre Marie. Finally, the publication of Dr. Pierre Janet's lectures at the *Collège de France* records the immediate adoption of the conclusions of my research by the author of *Intelligence before Language* (*L'intelligence avant le langage*).[5]

Thus used, tested, and validated by these many specialists of geste and language, my anthropological work came to serve with ever-increasing authority as a point of departure for new research. The anthropology of

1. "Le Langage", in *Traité de psychologie*, edited by George Dumas (Paris: Alcan, 1923) 1:733–57.

2. "Le langage, gesticulation significative, mimique et conventionnelle," in *Nouveau traité de psychologie*, edited by Georges Dumas (Paris: Alcan, 1933) 3:363–79.

3. Paris: Legrand, 1928.

4. *L'Encéphale* 3 (1935) 197–208.

5. Paris: Flammarion, 1936.

language should be the poorer for the methods of linguistic philology; let rather the *living* facts discovered by the anthropology of language enliven the all too often overly bookish methods of linguistic philology. What I put out here in summary are a number of such anthropological facts and their interlinking, with a focus on *human mimism, cinemimism* and *manualage, phonomimism* and *langage.*

## Human mimism

Compared with those anthropoids most highly endowed with "operative mimetism," the young anthropos appears before us with a singular, yet insufficiently emphasized characteristic: *mimism.*

During the first months of his life, young anthropos is undoubtedly, like any animal, capable of a few reflex gestes such as breathing, eating, random movement, crying, etc. However, gradually, as his gesticulation becomes more richly informed, a certain number of his gestes take on a strange and wholly new orientation. It is as if he grows by the day into a living, plastic, cinemimic and phonomimic motorcamera in which all the visible and audible actions and interactions of the animate or inanimate beings around him reflect, re-sound like an echo and re-play.

The child does not indeed confine himself to the handling of objects the way he saw other human beings do around him. Such handling of a "real tool" according to a previously perceived gestual prototype is what I earlier called "operative mimetism," and anthropoids prove to be quite adept at this. What the young anthropos does however, is something wholly different, and I differentiate this "something else" by calling it *mimism,* and within mimism I distinguish between *cinemimism* and *phonomimism*—mimism of movement and mimism of sound.

## Cinemimism and *manualage*

In mimism, the cinemimic geste can "be detached" from the object in order to "re-play all-by-itself." This unattached replay expands gradually to the point of monopolizing the gestual activity of the young anthropos. It is as if the visible actions and interactions of the universe, reflected in his eyes as ocular microscopic mimemes, extend and irradiate, one by one, through his entire global musculature as *corporeal* and especially *manual* macroscopic mimemes.

It must be stressed from the outset how extraordinarily important the young anthropos' hands are in the operation of mimism. As a logical means of intercommunication between one anthropos and another, *mimage* always and spontaneously tends to be cinemimic *manualage* rather than phonomimismic *langage* (to be scientific and thus precise, I here give the word *langage* its proper and normal meaning of "lingual gesticulation"—gesticulation of the *langue*, the tongue). Remember how, when meeting, two men who do not speak the same language but who nevertheless wish to communicate intelligibly, resort at once to *plastic, manual* mimage and only very rarely to *sounded, oral* mimage. During the last war, communication between French and American soldiers brought daily proof of the invincible propensity of "eternal anthropos" to manual mimage.

I might be tempted to add that the anthropos is endowed with mimism because he has two hands—a titillating aphorism modelled on that of an old Greek philosopher—but further observation prevents me from doing so, seeing that the anthropoid, with his . . . four hands, is not endowed with mimism. His mimic deficiency when compared to the young anthropos can clearly not be imputed to a lack of gestural organs of intercommunication.

In young anthropos, whenever irradiating ocular mimemes encounter sufficiently developed gestual elements at the ready, they combine and a mimismic synthesis ensues. The combination is progressive: there is always an indispensable prior limbering-up of the mimismic system. From non-existent or almost non-existent in the first months of life, the irradiation of ocular mimemes expands in keeping with the mounting of corporeal and manual gestes, culminating in an infinite wealth of re-played gestes. What the human musculature replays in synthesis it has first played out in fragments.

The mimismic replay of the young anthropos is indeed at first fragmentary and erratic. It is not so much a first maladroit outline of a gestual ensemble as a whole, but rather the replay of one or other feature of this ensemble—usually of its most salient feature. Then slowly, progressively, this particular point stretches into a plain line as the gestual phase extends into a multi-phased gesticulation that assigns to each feature its true place and function in the global replay of the interaction.

It soon seems as if the preoccupation of young anthropos is no longer with the real objects around him but rather with the arrangement of the interactions of his subjective mimemes. It is essentially in this re-arranging that his "all-by-itself" mimism differs from the operative mimetism of the anthropoids, which cannot be separated from the object. It is as though the young anthropos is constrained to act, no longer just in *our* world of objects, but in *his* universe of interiorized, intussuscepted mimemes. The function of the exterior world is solely to furnish his intussuscepting curiosity with a continuous stream of new mimemes which set about by themselves to replay and combine in all his muscles, variously and ceaselessly.

***

So intense is the energy of the child's mimemes that they soon seem as real as and even more real than the things they represent. He is "acted upon" by them and by their interactions, just as we adults are ourselves "acted upon" by the interactions of the external world. We cannot overemphasize the all-pervasive power of these mimismic interactions. Whenever an elementary gesticulation has reached fullness, it will replay as part of a dynamic, extremely complex set of interactions and not as an isolated intussuscepted mimeme in the way of artificial words of a dictionary. The interaction is the unit of mimismic re-play. Intelligized, it becomes the propositional geste—the generally tri-phase propositional geste:

*an* acting *one*—acting *on*—*an* acted *upon*

It is through this spontaneous drive of his interactional mimemes that the young anthropos becomes a mimodramatist *malgré lui*. He enters into what the old psychology used to call the *stage of play*. The often heard claim that "children always *want* to play!" is anthropologically inexact, at least in the beginning, because children do not "want" to play any more than they "want" to be hungry or thirsty. Close observation demonstrates rather that the young anthropos "is being played," just as he "is made hungry," just as he "is made thirsty." There is in him a genuine anthropological urge that arises from the law of mimism and that impels him somehow to become all things, and all things as they manifest in their spontaneously imbricated interactions.

The child does not become, as is the case with independent "plastic poses," a living but immobile statue, then another living but immobile statue, and another living but immobile statue, all without any link from one to the other. No, there is not fragmentation but vitally and muscularly fluent "successivization": by virtue of a dynamic and muscular flow, the successive interactions of the universe incarnate within him without any break in continuity. He infinitely replays, as a matter of course, what has been finitely played within him. His ability to "compose," to "de-compose," to "re-compose" gestual interactions is infinite. Quite unlike that of the anthropoid, his curiosity is universal and mechanical, in the sense that he is despite himself impelled to become aware of *how* everything plays before him so that everything can faultlessly re-play in him. This is science before con-science.

Because it is so automatic and constraining, young anthropos is at first only very confusedly conscious of this unabated and global corporeal-manual mimodramatic play—a play that engages all his muscles as in some kind of "awakened sleepwalking," not unlike the tyrannical "ocular mimodramatics" in the adult anthropos that is quite inexactly called "visual reverie." As psychological and psychiatric research on "daydream" has shown, such involuntary and nearly always unconscious re-play continues unabated in our ocular gestes even when we are awake and even when we are at our most attentive.

It is replay directing us rather than we directing replay. It is a rare anthropos—if he exists at all—who could claim that it is he who choses which mimemes will be allowed to replay in him. As our ocular gesticulation replays more often involuntarily than voluntarily, it is near impossible for us to choose which ocular mimismic interactions to allow. This might be so because we failed to exercise or develop our power to inhibit this subtle mechanism. It is a fact that even our most intense purely ocular gesticulation is no more disturbing to the people standing closest to us, than our auricular gesticulation. Which is why no one cared about controlling this particular replay and neither did we: *de minimis non curat praetor*—the praetor does not concern himself with trifles.

Yet we do exercise partial control and we do partially inhibit the spread of our ocular mimemes through our corporeal and manual musculature: the unrelenting constraints of social convention imposed on us from early infancy taught us to do so. We should however not delude ourselves too much, because, even if "we think with our entire body," as Pierre Janet reiterated, what used to be spontaneously macroscopic in us has become artificially and painfully microscopic.[6] Our so esteemed education has seen to this, leaving us with an atrophied memory so that, in its present state, our poor human thought amounts to no more than a moderately clear consciousness and propositional intellection of our mimemes. Memory being the more or less free replay of one's mimemes, atrophied memory results in equally atrophied replay.

This reduction in our expressive capacities notwithstanding, we all know how some mild depression, or even just a few glasses of champagne, suffice to break open the straight-jacket of social restraint and to restore the corporeal-manual mimemes in all their splendid and anthropologically ordinary amplitude. All of us, both young and adult anthropoi, remain against all odds what we are essentially in all our fibres: wholly global mimodramatists.

***

6. Frédéric Lefèvre, "Une heure avec M. Pierre Janet," *Nouvelles Littéraires*, 17 March 1928, p. 9.

The mimodramas of young anthropos are organized and structured, and not mere physical fluster, because he always "plays at something." This internal organisation does not mean that each of the mimismic interactional gestes that constitute their framework is consciously premeditated and composed, but it does mean that they are all logically—quasi-grammatically—de-composable.

The anthropoid on the contrary, unless he physically handles some object or other, "plays at nothing." He gambols about and wiggles around in an inchoate commotion that resist mimismic analysis. Even when he seems to be "playing with" something, we are punting anthropomorphism if we imply here by "play" what play means when applied to the young anthropos. The anthropoid's apparent "play" is nothing but repetition of gestures characteristic of *operative mimetism*. He is moulded and directed by the object as it is actually perceived or actually handled, whereas an object used for play by a young anthropos becomes a mere support for interactional mimemes that bear no relation to the normal usage of this object. Moreover, the mimemes drawn from the real object can vary indefinitely: the young player's mimismological gestes will transform a stick used for hitting into a gun, into a horse, etc. The young anthropos can play at just about anything with just about anything.

We never see an anthropoid behave in this way. His operative mimetism cannot "abstract" his gestes from the here and now—from the *hic et nunc,* to use the very correct phrase of our old philosophers. On the other hand, the *mimism* of young anthropos continuously "abstracts" and "detaches" the characteristic and transitory mimemes that he intussuscepts from the surrounding actions and objects. Once he has these mimemes within him, he replays them all by themselves, regardless of time or place. From the platform of present space and time, he manages, on his own, and unknowingly, to leap beyond space and time.

Such abstraction triumphs over space and time without any diminution of the mimemes' plasticity and concreteness. Our empirical vocabulary all too often unduly confuses *abstraction* and *algebrization*. Where, with his whole being full of mimemes, the young anthropos can play in abstract concretism, the anthropoid handles only the concrete objects, without ever being able to abs-tract or ex-tract his operative gestes from them.

Unlike the anthropoid then, the young anthropos, placed in the midst of the countless interactions of the universe, is not the inert contemplator he might seem to be at first glance. These interactions of the external world reflect, not only in his eyes but also, thanks to the globalizing irradiation of mimism, in his entire being. They replay in all his fibres and he is replayed by them, in all his fibres, voluntarily or involuntarily. Unable to inhibit the interactional geste that has spontaneously begun in him, he replays the three phases of all interaction, i.e., the mimodrama of an *acting one—acting on—an acted upon.*

For example:

*The riding whipping the galloping*

The horseman whips the horse

Naturally, young anthropos has neither a real horseman, nor a real horsewhip, nor a real horse at his disposal. He has only the characteristic and transitory mimemes, but they are *really* in him and *really* active. Replayed microscopically or macroscopically, this little mimodrama is initially, and for months thereafter, only vaguely conscious. One day however, the young anthropos becomes more clearly conscious of this interactional replay of mimemes and that day, he intelligizes the repay and directs it.

Having seen a locomotive go by, for example, he runs to his mother in order to replay for her and to "recite" for her cinemimically, with both arms alternately extended and retracted, the characteristic back and forth movement of the wheels' connecting rods. Of such spontaneous action the anthropoid is wholly incapable, although, like the young anthropos, he sees the locomotive and he has arms and hands which could gestually execute the movement of the connecting rods. He has all the organs and all the gestes, but lacks the intelligizing mimism.

Now, give or take a few years and our social milieu will have succeeded in inhibiting the child's spontaneous, significative, cinemimic gestes. Our social milieu will have forced him to transpose his manual gestes onto his laryngo-buccal muscles in the algebrized and today seemingly conventional guise of *the locomotive propels the wheels' connecting rods.*

Later again, when our young lad, now grown into a serious adult, tries to make a foreigner understand what *propels the wheels* means, the repressed mimemes of the characteristic back and forth motions will be forcefully re-played all by themselves in the muscles of this "eternal anthropos" and eternally miming anthropos. Now the grown-up anthropos "does" himself by *imitation,* i.e., consciously and voluntarily, what "was done" earlier in him as a child by *mimism,* i.e., unconsciously and involuntarily. He now masters the expressive tool mounted in him previously, pressing out what had been pressed in and reproducing it at will in order to signify. Thus is born the *propositional geste.* Logical human expression has found its fundamental unit of oneness.

From now on, the ceaseless drama of the interactions of the universe is left literally in the conscious and deliberately knowing hands of the awoken mimodramatist. From the very first months of his existence, a number of animate and inanimate beings had come to mount in-him their character-istic geste, their "gestual name," without-him. What the young cinemimer has grasped that this characteristic geste, pregnant with multiple transitory gestes, acts in multiple ways on other beings who have equally been received in his manual musculature through their characteristic geste.

This is how manualage, or manual mimage, emerges from the an-thropological playing field with a methodologically clearly defined propo-sitional stylistics. For a great many thousands of years to come now, our indefatigable human mimodramatist will extend his natural mimism and *imitate* voluntarily what *had been mimed* spontaneously. That is the path followed by the anthropos, a path that will lead him to develop the immense significant corporeal, and especially manual, gestual expression recorded by Mallery in his acclaimed anthropological study of the Amerindians.

## Phonomimism and *langage*

The instinctive tendency to mime the actions and interactions of the uni-verse corporeally and especially manually may be psycho-physiologically dominant in spontaneous anthropos, but it is not his only tendency. Besides plastic and visible actions and interactions, the animate and inanimate be-ings of the universe have also sounding and audible actions and interactions that reverberate mimismically on the subtle muscles of the anthropos' inner ear in the form of auricular mimemes. It is *auricular* phonomimism.

Like ocular cinemimism, auricular phonomimism plays out secretly in microscopic gestes on organs that remain inaccessible to outside observa-tion. As only the subject himself sees mimismic ocular replay and hears au-ricular replay, no direct experimental recording from the miming muscles is possible. Fortunately, the conformation of the anthropos' respiratory and laryngo-buccal system is such that under the pressure of breath, the most diverse sounds can be emitted with an almost infinitely variable range of intensity, duration, pitch and tone.

Thus comes about a new specialization of the general law of human mimism: just as ocular cinemimism irradiates and amplifies into corpo-real and manual cinemimism, so too does auricular phonomimism have its spontaneously amplifying irradiation echoed on the laryngo-buccal muscu-lature. The sound that is played mimismically and microphonically in the inner ear tends to be replayed mimismically and megaphonically on the lips. It is *oral* phonomimism.

\*\*\*

Compelled by this auricular and oral phonomimism, any child raised freely in the countryside "names" naturally, by himself, a number of animals and objects by the characteristic sound they emit. This is evidenced on a farm in the Sarthe where a barely articulate child runs to his mother, with his hand rhythm-mimically to his mouth, shouting with startlingly accurate melodious intonation and timbre:

*Miaou ham cô! Miaou ham cô!*

The cat has eaten the rooster!

Indeed, a large and formidable neighbourhood cat had just strangled a cockerel . . .

Compared to this rich phonomimismic spontaneity of young anthropos, the laryngo-buccal expression of the anthropoid appears even more obviously devoid of phonomimism than he was of cinemimism.

Not that the young rural anthropos, brought up in free contact with the countless sounds of the countryside and of nature, proves to be an incomparably greater phonomimer of things than the young "cloistered" city dweller who lives with his mother between four walls. Obviously, our learned pedagogues only ever studied the latter, and with savant complacency. Deprived of nearly everything that could spontaneously multiply within him the rich phonomimemes of sounding, moving and living things, this city child has his ears almost exclusively bathed—or rather drowned—in the very poor sounds of human speech. No surprise then the following naive and significant response of a little five-year-old Parisian who told me: "My ears, they are for listening to mouths." What the ears of a country child are much more likely to hear are "the sounds of things" and it is such sounds that will re-play like an echo most spontaneously and most clearly in his auricular and laryngo-buccal gestes.

Not that oral phonomimism always reverberates with the mechanical precision of the case mentioned earlier. Human mimism is not brutal machinism. In the gestual replay of the young anthropos, there is a "personal equation" to take into account that is alive, that very soon intelligizes and thus interpretes. Between the sound emitted by the object and the sound re-played by the mouth, there is at times no more than a relatively obvious analogy. Phono-mimism then becomes phono-analogism and from phono-mimeme to phono-analogeme there is a wide range of possible intermediaries.

The phono-analogeme is not always and not as a matter of course directly borrowed from the object itself or from its transitory actions. While making a spontaneous or mimismic geste, the anthropos tends to emit himself a sound that may become semantically characteristic of that geste. Such is the *ahan* sound which becomes as it were the audible, phono-analogical geste of the visible and corporeal geste of the woodcutter.

It is the anthropologically instinctive and forever tenacious pressure of phonomism, now reduced to phono-analogism, that drives the writers of our algebrozed tongues to create, pen in hand and with varying success, their individual "imitative harmony":

> *Pour qui sont ces serpents qui sifflent sur vos têtes . . .*
> For whom are these serpents which are hissing on your heads?
> *Les souffles de la nuit flottaient sur Galgala . . .*
> The breath of the night floated over Galgala
> *L'insecte net gratte la sécheresse . . .*
> The brittle insect scrapes at the dry loam . . .

This shows just how difficult it is for even the most graphically algebrized anthropos to rid himself of what comes naturally, i.e., human mimism!

***

By its very nature fluid and unstable, the audible mimeme proves to be less constraining and so less precise than the visible mimeme. Thus each human grouping, independently of all others, choose by itself and for itself from among the many sounds emitted, its own perceived characteristic sound of an object or of a geste. If only the past had done what the present-day talking movies are doing, which is to record meticulously each of men's gestes—of hunters, warriors, pastoralists, agriculturalists, etc.—and how that *one particular* geste would translate spontaneously in that *one particular* characteristic sound in the throat of that *one particular* human grouping.

Progressively and lazily, the phono-mimeme, and even more so the phono-analogeme, being further removed and thus less conform with the original object than the plastic cine-mimeme, lost contact with the object that had given them shape and that held them to that shape. At some point, no perceivable relationship with the originating sounds or actions of the object is left and to the speaking subject, the phono-analogeme has become no more than an artificial phono-algebreme—a sound that must have once been conventionally uttered and conventionally assigned to the object. For thousands and thousands of years and from generation to generation, this sounded algebreme took on a life of its own in each particular human group, subject to the strange deforming psycho-physiological laws of ear and mouth, audition and diction.

Scientific analysis of these gestual, auricular or laryngo-buccal defor-
mations would demand a knowledge and determination of all the influences
of atmospheric and climatic elements, altitude, food, drink, the contamination of one language on another, etc. In addition, there are in any given
region of any given country no two throats or palates that are identically
conformed and therefore capable of uttering a strictly identical sound.

It is from countless, and as yet only partially studied factors such as
these, that arises the continuous evolution of laryngo-buccal articulations
in the official and provincial languages and in the dialects and patois so
cherished and so brilliantly studied by my master, Jean-Pierre Rousselot,
with the help of the recording apparatus of experimental phonetics.

The slow transformation of *manualage* into *langage* I have just described took place over a great many thousands of years, with a concomitant
change in the anthropological evolution of writing, from mimo-graphism
into phono-graphism.

## Conclusion: human expression, from *manualage to langage*

At first phonomimically emitted through the laryngo-buccal geste, sound
serves to reinforce, specify, and perfect the audible signification of some
manual mimismic and visible geste. Later, little by little, a sounding adjuvant duplicates each characteristic or transitory manual geste. Still later, the
manifold sounding gestes decode and counterbalance in equal numbers the
manifold manual gestes. At this stage, corporeal-manual gestes and laryngo-buccal gestes are on a par. Finally, less expressive than the corporeal or
even the manual geste, but demanding less energy, the sounding laryngo-
buccal geste begins to dominate, with a concomitant reduction of now
increasingly dispensable corporeal-manual gestes. Laryngo-buccal geste
increasingly prevails and begins to gain a life of its own and *manualage* and
*langage* switch roles, with the once all-powerful *manual* geste now become
an adjuvant to the *oral* geste. Useful still but no longer indispensable, this
aid falls progressively into neglect, abates and almost disappears.

Today, the original importance and past dominance of significant corporeal and manual gesticulation can only be rescued from oblivion through
specialised studies and meticulous anthropological and ethnic research. Yet,
its transfer into the laryngo-buccal system did not alter the profound nature
of expressive corporeal-manual mimage and its roots remained intact. We
find ourselves to this day in the realm of the anthropology of significant
geste. The phases of a manual propositional geste, transposed into the corresponding phases of a laryngo-buccal propositional geste, retain their

original concretely cinemimic meaning for a long time. In a great number of ethnic milieus, the significative laryngo-buccal gesticulation is indeed comprehensible truly and totally only when one knows the manual gesticulation from which it derives and upon which it continues to depend semantically.

Hence the tremendous anthropological importance of seeking out the first and cinemimic meaning of the so-called *roots*. These roots are quite simply the sounded transposition of the ancient cinemimic gestes of manualage. In this search for original meaning, mimograms and their subsequent manifestation as phonograms are an inestimable aid.

Indo-European, Semitic, or Chinese roots, we were told repeatedly in the course of our studies in grammatical linguistics, all had concrete meanings. We now know why this is so, and only the anthropology of language could give us the reason, not philological linguistics. Under the gaze of the law of mimism and its compelling findings, that old chestnut, the "problem of the origins of language," shows up as what is truly is, a "pseudo-problem" caused by ignorance of the anthropological laws.

Endowed with his essential and intelligizing mimism, the first anthropos expressed himself through mimismic propositional gestes as spontaneously as he walked on his two legs.

Others now, the Boule and the Teilhard de Chardin, need to explain to us why the anthropos alone is endowed with mimism.

ESSAY 3

# From Mimism to Music in the Child

## *The Development of Human Expression — 2 — Mimage, from Manualage to Langage*

### Outline

Corporeal and manual mimism
Propositional parallelism
From mimism to mimography
Auricular phonomimism
Oral phonomimism
From mimage to *langage*
From *langage* to oral style
From oral style to music

### From mimism to music in the child

#### Corporeal and manual mimism

A CHILD RECEIVES THE characteristic and transitory actions of the animate and inanimate beings of the exterior world through the gestes of his whole instinctively miming body. Surrounded by the ongoing mimodrama of the universe, the "human compound," made of flesh and spirit, behaves like a strange, sculptural mirror, infinitely fluid and incessantly remodelled.

A child *registers* this complex and multifold universal mimodrama gesturally, in the manner of a plastic, living and fixing film. Without consciously realizing it, he becomes a complexus of mimemes or intussuscepted mimismic gestes, the richness of which increases with each new intussusception.

A child *replays* the phases of each of the interactions of the universe mimismically through the gestes of his whole body, and above all through the countless gestes of his hands. What is created physically and unconsciously in the universe is psycho-physiologically and consciously re-created in the child.

This re-play of corporeal and manual mimemes is neither scattered nor incoherent but happens spontaneously in the intelligent and logical form of a generally tri-phase propositional geste:

*an acting one—acting on—an acted upon*

Of necessity successive, these three natural phases of the mimismic propositional geste are also biologically imbricated: they make up a tear-proof muscular and semantic "whole."

Thus, a child's living thought has its own living tool for the conquest, preservation and expression of what is real: *mimage* or language by gestes that are corporeal and manual, mimismic and propositional.

Propositional mimismic re-play is the intellectual and living basis on which to build pedagogical anthropology.

From now on pedagogy has to be mimo-pedagogy.

## Propositional parallelism

Because of the human body's bilateral conformation, the propositional gestes of the corporeal and manual style tend to replay in rhythmic balancing, two by two, or, less frequently, three by three.

This is the important anthropological law of the *parallelism* of propositional gestes, the influence and survival of which can be found everywhere, but particularly in the following intellectual activities:

- In the alternating balancings of what we call "folk dancing," those relics of thought, the purely gymnastic minimally recognisable residue of *ancient* propositional and pedagogic rhythmo-mimisms. These corporeal balancings alone survived centuries of progressive degradation and degeneration of the propositional rhythmo-mimisms precisely because they are so irradically physiological. Yet, it was their propositional element that had accounted for the supreme greatness of these human gestures. While animals do dance gymnastically, man alone has propositional rhythmo-mimisms. Man alone has the mysterious privilege of "propositioning" his gestes. Proposition is the miracle of human life.

- In the isosyllabic and balanced hemistiches of our so-called "folk songs," which are no more than the trivialised residue of the ancient recitatives of rhythmo-pedagogical oral style. The misfortunes of the oral style in our written-style ethnic milieus are well known. At some point in history, writers—some gifted with intellectual brilliance—graphically and slavishly imitated the traditional balanced forms of the oral style. They did so without truly understanding the full significance of the psycho-physiological and mnemonic nature of these monotonous balancings and their mnemotechnical linking by rhyme. They sought, and therefore found in these rhymes no more than aesthetic pleasure, of which they inevitably and predictably soon tired. There followed, in the last century, a very tardy revolt of these scribes against the monotony of the traditional balancing of isosyllabically parallel hemistiches and in its wake came rhymeless free verse, the perfect "enemy of memory." Abandoned and scorned for centuries by the intellectual elite, the mnemonic and mnemotechnic oral style of our druids and minstrels found refuge in our folk songs—where it awaits rehabilitation and pedagogical application.

- In the balanced sentence parts of the traditional melodies that to this day animate rhythmopedagogically the oral propositional balancings of these folk songs, transmitted by memory. Stripped of their lyrics, these living melodic balancings became our instrumental, increasingly algebrized music.


## From mimism to mimography

The corporeal and manual muscles of a child overflow with mimemes moulded in him by his mimismic intussusceptions of the actions of the universe. We readily repeat that children "play" at everything. We are wrong: children "are played" by everything. What we could say is that these cinemimemes pour out of the child through all his gestes:

- through his ocular gestes, in a manner invisible to us. We call this spontaneous re-play of ocular mimemes: "the child's dream."

- in all his corporeal and manual gestes, in a manner visible to us. We call this spontaneous replay of corporeal and manual mimemes: "the child's instinctive play."

This distinction between dream and instinctive replay is in fact misleading because their psycho-physiological mechanism is identical in nature: it is a gestural replay of previously intussuscepted mimemes.

Moreover, these two registers of re-play are functionally interdependent. The microscopic ocular mimemes irradiate and amplify in the macroscopic corporeal and manual mimemes. We daily express our understanding of this process when we say: "The child plays out his dream." We could just as well say: "The child dreams out his play." What is manifest here is the compelling anthropological law of ocular and corporeal mimism, which drives the child to grasp—i.e., to take in and to understand—the interactions of the universe through his own propositional re-play. Play is the science of the child.

Such is the child's gestural overflow of mimemes that he cannot resist projecting them mimismically onto the walls in the form of a miming "shadow theater" in which he has the shadows fighting each other. Better even, as soon as he has a piece of charcoal or a pencil in his hand, he "reifies" these evanescent propositional mimemes in the shape of *mimograms* or spontaneous drawings. That is how early Man at the mimage stage started to write in pictographic propositional mimograms.

A born mimer, the child is also a born drawer. Far from inhibiting the child's instinctive *mimographism* by condemning him prematurely to our algebrizing and to him repulsive writing, mimo-pedagogy strives to draw from this instinctive mimogaphism the maximum intellectual and scientific benefit possible. Drawing is the child's writing.

## Auricular phonomimism

In addition to their plastic and visible actions, animate and inanimate beings of the universe also have voiced and audible actions which are mimismically echoed in the microscopic gestes of the inner ear in the form of auricular mimemes. This is *auricular phonomimism*.

Until recently, in our ethnic milieu that tends to be overly bookish and artificial, a child's ear has seldom been initiated in listening and discriminating the subtle sounds of things. His auricular gestes are modelled only by the few stereotyped sounds of our algebrized Greco-Latin languages and the handful of mechanical notes of our instrumental music.

Language and music of this ilk all too soon undermine the rich potential of the young ear. Recordings of experimental phonetics have shown us that an adult's ear is no longer capable of "hearing" objectively the phonemes of an unknown or unfamiliar idiom. The adult ear subjectively deforms unfamiliar sounds by reducing them to crude approximations of the phonemes of those languages learnt in childhood. European specialists in Eastern melodies have similarly told me of their inability to "capture" the characteristic sounds of these melodies. At some stage, the plasticity of the auricular gesticulation hardens into a limited number of receptive gestes that become fixed and fossilised.

It is clear that our language and music focus the young ear too exclusively on the voiced algebremes of signs, instead of allowing it to become supple through the auricular mimemes of the things surrounding us. We are utilitarians, artists with tunnel vision, and impatient to teach the child the social labels for things and the serial notes of our musical scales. In so doing, we fail unfortunately, to make him hear the characteristic timbre of the things themselves. Because the socialised word and the algebrozed note are so easy to access, they soon kill any spontaneous curiosity about the concrete sounds of the wider and truer real.

Yet, both intellectually and aesthetically, the surprising harmony of nature's sounds is no less educational than the stylised harmony of an orchestra's notes. Did Aeschylus's ear not render unforgettable "the infinite burst of laughter of the ocean's waves"? The sounds which a human ear has already heard may be pleasing, but how much more pleasing would be those sounds no ear managed yet to hear! Far richer is the harmonious real than our dictionary and far more nuanced than our music.

## Oral phonomimism

Like ocular cinemimism, auricular phonomimism is played secretly in microscopic gestures and on organs yet inaccessible to outside observation. The teacher cannot see the child's ocular re-playing; he cannot hear his auricular re-playing. Direct pedagogical control is therefore not possible.

Fortunately, just as ocular cinemimism is amplified in corporeal and manual cinemimism, auricular phonomimism has its own spontaneous amplifying irradiation—it is re-played in echo on the laryngo-buccal musculature. The sound which has been mimismically and microphonically played in the inner ear tends to be mimismically and megaphonically re-played on the lips. This is *oral phonomimism*.

By virtue of this further specialisation of the general law of mimism, a young child, raised predominantly by her mother, will unconsciously reflect the typical timbre and inflections of her mother's pronunciation. One hears the mother's voice in her daughter's voice just as one sees the mother's gestures in her daughter's gestures. In this, we find ourselves gazing at the profound and vital source of what has so judiciously been identified as the "contagion" of the example.

A natural result of this propelling compulsion of auricular and oral phonomimism is that any child brought up in the freedom of the countryside begins, of his own accord, to call a certain number of animals and objects by the sounds that they typically make. Witness the young child from a farm in the Sarthe region who, although barely of talking age, runs toward his mother and, with his hand rhythmically to his mouth, cries out with melodious intonations in surprisingly exact tones:

*Miaou ham cô! Miaou ham cô!*

Le chat a mangé le coq

The cat has eaten the rooster!

When a large and formidable neighbourhood cat had in fact just strangled a cockerel . . .

If a child is gifted with very precise auricular phonomimism, he intussuscepts and auricularly re-plays, with uncanny accuracy, the distinctive sounds made by each thing, including its intensity, duration, pitch and tone. Such a child is usually blessed with particularly precise oral phonomimism. But such oral phonomimism in echo can present flaws of its own. While the ear may be true, the laryngo-buccal apparatus may be false. The latter may even, in a type of reverse mimism, manage to distort the auricular phonomimemes.

Mimo-pedagogy must therefore intervene from the earliest years to verify and align these two phonomimismic systems.

## From mimage to *langage*

However unaware our young Sarthois child may have been of human mimism, he was nonetheless just a plastic and "voiced echo" of a plastic and voiced action of the universal interactional formula: *an acting—one acting on—an acted upon.* This mimodrama was re-played within him, intelligized and expressed in the three imbricated phases of a geste that was propositional, manually and orally mimismic and bilaterally balanced.

We saw the child "being played by" far more than himself "playing" the corporeal and manual mimismic gestes that are modelled within him by his intussusception of the *plastic* actions of things. We now see the same spontaneous impulse in the oral mimismic gestes of the child interacting with immediate and living *vocal* actions of things. Now, oral play is as important as corporeal play for the education and enrichment of a child's thoughts. This is proved daily by observing a child left to his instinctive devices: he proves to be as spontaneously curious to listen to and re-play the typical *timbre* of things as he is spontaneously curious to look at and re-play their characteristic *forms and actions.*

It was this same spontaneous curiosity which, in earlier times, enabled corporeally miming Man to become phonetically, lingually miming. *Mimage* (or the intellectual expression by the plastic gestes of the body and the hands) thus yielded its admirable meaning-giving powers gradually, but never completely, to *langage* (or intellectual expression through the voiced gestes of the tongue). It is the very voice of things that dictated to the various ethnic groupings of corporeal-manual style men the first oral languages, with dynamic variants due to the naturally variable replay by living and intelligent receptor organs: human mimism is not brutish mechanism. That fresh sample of "eternal anthropos," our young Sarthois child, gave us empirical proof of the authenticity of such dictation to spontaneously attentive human ears.

We find another proof in the numerous phonomimemes or "onomatopoeia" which have withstood the degradation of ravages of time and evolution upon their articulatory and phonetic systems in languages less algebrized than our own. Among many others, the Chinese and the Annamites list, with legitimate pride, the richness and subtle refinement of the countless onomatopoeia which are still alive on their lips and still sensed in their ears. The concrete mimograms or "shadow plays" of their former manual style can similarly be perceived and admired in their algebrizing brush tracings.

## From *langage* to oral style

Corporeal and manual propositional gestes, bilaterally propelled by the successive explosions of living energy, are balanced by means of binary, or, less frequently, ternary movements, in a spontaneous rhythm. In living matter, rhythm is the repetition of the same physiological phenomenon at biologically equivalent intervals. When regularised, it becomes meter.

Each propositional balancing of the binaries and ternaries generally has three phases, since within each balancing are re-played the mimemes of the *acting one—the acting on (or interaction)—and the acted upon.* Within each balancing, these three gestual elements are individually propelled and measured by the successive intensification and relaxation of energy that expands in duration. We find ourselves at this point in the presence of the two basic rhythms inherent in any series of living gestes: the rhythm of intensity and the rhythm of duration.

Transposed onto the laryngo-buccal muscles, the propositional gestes remain balanced and retain perforce the two basic rhythms of intensity and duration. However, the laryngo-buccal gestes become the emitters of sounds that may differ in pitch and timbre. There will then, in each of the balancings of the oral binaries or ternaries, be four rhythms: the rhythm of intensity, the rhythm of duration, the rhythm of pitch and the rhythm of timbre. Any one of these four omnipresent rhythms may become spontaneously predominant in any language depending on its specific phonetic evolutions. Not only will the dominant rhythm impose its regulating structures on all the propositions of that language, but its automatic nature will also greatly facilitate improvisation, memorization and rememorization. So develops by degrees a traditional mechanism of rhythmo-pedagogic oral style that models on its own rhythmic structures the rhythmic structures of its melodies. Melody originally wells up from the very depths of a language.

Yet, language is a living and changing thing. Melody, without being immutable, has greater rhythmic stability. Melodies formed over time may impose their archaic rhythm and so, ironically, distort the new rhythm of the propositions they should reinforce. For example, if we analyse the phonetics of our folk songs, those precious residues of our ancient oral style, we will find that the rhythm of intensity of the melodies rarely coincides with the rhythm of intensity of the words. The phonetic evolution of our language is the cause of this.

## From oral style to music

The oral style of popular Latin, as it was brought to Gaul, was verbally balanced in a rhythm of intensity, expressed in iambi and trochees. Generally, this oral style and its accompanying melody scanned according to this rhythm. With time, it would seem that the energetic explosion of Latin articulation became gradually less intense in the mouths of its speakers. With the exception of the end of each balancing, even the weakest syllable could be consistently intensified and strongly defined by the energetic inner explosions of the traditional melody. This is still the case. Probably no Frenchman, not even our poets or musicians, truly feels or knows accurately, the rhythm of the phrase he utters. Recent recordings of experimental phonetics were necessary to prove to us that the dominant rhythm of present-day French is still the rhythm of intensity tending towards the anapaest. But this intensity is always so soft and so suffused that even phoneticians born in Paris consider that the dominant rhythm in French is the rhythm of duration.

A born mimer, a born drawer, the child is also, like our young child from Sarthe, a born improviser-rhythmer, whether he re-plays the sound of things in unfailingly parallel melodious onomatopoeia, or whether he comments on the balanced gestes of his rhythmo-mimisms in his own consistently rhythmic and melodious French oral style. Let us capture these verbal rhythmo-melodic replays so that they may live on subtly and pedagogically in the short rhythm-melodic phrases of our folk songs in which our oral style survives. However, let us, simultaneously and carefully, rectify the words of these songs so that the two rhythms of intensity, the verbal and the melodic, coincide. The intimate rhythmization of the child by the *exact* and melodic rhythm of his language, irradiating in his corporeal and manual rhythmo-mimismic geste, should be the primary concern of our educators. The harmonious Greeks understood this, and therefore made their children melodically rhythmo-mime Homer's dactylic oral style. Let us, likewise, base all initiation in music on the rhythm of that language from which, historically, the music has sprung. The real problem does not lie in teaching the child prematurely how to read, write and play empty sounds. No more than humanity in its early stages should the young human dissociate, without a slow process of transition, pure music from speech that is anthropologically both signifying rhytmo-mimismic geste and melody.

Once he has mastered the complex and living lyre of his own body, the child will master, effortlessly, the most algebrized techniques of our inert musical instruments. His musical hand will make all things musical.

ESSAY 4

# The Psycho-Physiological Laws of Living Oral Style and Their Use in Philology

*Language Takes Form — 1 — Propositional Patterning and the Formula*

## Outline

The human compound, balancing and the propositional geste

Melodic and rhythmic patterning

Improvisation and memorization

Oral style and present-day didactics

### The psycho-physiological laws of living oral style and their use in philology

#### The human compound, balancing and the propositional geste

THE FOLLOWING PAGES ARE an attempt at bringing experimental phoneticians, linguistic philologists and ethnographers to closer collaboration on existing common ground between their disciplines.

My scientific studies led me, some twenty years ago, to pose the following problem of experimental and ethnic psychology: "How does man, placed at the heart of all the countless *actions* of the universe, manage to conserve the memory of these actions within him, and to transmit this memory faithfully to his descendants, from generation to generation?" What this amounted to was nothing less than finding out how the psycho-physiological tools developed for the conservation of the great human *living tradition*.

Slowly and methodically, taking special care not to invent anything, I set about gathering *facts*. I investigated the greatest possible number of ethnic milieus, from one end of the world to the other. Obviously, I chose to focus my attention primarily on those human groups that remained shielded from the printed word. It would have been singularly anti-scientific to gauge the potential of the human memory by studying subjects who strive to bypass memory, secure in the knowledge that, if need be, everything would be found in an appropriate book or encyclopaedic dictionary. Yet, how many serious scientific questions have not been psychologically distorted, and even rendered insoluble, by the inappropriate and erroneous attribution of our growing amnesia to individuals belonging to milieus that are profoundly different from ours in this regard.

To my personal ethnographic observations, I have added information gathered during numerous conversations with explorers and missionaries. The written accounts of acutely perceptive observers of the "ethnic laboratory," especially those of the last three centuries, have been equally valuable in guiding my research.

The cinematograph, the phonograph, and the marvellous recording apparatus of that much-lamented genius, Abbé J.-P. Rousselot, Professor at the *Collège de France*, have added their objective and experimental precision to this research—which was complex, as is everything that touches upon life.

After eighteen years of strenuous and passionate investigation, I published in the *Archives de Philosophie* an outline of my experimental method and some of the results that had emerged. This essay appeared early in 1925 under the title: *Studies in linguistic psychology: the rhythmic and mnemotechnical oral style among the verbo-motors*. Each chapter was a summary of my future studies, which came about quite naturally, gelling logically around the facts provided by living material. I refer the reader to this earlier essay for a more detailed, psychological explanation of the facts that I can only briefly set out in the following pages. When "summarizing summaries" in a matter as complex as the one in hand, one does indeed run the risk of presenting unwittingly a distorted idea of the reality.

***

In the first chapters of my 1925 essay, I stated that any study on the psychology of language must start with an in-depth examination of the living proposition, of the propositional geste. A brief analysis cannot do justice to a matter as complex as the experimental examination of Man's expressive process:

- firstly, I would indeed need to embark on a cinematographic study of the admirable languages of geste that formed basis, as yet unexplored, of so-called "hieroglyphic" writing (more accurately: "mimographic" writing);

- secondly, I would need to study of the intermediary, always still concrete, languages, such as Chinese;

- thirdly, reaching beyond the algebrizing syllogisms of Aristotle and the like, I would have to dwell on the relational formulas of Henri Poincaré and Einstein's higher mathematical analyses.

Such a three-stage journey "from concretism to algebrism" would be an exciting topic for a lifetime of study, but well beyond the limitations of the present outline.

I will limit myself then to stating that my research has allowed me to identify the psycho-physiological origin of the linguistic phenomenon of propositional parallelism, acknowledged since Lowth. What Lowth could not have suspected in his lifetime, however, was the enormous psychological importance of this phenomenon. It is no exaggeration to assert that the central role played by the proposition in the world of human thought and memory is akin to the role played by gravity in the physical universe.

The profound laws of the "human compound" made of flesh and spirit, cause each improvised proposition to have the curious tendency to trigger in the speaker's phonatory system, one or two other propositions, parallel in construction and analogous or antithetical in meaning. Phonograph records of the delightful improvisations of an oral composer of the Emyrna region in central Madagascar illustrate this process. Linguistic analysis of the recorded propositions reveal striking parallelisms that can be felt rudimentally, even in inevitably distorted translation:

*Money is the horn of the rich,*
*the spade is the horn of the poor.*


*You are in the midst of a thousand lemon trees,*
*I am in the midst of a thousand crowds.*


*I am not the insouciant wild cat,*
*but the cat that obeys a law.*

Parallelism appears in any oral-style milieu—which is any ethnic group unacquainted with writing or composing without recourse to writing. It comes in a great many variations, due to the suppleness of life, the diversity of language mechanisms and Man's free will capable of breaking with any automatism. As a phenomenon, it is universal.

Another phenomenon too proves to be universal: balancing. Balancing is equally psycho-physiological in nature and compels the whole body of the reciter to oscillate in tune with the delivery of each proposition. Balancing is variously referred as the rolling gait of a camel loaded with a burden, the strutting of the cooing dove, and so on.

Every parallel proposition, or balancing, as I will call it from now on, is modulated on a simple and rather monotonous melody. The melodic members of this psalmody also balance naturally, in accordance with the parallelism of the propositions that they animate. Thus two or three semantically and melodically parallel vocal emissions constitute a complex whole, a kind of binary or ternary living schema which I have called a rhythmic schema.

The following is a concrete example of such a binary rhythmic schema, i.e., a rhythmic schema composed of two balancings:

> *They do not at first give counsel,*
>> *but they poke fun later on.*

Here, a ternary rhythmic schema—a composition of three balancings:

> *We do not chase them before us like sheep,*
>> *but they follow us like dogs,*
> *they balance from the rear like the tail of a sheep.*

The presentation of the texts with indented lines makes it clear that the two or three balancings of the rhythmic schema are not two or three erratic fragments, but a unit of recitation, a living, melodic and balanced unit. It is a rudimentary indication only, one that can never replace the performed life recitation, nor even its melodious phonographic echo.

## Melodic and rhythmic patterning

Let me emphasize from the outset that the question of melody and rhythm of the oral propositions is crucial. Ethnographers will render an inestimable service to the sciences of psychology and rhythmics by collecting on phonographic discs, or better still on Rousselot's phonetic apparatus, large numbers of living elements of spontaneous ethnic propositions. This will allow the objective, microscopic analysis of all the phonetic elements—so much alive and so intricately complex—of each and every balancing of each and every improvised rhythmic schema. They are: the rhythm of intensity, the rhythm of duration, the rhythm of timbre, the rhythm of pitch, the alliteration of consonants, the assonance of vowels, the exact number of fully pronounced syllables, the average tempo of delivery, and so on. Each of these numerous elements is present and active in the mysterious genesis and the mnemonic conservation of every oral proposition. Only the recording apparatus of experimental phonetics can detect and measure with mathematical precision to what degree.

Since Rousselot's wonderful discoveries, one can no longer afford to study this intricately complex play of living energy called rhythm (the term is an excessive simplification) at one's desk and with pen and paper only. It was psychologically inevitable that, in the past, rhythm was no more than a preconceived idea of some or other German, English, French, Italian linguist, unconsciously foisting his own habitual ethnic distinctions on inert lines of writing.

It comes as no surprise that in a doctoral thesis presented at the Sorbonne, a French "syllabic metricist" tried his utmost to reduce each of the supple balancings of our Basque improvisers to eight syllables, when in the course of a single improvisation these balancings vary freely between approximately five and fifteen syllables. The Basque improvisers railed against such bookish vivisection. Some German metricists, accustomed to regular intensive stress, similarly tried to convince us that Racine should be rhythmed according to the stress accent in their language:

Oui, c'est Agamemnon, c'est ton roi qui t'éveille.

As French speakers, we can only smile at those three all too regular stresses on each of the recited units, such rhythm being foreign to our lips. However, whether one smiles indulgently or protests loudly—which is much the same, somehow—one must be alive. Written texts no longer possess life, especially written texts of past or extinct languages: quiet, yet objective and critical life. Anyone versed in Palestinian studies knows to what metrical surgery the traditional but docile propositions of Israel's psalmists and prophets were subjected—*metri gratiâ*. Open any such study at random, and read aloud some of these merciless "rhythmizations," often several to a single page, and listen to the lugubrious sound of the blade coming down: "Retrench this word for the rhythm! Add this word for the rhythm!" Shouldn't that be translated rather as: ". . . to suit *my* rhythm?"

Clearly, prior to dare touch ever so slightly on such traditional texts in the name of rhythm and of rhythm alone, one should analyse scientifically the psycho-physiological nature of this mysterious and, in this case, devastating rhythm. This should be followed by meticulous ethnic research on the largest possible number of living and spontaneous rhythms. Such preliminary research was never undertaken, to my surprise both as psychologist and as experimental phonetician. Had it been done, ad broadened to a hundred or so ethnic milieus, living and supple rhythmic laws would have emerged that would have accommodated quite naturally and without mutilation the ancient propositions of the Hebrew psalmists and prophets.

This demonstrates how dangerous it is in scientific matters to imagine instead of observing and how quickly lack of objective information results in pseudo-problems and apparently disconcerting difficulties. Present-day scientific specialization progresses inexorably and modern researchers are faced with increasingly complex questions that can only be solved by close, constant—and fraternal—collaboration of the various rational and experimental disciplines.

In the very new branch of scientific investigation that concerns us at present, the majority of its ethnographers and linguisticians were confronted by unique living documents, now disappeared forever. These scientists, lacking material means and experimental skills and methodologies, could provide us with only approximate graphic transcriptions of melodiously and rhythmically balanced words. Subsequently, each German, English, French, Italian, etc. linguist would then transpose and rhythm them on his own lips and in his own ethnic, and invariably distorting fashion.

What a great many technicians dreamt of for so long has now fortunately opened up to phoneticians, linguists and rhythmicians: the establishment of the archives of the spoken word and of the geste. Here recordings by great teams of intelligent ethnographers and missionaries recall and recreate the living melodies of ethnic recitations previously found in ethnographic journals, invaluable but disincarnated graphics. We must remind ourselves continuously that our dreadful modern "graphism" all too often causes us to forget, and renders us incapable of solving, complex and dynamic linguistic problems: real human language does not have words on the one hand, melodies on another and rhythms on yet another, and so on. All parts come into play and interpenetrate intimately in order to set off and steer subtle parallel balancings within the organism.

In each ethnic milieu, this living and active parallelism, which is simultaneously physiological, semantic, melodic and rhythmic, leads to a kind of "patterning" of the musculature in a number of choice proverbs. Take for example an ethnic milieu in which the oral tradition has fixed forever some four to five hundred of such typical proverbs. The improvisor's personal invention consists in taking, more or less consciously, these four or five hundred typical rhythmic schemas as models and to adjust on them other rhythmic schemas of identical form, equal in structure, in the number of words, in rhythm, and even, if possible, with equivalent meaning.

The following is an example taken from the four or five hundred sample proverbs of the Merina oral-style milieu:

*It is not the rain which comes little, little,*

*but it is this conversation of the two of us which is little, little.*

We can hear from the lips of the improvisors imitative rhythmic schemas such as:

*It is not the rice-fields of which the rice is little, little,*

*but it is our affection of us both which is little, little.*

That is how typical rhythmic schemas shape rhythmic schemas improvised in the course of oral composition. Improvised rhythmic schemas are reproduced in their hundreds—expanded, or shortened sometimes, or framed by differently rhythmed propositions transferred from other model-proverbs. This gives us an accurate idea of how rhythmic improvisers operate in an oral-style milieu.

The psycho-physiological operation of parallelism plays normally and habitually from balancing to balancing within a rhythmic schema, but it is not unusual for parallelism to influence the rhythmic schemas themselves, in which case these schemas become themselves parallel, as in the following binaries and ternaries:

*This smoke from the west,*

*it is not smoke but coquetry.*

*This rice being pounded toward the east*

*is not rice being pounded but a whim.*

*—The tubers precede the ambiaty:*

*am I the girlfriend who is not loved*

*that you should wake me when the sky at the horizon is dark?*

*—The tubers precede the ambiaty:*

*you are not the girlfriend who is not loved*

*and I would wake you when the sky at the horizon is dark?*

So active is parallelism in all the human fibres that it tends to balance even whole groups of propositions that are sometimes already parallel among themselves, two by two or three by three. It is in such instances in particular that the deep and decisive role of melody, of the modulating tune of these grouped parallel propositions, manifests itself. Parallel recitatives formed by such instinctive grouping of evenly numbered rhythmic schemas are found on the lips of improvisers the world over.

The following is an example taken from the Merina oral-style milieu:

### Recitative one

1. *May I come in Rosoa-the-precious?*

—*Who asks?*

2. *It is I, Andriakato-of-life,*

*little one who wears the red lamba*

*with the purple fringe.*

3. *I have a salaka of silk,*

*my teeth are deforested.*

4. *I mount the Beautiful-one-who-looks-at-the-sky,*

*I make gallop the Tall-one-breath-of-life.*

5. *I wash my feet with milk,*

*I wash my mouth with honey.*

6. *I bring silver* of exact weight,

*if you bring* piastre coins.

7.—If *you bring* silver of exact weight,

*if you bring* piastre coins,

8. *Our calf* is badly *tied up,*

*our door* is well closed,

*father and mother sleep here.*

### Recitative two

1. *May I come in Rosoa-the-precious?*

—*Who asks?*

2. *It is I, Andriakato-of-life,*

*little one who wears the red lamba*

*with the purple fringe.*

3. *I have a salaka of silk,*

*my teeth are deforested.*

4. *I mount the Beautiful-one-who-looks-at-the-sky,*

*I make gallop the Tall-one-breath-of-life.*

5. *I wash my feet with milk,*

*I wash my mouth with honey.*

6. I bring well-fattened meat,

I bring *small balls of fat.*

7.—*If you bring* well-fattened meat,

*if you bring small balls of fat,*

8. *Our calf* is well *tied up,*

*our door is* badly *closed,*

*father and mother do* not *sleep here.*

It is possible to improvise successfully such curious and universal parallel recitatives in indefinite numbers, much to the joy of audiences who do not tire, as we do, of such monotonous rocking. The substitution of even a single word, the addition or the exclusion of a negative, is enough to create a new parallel recitative.

Recitatives can also be paralleled two by two only, each pair consisting in a recitative #1 and a recitative #2 and separated from the following pair by an independent recitative which has no parallel and which I therefore call recitative #0. A recitative #0 may set off a series, whilst another recitative #0 may conclude it, the order being:

$$R°. R^1. R^2. R°. R^1. R^2. R°.$$

A simple random collection of one or two improvisations from each oral-style ethnic milieu will have us wonder how men, women, young girls—mere children almost—can improvise oral rhythmic formulas of such grace, perfection and fullness that they command the admiration of people as refined as we, even.

If we continue, psychologicaly and methodlogically, with our research in the same ethnic milieu, the mystery lessens, not however our admiration. As the improvisors follow each other up before us, one by one, but in varying contexts, we hear yet again the formulas originated on the lips of earlier improvisers. It is not unlike a marvellous game of living dominoes: the tiles remain roughly the same with equal mutual appeal, but their combinations are quasi-indefinitely renewed.

Delving deeper into the psychology of a chosen ethnic milieu, we discover several literary oral-style genres: history, law, cosmogony, ethics, philosophy, theology, medicine, etc.—in sum: the entire science of this particular ethnic oral milieu. A science no doubt not as advanced as ours, nor expressed in our algebraic terminology, but to the individual members of this ethnic milieu, it is science and not, as we are wont to say, poetry.

Some genres are by reputation so learned and so technical that they are the exclusive reserve of the most gifted and the best-trained minds. Each of these scientific genres develops its own specialised clichés and boasts its own virtuoso improvisers, some of whom, as happens everywhere, attain the heights of genius.

## Improvisation and memorization

Such customary patterned associations, verbal imbrications, clichéd parallelisms, balanced and measured recitatives obviously greatly and spontaneously facilitate the memorization of long improvised series. Man however was always and everywhere too intelligent and too industrious not to recognize, exploit and develop optimally the resources put at his disposal by this marvellous ingrained spontaneity.

That rhythm, melody, and word and sound association greatly facilitate the conservation and recall of verbal material through memorization was noted long before it was proved by modern day laboratory tests in experimental psychology, all the more so because memorization could not rely on outside memory-aids.

Proper analysis of the marvellous techniques developed by Man to maximize his verbal re-call in the absence of writing will require encyclopaedic volumes. We, bookish amnesiacs, would happily deny the eminence of mnemonic power if ethnic psychology were not daily informing us of its capacity and so prod us into humility. One example quoted from among thousands will suffice.

The *guslars* are the southern Slavs' strolling reciters. They are illiterate, as are nearly all improvisers and reciters of oral-style milieus. In this environment, illiterate does of course not mean ignorant, on the contrary: popular opinion endows these *guslars* with astounding feats of memory, some are said to know thirty thousand, seventy thousand and even over one hundred thousand rhythmic schemas. The facts prove the people right and I explained why: the recitations of the *guslars* too are juxtapositions of a relatively small number of clichés.

The development of each of these clichés happens automatically, in accordance with fixed rules. Only the order may vary. A good *guslar* is he who plays these clichés as we play cards, arranging them variably according to the manner in which he will put them to use. Moreover, each *guslar* develops his own personal genre: one specialises in the history of Marko, another sings the praises of a famous heyduck. In addition, everyone creates a sort of personal oral and mnemotechnical catalogue: the individual arranges his "provision" of clichés in the manner of a litany or didactic rosary, comprising the opening recitatives of the various recitations. A certain Milovan, one of the *guslars* who was studied experimentally, and whose memory was considered merely average, recited forty thousand rhythmic schemas in a row.

Further, the following fact is as instructive as it is conclusive about every type of traditional oral-style teaching. On 18 March 1885, researcher Fr. S. Krauss had a certain *guslar* dictate to Milovan, in his presence, a recitation of four hundred and fifty-eight rhythmic schemas. Seven and a half months, later on 4 October 1885, Milovan repeated the four hundred and fifty-eight schemas word for word. Another nine months later, Krauss had Milovan repeat the same recitation again: the variations were insignificant.

Moreover, when impeccable reciting of traditional, and especially religious recitation is deemed necessary, oral-style milieus know very well how to obviate radically even insignificant variations completely. Here is a quick example.

An anthropologist employed for sixteen years by the British government in the land of the Achanti on the west coast of Africa, Mr Rattray, recently published an account of his work. This publication contributes in an interesting way not only to the study of the regional languages and the science of music, but also to my outline here of the psychology of recitation.

I am concerned here with linguistics, suffice it to state that Mr. Rattray has an in-depth knowledge of the language of the Achanti, and that he has managed to develop a written form of the Achanti language, which is more than the indigenous people themselves achieved. The Achanti adopted him as one of their own and considered him a pious man to whom all could be said and shown. This is what enabled him to hear, write and translate their historical recitations.

Writing being foreign to them, the Achanti conserve their history through oral tradition alone and there exists among them a cast of professional historians who re-tell the glorious deeds of the kings in rhythmic schemas. They psalmodize their recitations in specialised melodies that vary with each reign. Their function is, overall, that of the reciters of any oral-style milieu. Each reciter has a number of disciples to whom he teaches his recitations, word for word, and the appropriate melody, note for note. There is no danger of distortion or corruption for, once a reciter is admitted to the caste, the slightest mistake in the text or psalmody is punished by death. This system has guaranteed that recitations composed more than eight hundred years ago, were handed down intact.

Languages undergo inevitable variations over the centuries, especially those that possess neither written grammar nor literature, which is why such languages evolve, generally, more rapidly than others. The Achanti language is no exception to this rule and the words of their oldest historical recitations are perfectly incomprehensible to the present generation. The reciters alone are able to clarify their meaning and to translate them into modern Achanti.

The singing of the historical recitations is a sacred function and the sole preserve of the reciters. Mr. Rattray needed the king's special permission to record, by phonograph, the precious rhythmic compositions of the Achanti's reciters.

It is such ethnic observations that make it clear why one should not call these rhythmic oral recitations and their constituent elements poetry, stanzas, or verse—particularly because of the meaning that the latter words have acquired in our current usage, whether for better or worse. It would be an enormous psychological mistranslation and one with considerable consequences, tantamount to calling "idols" the sculptures in our catholic churches. Of course, the physical materials used and their external forms are similar to a point, but the mental attitude of the people is entirely different, opposite, even. The historical, philological, theological, etc. science of the oral-style recitations is expressed in concrete formulas because the languages of the ethnic milieus are restricted to concrete expression. Their rhythmic schemas are necessary because all these recitations have to be retained scrupulously by heart, and the rhythms, melodies, etc. are considerable aids to memorization.

We on the contrary proclaim pedantically that "to know by heart is not to know," not realizing perhaps that in so saying we are denying the existence of the very real corpus of scientific knowledge of 99 percent of the people who have populated, and continue to populate, our planet.

## Oral style and present-day didactics

For better or for worse, our didactics have progressively abandoned the spontaneous processes of oral style and replaced them with our written style. The didactic and living ancient oral style has passed from the utilitarian domain to the purely aesthetic domain, far removed from the common crowd.

In the aesthetic domain, it has become the bookish, artificial, splendidly isolated configuration that we call poetry, and pure poetry, even. The most salient didactic aids (alliteration, rhyme, etc.) have completely changed in nature and have turned into ever more difficult obstacles to meaning, at times rivaling the "crossword" puzzle conundrum.

No present-day teacher of philosophy, theology, history, or astronomy would entertain the notion of teaching in the form of sonnets constructed out of propositioned parallels. This simple fact shows, experimentally as it were, the psychological and social abyss that exists between oral style and poetry. This curious metamorphosis of a human institution should attract the attention of both the psychologist and ethnographer: what was by nature essentially didactic and oral, became for us essentially aesthetic and written.

In oral-style milieu, recitations, orally composed and known by heart, may be put in writing, on steles, bricks, animal skins and so on. Let us not confuse such graphics with the present-day books we skim rapidly. Oral-style records are "standard-texts," "control-texts," so to speak, that serve to verify, confirm or rectify the traditional content of the living recitations. For this reason, these "testimonials" are often preserved in religious temples, under the secure guard of a sacerdotal caste.

The rhythmic recitations comprised in such oral texts "put-into-writing" and essentially made to be known by heart are not poems; their didactic recitatives are not stanzas; their frequent mnemotechnical repetitions should not be mistaken for "dittographies" or for "glosses by maladroit second-tier copyists." The living recitations that were never "put-into-writing," present similar repetitions and had the same didactic purpose.

Once living ethnic milieus have familiarised us with the psychophysiological and universal processes of oral style, we will be able to use our experimental discoveries to analyse the stylistic structure of texts emanating from oral-style milieus familiar with writing. I refer to Caesar on the Druids, in his *Commentaries* 4.14, or, on the Rabbis of Israel, Tuwa Perlow in *Education and Teaching among the Jews during the Talmudic Era* (Paris: Leroux, 1931) 37, 54.

To pure linguistic psychology, all ethnic milieus are intrinsically of equal interest. No civilization as great as that of the Incas of ancient Peru, with its traditional recitatives, can leave us indifferent, and neither should the Ancient Chinese, the pre-Islamic Arabs, etc. It is true though our classical and quasi-exclusively Greco-Latin training, it is the Homeric milieu that touches us most closely. After years of practicing Homer, one begins to recognize the Homeric milieu as one of oral style through its familiar oral-style formulas. Two of the purest masterpieces ever uttered by human lips—uttered, not written—were made by means of mosaics of ready-made expressions all αοίδοι had at their disposal.

I was particularly happy to concur with the great French linguist, Antoine Meillet, on this very point, even though the discovery was at first a

little disconcerting: Homer's recitations are made up of a few hundred ethnic and impersonal formulas. So striking is this fact that anyone alerted to it
will unfailingly rediscover the true Greek of Homer through a Latin translation, provided of course that the latter is very faithfully, and very literally
"encoded" (such as the Firmin-Didot translation). Once one has learned
by heart all the Greek formulas of the αοίδοί and their Latin encoding—the
encoding is at times synonymous—it is an intellectually fascinating exercise
to "reconstruct" Homer by substituting the encoding Latin expressions with
the hundred-odd corresponding Greek formulas.

The following are some random examples, such as this formulaic
Greek binary with its Latin encoding:

$$\text{Ὄφρ᾿ εἴπω τά με θυμὸς} \quad \text{ἐνι στήθεσσι κελεύει.}$$

*Ut dicam quae me animus in pectoribus jubet.* H 369.

It is easy enough to replace the dotted lines above each of the following
encodings by impeccable "Homer":

*Ut dicam quae me animus in pectoribus jubet* Θ 6

..........................................................................

*Ut dicam quae me animus in pectoribus jubet* μ 187

..........................................................................

*Ut dicam quae me animus in pectoribus jubet* θ 27.

The following is a new formula:

$$\text{Ὣς ἔφᾳτ᾿ ·οὐδ᾿ ἀπίθησε}$$

*Sic dixit : neque inobsequens erat* H 43.

The original Greek formula transposes itself automatically and faithfully to Homer, congruent with the identical or synonymous original Latin
encodings:

. . . . . . . . . . . . . . . . . . . . . . . . . . . . .

*Sic dixit ; nec non paruit* B.166.

. . . . . . . . . . . . . . . . . . . . . . . . . . . . . . . . . . . . ...

*Sic dixit ; nec non obsecutus est* ε 43.

The same holds for this other Greek ethnic formula, one with which we too are familiar:

θεὰ γλαυκῶπις Ἀθήνη

*dea caesiis oculis Minerva!* A 206.

and whole Latin encodings appear all the time:

*dea caesiis oculis Minerva* B 166.

*dea caesiis oculis Minerva* α 44.

The last two formulas even allow us to grasp from life, and to re-play in our laryngo-buccal organs the psycho-physiological mechanism of oral "linking," as they played in the organs of the great Greek rhythmer. Indeed, faced with the following Latin encoding,

ἀΩς ἔρᾳτ᾽·οὐδ᾽ἀπίθησε θεὰ γλαυκῶπις Ἀθήνη

*Sic dixit : nec non paruit dea caesiis oculis Minerva* B 166.

We notice immediately that it is no more than the "linking" of two already well-known formulas, and we are thus able to reconstruct the original Homeric whole without fault.

Milman Parry studied in detail the numerous questions raised by this oral-style methodology when applied to the Homeric compositions. I challenge our ethnographers to read the very provocative works of this student of Antoine Meillet. Ethnic psychology and philological linguistics could hardly be working together under more favourable auspices.

# Human Bilateralism and the Anthropology of Language

## Language Takes Form—2— The Construction of an Oral Text

### Outline

### Human bilateralism and the anthropology of language

### Introduction: the gestual portage of the yoke and of the burden

The anthropology of mimism provides an insight into the spontaneous elaboration of the interactional or propositional geste in all the fibers of the global anthropos. It is the anthropology of mimism again that will explain to us the tendency of the anthropos to *balance* the interactional geste in accordance with the bilateral structure of the human body.

Physiologically speaking, there is a "right man" and a "left man," a phenomenon familiar to psychiatrists and a focus of Dr Morlaâs's research for many years. I would go further and add that in the anthropology of geste and rhythm, there is a "front man" and a "back man." The Palestinian ethnic milieu had a deep understanding of this double bilateralism and expressed it concretely by distinguishing between the geste of balancing, the *yoke* (left-right), and the geste of carrying the *burden* (up-down). Mothers cradling their infant to lull them to sleep give us timeless examples of such double gestural front to back, right to left bilateralism, examples all the more striking for being wholly unconscious!

The following diagram is a concrete instance of this intriguing human mechanism of the *berceuse*:

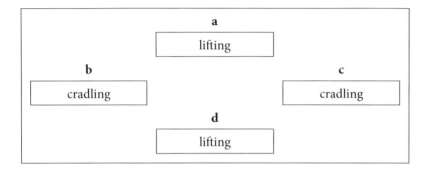

We will further on come across many such anthropological cradling and its balancing pull on the rhythmic and semantic structures of propositional gestes as a whole or in parts of their constitutive phases. In the meantime, let us acquaint ourselves with the mechanism of facts through another, more elaborate example: *the pedagogical cradling of the yoke and of the burden*:

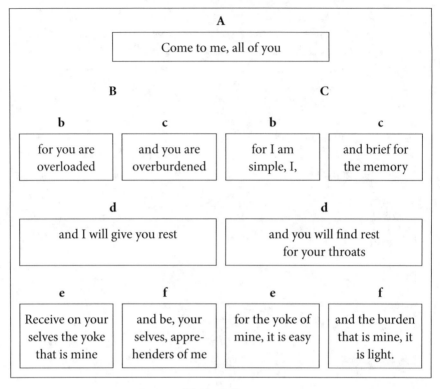

**A**

Come to me, all of you

**B** **C**

| b | c | b | c |
|---|---|---|---|
| for you are overloaded | and you are overburdened | for I am simple, I, | and brief for the memory |

**d** **d**

| and I will give you rest | and you will find rest for your throats |
|---|---|

| e | f | e | f |
|---|---|---|---|
| Receive on your selves the yoke that is mine | and be, your selves, appre-henders of me | for the yoke of mine, it is easy | and the burden that is mine, it is light. |

Matt 11:28–30

When the anthropologically original corporeal-manual geste is trans-posed—progressively and perhaps rather belatedly—onto the laryngo-buc-cal muscles, its gestual nature or its tendency to bilateralism remains intact. The original manual expression, *manualage,* and the subsequent lingual expression, *langage,* are simply two specific instances of mimismic expres-sion or *mimage*: one is cinemimismic, the other, phonomimismic. Language never frees itself completely from manualage and thinking Man, whether we like it or not, expresses himself *with his entire human compound;* he never speaks simply "from the tips of his lips," nor does he ever write simply "from the tip of his pen." A Man who *truly understands what he expresses,* finds his entire global being sculpted mimismically, successively and fluidly by the insuperable hold and spread of the particular mimeme that underlies *each* of the semantic phases of his propositional gestes. Palestinian anthropology puts it most gestually:

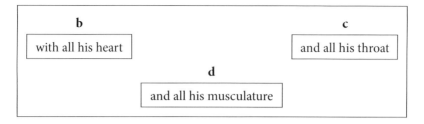

**b**

with all his heart

**c**

and all his throat

**d**

and all his musculature

*Manualage* invariably structures all expression in *langage* bilaterally. In whatever form and length and at any given moment, manualage is at the ready to reclaim its original dominance. Man cannot rid himself of his doubly bilateral globalism. A single visit to the Wailing Wall in Jerusalem or to one of our schools at the time the children recite their lessons balancing from one foot to the other, constitutes sufficient proof. More profoundly than Buffon thought, "style is Man himself." The study of style proves to be one of the major branches of dynamic anthropology.

I have demonstrated in my essay on *Human mimism and the anthropology of language* that the anthropology of mimism needs to focus exclusively on methodology. The task of anthropology is to discover the fundamental laws of the interacting mimer-anthropos and to create a clear, precise terminology to deal with these laws as and when they are discovered. The other, increasingly specialized scientific disciplines (psychiatry, psychology, pedagogy, linguistics, philology, etc.) are responsible for the meticulous and thorough scrutiny of the play or disarray of these great laws in their numerous and varied specific applications. *Cuique suum*: to each its own.

I was pleased to find precisely such meticulous pursuit of the great anthropological laws of mimism right down to the innermost depths of the minutest details of certain ethnic gestes in *The typological reconstruction of the archaic languages of humanity*, a remarkable study by the renown Dutch linguist Van Ginneken. It is such intellectual sympathy and expert collaboration that will enable the anthropology of mimism to observe with increasing confidence the numerous "spontaneous experiences" that have been played in the past and that are still today being played tirelessly in the world-wide "ethnic laboratory."

The problem of "portage"—the portage of *corporeal-manual* and of *laryngo-buccal* propositional gestes—needs to be tackled first and all-round in this vast ethnic laboratory. Pierre Janet was the first to identify the problem. Here I deal with the portage of *laryngo-buccal* propositional gestes only. With the algebrozed residue and desiccated stumps of the portage of *corporeal-manual* gestes in our present-day liturgies I will deal in another essay.

This problem can be looked at from two perspectives:

- the transmission or "oral tradition" of laryngo-buccal propositional gestes in a specific ethnic milieu, one clearly privileged in this respect;

- the anthropological tendency of these linguistically ethnicized propositional gestes to *structure themselves* in accordance with the double bilateralism of the anthropos.

The focus in my present anthropological research is on the ancient Palestinian ethnic milieu because it is so particularly suffused with the experiences of secular oral portage and because, ironically, it remains wholly ignored by anthropologists. Until recently, the study of all the prodigious successes of Palestinian oral portage resulted in bizarre ethnic misinterpretations or insoluble pseudo-problems created by "papyrovorous" Greco-Latinicists of exclusively bookish educational background. Let us be clear: humanity's expression was neither immediately nor globally sclerozed and necrozed in the pen-pushers' *written civilization*. Humanity expressed itself for a very long time and dynamically as a *global-gestual-oral civilization*. To study a Hillel and a Mohammed as one habitually studies Plato or Cicero would therefore be completely unscientific.

In the slipstream of the first publications by the anthropology of geste, historical psychologists such as Léonce de Grandmaison, Maurice Goguel and Giuseppe Ricciotti immediately understood the stupefying deficiency of the earlier approach. As an anthropologist of the laryngo-buccal geste and of its portage, I cannot praise enough Ricciotti's *History of Israel* and its fresh and frank exposition of oral-tradition methodology.

## Bilateralism and traditional Palestinian oral style

In his preface to Dottin's *Grammaire gauloise*, and especially in the second tome of his voluminous *Histoire de la Gaule*, Camille Jullian has given us much information on the *exclusively oral* pedagogical method used by the ancient Druids, those famous instructors who were philosophers, historians, theologians, and so on. It is quite certain that the Druids were perfectly acquainted with writing, for the Greek alphabet's letters were in use all around them, on a daily basis, for all the public and private matters of Gallic life. This notwithstanding, we are informed by Caesar that the Druids outlawed the use of writing in the transmission of their lessons which they presented in "rhythmo-catechetical" form, demonstrating thereby their particular pedagogic wisdom. From a purely anthropological point of view,

I give "oral-repetition-like-an-echo" as the full etymological meaning of the word "cat-*eche*-tical."

While the Druid instructors were handing on their lessons in this very "rhythmo-catechetical form" in ancient Gaul, in Palestine, the *Abbâs* or *Rabbis* or *Mâris* were simultaneously "traditioning" their lessons to their *Berâs* or *Talmid* or *Abdâs* in the very same form.

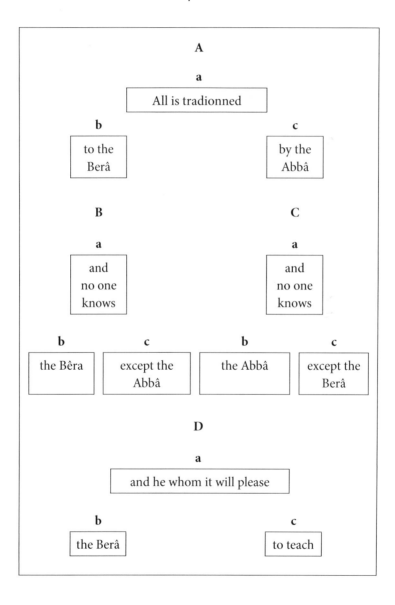

In our bookish language, the word "catechism" proves to be the most exact translation of the pedagogical term "mishnâh" or "oral-repetition-like-an-echo."

The *Abbâs* or *Rabbis* or *Mâris* were mishnaïsts, catechists, and more specifically, rhythmo-catechists. I analyzed their traditional pedagogical method anthropologically in *Les Rabbis d'Israël*. Since then, this anthropological analysis has been verified and adopted by experts of Palestinian style, such as H. Fleisch and R. Pautrel. These specialists know, moreover, that the amiable, young German philologist, Paul Gächter, has made the characteristic features of my anthropological discoveries in Palestinian oral style his own. He did this in rather totalitarian fashion, having translated them faithfully in beautiful Latin: primacy of oral tradition in Palestine, *even at the beginning of our era*; pedagogical utilization of rhythm; amplitude and fidelity of the reciters' memory; capital role of the Aramaic-Hellenic metourguemâns or *sunergoi*—translator-interpreters, etc. The anthropology of geste and rhythm then succeeded, in sometimes unexpected ways, in restoring to its rightful place the primordial importance of the ancient "oral tradition" of the Palestinian Abbâs or Rabbis.

The greatest of all these rhythmo-catechist Rabbis—if not the one most studied as such—is unquestionably Rabbi Ieshua of Nazareth, the Palestinian initiator of what we call *our* Western civilization. However, what characterizes Rabbi Ieshua is that he was essentially a *popular* rhythmo-catechist. Stylistically, he can be compared to the prestigious Finnish peasants, oral rhythmers of the parallel balancings of the Kalevala. The Galilean paysan-cartwright did not rhythmo-catechize *in scholastic Hebrew*, the language of the academies of the learned or for the learned, but *in Aramaic*, the language of the synagogues and in the open air for the people—those "poor in knowledge," which poverty it so distressed him to see, catechistically

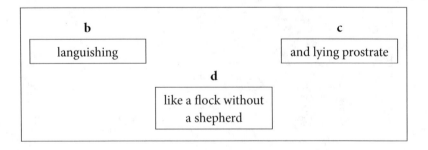

At that time, and probably since Esdras, the rhythmo-catechism of the Palestinian people was the Targum or the Aramaic *oral* encoded translation of the formulae of the Hebrew Tôrâh put-into-writing. The learned "read" the Hebraic *Tôrâh*, but the people "listened" to the Aramaic *Orâyetâ*. Here, "listening to" signifies "memorizing through listening."

I have outlined the gestural methodology in my essay on *The Aramaic formulism in the historical gospel stories*. Here I treat the oral and targumically formulaic rhythm-catechism of Rabbi Ieshua of Nazareth *exclusively* as anthropologist of the oral, propositional and formulaic geste and of its Palestinian semantic balancing.

***

At a decisive moment, we hear this prodigious popular rhythm-mimer recite the following formula, a formula that by a quasi-uniquely stroke of fortune came to us put-into-writing—"scriptured"—as an aide-mémoire in its targumic Aramaic:

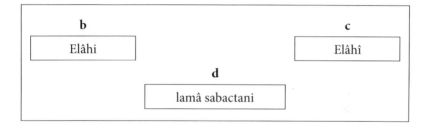

The double and "synoptic" Greek encoding of this formula, transmitted by our Gospels, gives us a priceless indication of the method to use in the investigation of the Aramaic formulaic *balancings*, particularly when no original targumic formula directly accompanies the Greek encoding.

This is the case, partially at least, for another such formula (graphically abbreviated by certain "copiers"), so frequently found in the mouth of this popular rhythmo-catechist who knows his metier:

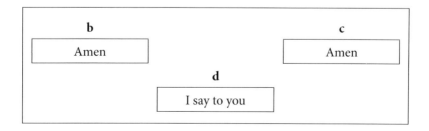

This is also the case, but this time wholly, for the third formula where I strove to reproduce in our language the balanced rhymes of the Aramaic:

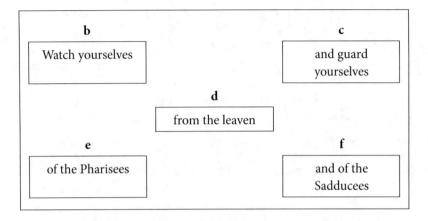

To my regret, I must admit that it is not always possible to *rhyme these semantic balancings phonetically* in French because our French endings are so variable. The very opposite is true of the Aramaic tongue where morphological endings coincide identically with grammatical functions. This makes rhyming not only easy, but also quasi unavoidable. While rhyme at the end of, or even within, the semantically parallel balancings in Aramaic was at first spontaneous, it was later prized for its utilitarian and mnemotechnical qualities, features strongly favoured universally in the popular rhythmo-catechesis. Let us reflect for a moment here on the similar role played by our own admirable and inexhaustible popular rhythmo-catechetical system of proverbs, ignored, of course, and neglected by our armchair pedagogues:

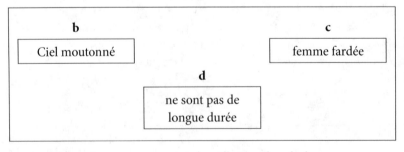

A fleecy *sky—a woman painted—will not endure for long*

Alternatively, with one of the recitational "synoptic" variants, which are as numerous in our oral-style proverbs as in the Palestinian oral style, although far less learnedly and obsessively commented on:

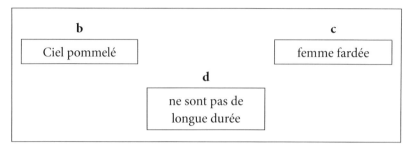

*A* dappled *sky—a woman painted—will not endure for long*

To have a quite exact, if very partial sensation of the Aramaic morphological tendency toward rhyme, a French catholic only needs to recite the remnants of a curiously compelling, if overly-bookish and algebrozed attempt at an entirely syllable-ized and rhymed (I wouldn't call it rhythmed) French rhythmo-catechesis: our "Commandments of God and of the Church," very neatly arranged in octosyllables "after the manner of" the instinctive, traditional octosyllabification found in oral-style French. Our bookish rhythmo-catechist greatly facilitated his mnemotechnical rhymes by using almost throughout the ending /*ras*/ of the second person singular of the future tense throughout, and the ending /*ment*/ that belongs to adverbs of manner.

There is more, and that unwittingly: in spite of and through the restricting graphic octosyllables, the formidable anthropological law of double bilateralism forced him to balance certain of his propositional gestes according to the fundamental norms that we see fully and freely at play all the time in the—in this case purely oral—Palestinian popular rhythmo-catechesis. It is this that "la mère Guespin" felt so sensitively. La mère Guespin was a wonderful old woman, a Sarthois reciter, totally illiterate and therefore not contaminated by the visual formation of the typographical arrangements of our "verse." She knew of course faultlessly by heart both of the greater and the smaller diocesan Catechisms, "even better than Monsieur le Curé," the Gospel readings for Sundays and feast days, and many other traditional recitations. Her memory was vast, sharp and sure, as is normally the case with the memories of intelligent illiterates. One evening, she made me recite my first memorizations of the well-known "Commandments," which I had learned from my catechism book but which I had sprinkled with enough

recitational variants to create a new synoptic problem. I remember very
well and in all the muscles of my miming and formerly mocking body: the
wonderful old "mère Guespin," the so intelligent and so delicate Sarthois
illiterate, remarked to me that one *cannot* make a mistake when reciting the
first and seventh commandments of God, because they "are made in similar fashion." Then, in the same way that she had slowly and gently cradled
her little "brood" in earlier times, she recited for me, or rather "rhythmo-
melodised," by balancing from front to back and from right to left, in an old
familiar and very mnemonic tune:

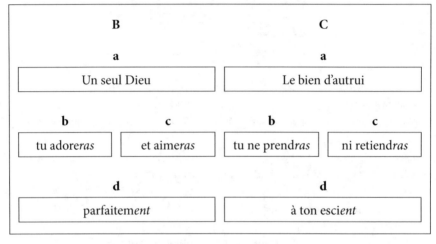

*One God only—you shall adore—and shall you love—perfectly*

*The good of others—you shall not take—nor shall you*
*keep—knowingly*

She was, along with my mother, one of those people who very simply
but very experientially helped to awake in me from early childhood what
today I call by a grand sophisticated word the *prise de conscience*—the
"bringing-into-consciousnes'"—of rhythm and of double human bilateralism. Here, as anthropologist of the propositional, balanced and rhythmed
geste, I would like to associate the memory of another master, the brilliant
creator of experimental phonetics, J.-P. Rousselot: he too was formed from
early childhood at the same old school, the school of real life and of real
people.

\*\*\*

The deeper my awareness, as anthropologist of geste, of the semantic balancings of the Aramaic Besôrâ with their habitually homophonic

rhyming final syllables, the more acute my regret for being so often able to transpose in my own language only part of what constitutes a living wholeness: the balancings. Compare with what would remain of the biting, so expressive and so mnemotechnical incisiveness of our best-balanced proverbs if we were to extinguish in them the echo of their rhymes, however banal? Consider the two following examples:

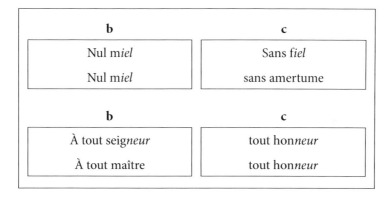

|    b    |    c    |
|---------|---------|
| Nul m*iel* | Sans *fiel* |
| Nul m*iel* | sans amertume |

|    b    |    c    |
|---------|---------|
| À tout seig*neur* | tout hon*neur* |
| À tout maître | tout hon*neur* |

*No honey without bile*

*No honey without bitterness*

cf.

*No joy without annoy*


*To every lord all honour*

*To every master all honour*

cf.

*Honour to whom honour*


Let's not forget that when transferred in French, some foreign language sentences rhythmo-catechized more easily than others on our lips simply because of just such fortuitous mnemonic echo:

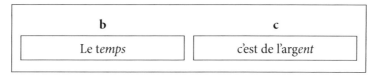

|    b    |    c    |
|---------|---------|
| Le t*emps* | c'est de l'arg*ent* |

*Time is money*

It is very important to note that this applies even when this echo plays internally within the two parts of an apparently indivisible composite expression:

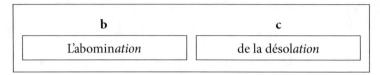

| b | c |
|---|---|
| L'abomin*ation* | de la désol*ation* |

*The abomination of desolation*

The following last, and precious example, allows us to experience within ourselves the rhythmo-catechetical abyss that exists between these two versions, in French, of the same Palestinian formula:

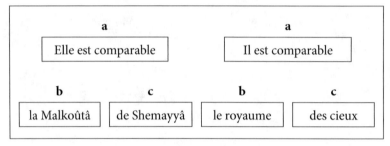

| a | | a | |
|---|---|---|---|
| Elle est comparable | | Il est comparable | |
| **b** | **c** | **b** | **c** |
| la Malkoûtâ | de Shemayyâ | le royaume | des cieux |

*It is comparable It is comparable*
*the Malkoûtâ of Shemayyâ the Kingdom of Heaven*

A rhythmo-catechetical analysis, such as I am pursuing here, should therefore account meticulously for such internal homophony in composite expressions—homophony so resonant and so frequent in Aramaic words that end "in the emphatic mode" with the final [â]. Such analysis should make ingenious use of clear highlighting typography to make feel or at least suggest the presence of internal homophonies. It is fortunate that the random incidence of French word-endings, the choice of possible if not common synonyms, the use of a part of the Aramaic formula itself, will help the transposer-analyst in his difficult task. Chance and effort thus unite to effect, from time to time, the whole sensation of the original homophony of the semantic balancings and of their constitutive parts. The following example allows one to evaluate this typographic procedure and its no doubt highly improvable outcome:

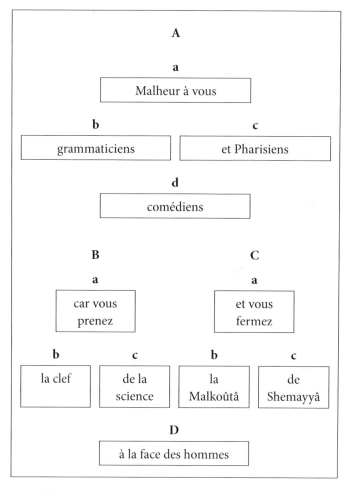

*Woe to you—grammarians and pharisees—comedians*

*For you take and you lock away—the key of*
*knowledge—the Malkoûtâ of Shemaiah*

*that lies before men.*

Whatever the rare successes and the numerous failures of this representation in French of concluding homophones, this typography is what I like to call a rhythmo-optic arrangement that at least attempts to render graphically the semantic or homophonic balancings. It is no doubt, speaking anthropologically, a truly perfect mis-presentation, since I am dealing with the purely oral lessons of a popular rhythmo-catechist who, *by common consent*, never put anything in writing. Further, as an anthropologist of geste, I greatly regret being obliged to present a rhythmotypographical arrangement on inert pages as a substitute for the normal, rhythmo-melodic and corporeally balanced method of revivification. It behoves me to thank here Mlle. G. Desgrées du Loû for her brilliant resuscitation of such a live method and for her precise and fine transmission of this method to a specialist in the anthropology of geste, Mlle. G. Baron, and to the students of the rhythm-pedagogic institute of Paris. Only life can understand life: to be understood, the rhythmic gestes of life need to be experienced.

In our rhythmo-pedagogical laboratory, we take this natural, indispensable revivification into account. We start from those Palestinian formulae that are of long established tradition and therefore relatively but vitally stable, balanced and rhythmo-melodized by the popular Aramaic encoded or midrâshized Targum. This is also how Léon Gry proceeded very recently and following my lead, in his *The Aramaic Formulaic Encoding of the apocalypse of Esdras* (I would rather say of Rabbi "Bar-Esdras"). Making the best of a bad situation, we try to highlight in static relief the dynamic, astonishingly new balancings of the old targumic formulae with which the great rhythmo-catechist himself had conformed. More profoundly even and more traditionally than our own André Chénier, Rabbi Ieshua of Nazareth might have summed up the method of formulaic balancings of his rhythmocatechism as

*On new thinking let us make old verse.*

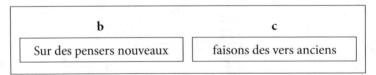

The altogether new and most important matter of the graphic abreviations that are customary whenever the various Greek encodings of the Aramaic Besôrâ (or Oral announcement) are put in writing, needed special prior treatment. My previous anthropological studies and the meticulous philological verifications by my faithful student R. Pautrel allow me to declare this matter finally settled.

Furthermore, my readers being familiar with Rabbi Iéshua's elementary and superior rhythmo-catechism, I will pare away and clarify my typography by dispensing with burdensome and in the circumstance unnecessary references.

## Bilateralism and semantico-formulaic structures

Comparison and opposition are two semantically balanced structures of propositional gestes that sprung up spontaneously from human bilateralism. One might say that they are congenital to Palestinian rhythmo-catechetics and, in fact, coupled antithetically, since opposition is simply a negative comparison. The following two propositional gestes for example, balance in two parallel recitatives, in accordance with the comparative formulaic structure at play in the targumic formula of Exod 16:4:

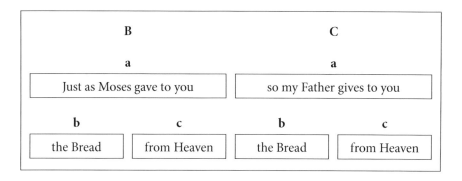

Balanced according to the formulaic structure of opposition, they become a negative comparison:

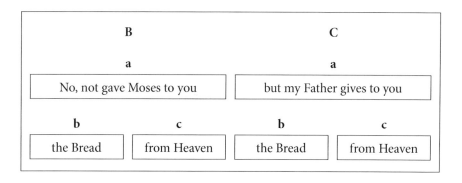

The Palestinian ethnic milieu, then, proves to be the ethnic milieu *par excellence* of comparison, of the mâshâl (= proverb or parable). This explains why, from earliest antiquity, the favoured Palestinian rhythmocatechists were called mâshâlists. Continuing the ancient tradition, Ieshua, himself a celebrated rhythmo-catechist, was really and essentially too, a mâshâlist, but a mâshâlist who targumized formulaically.

Unrelenting rhythmo-catechization from earliest childhood ensured the popular rhythmo-catechetical composer's mastery in the targumized Tôrâh or *Orâyetâ*. As a good Master of the House and of Instruction (the double Palestinian pedagogical meaning requires these two terms in French), he reserved within the treasure-house of his heart-memory all of 'the old,' that is: the entire immense stock of old targumic formulae. This prodigious formulaic wealth was however not scattered about chaotically. The formulas were recitationally enchained like a "sêder" (a pedagogical term encoded into Greek as *taxis*), that is, put in order or organised, according to the multiple structures of traditional didactic modules. When counted in "sêfer," this "computation" of the various elements, both great and small, arithmetically facilitated their preservation and rapid listing. Finally, these formulaic riches were not inert or dead as in the pages of a dictionary, but were constantly and intimately animated by the traditional rhythmo-melodies that "were breathed into them," and were, at the first beckoning of the "dictating breath," ready to "breathe them forth to the outside." In short, for the earthly Abbâ, as well as for the Abbâ of the Heavens:

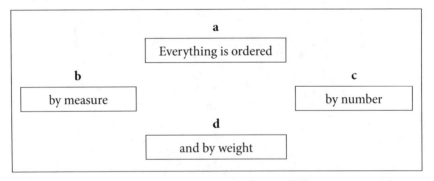

With all this "old," how will all the "new" be dealt with?

## Bilateralism and comparison

Thanks to the bilateralism of the formulaic structure of comparison: "As ...," or "Just as ...," "Thus ..." or, "So ...," it is very easy to take a formulaic recitative from the encoding or midrâshizing Targum and "to build" for it "a building" that would be symmetrical—a parallel recitative.

A pertinent, familiar example of this procedure relies on the recitation of the story of Jonah (2:1). The *strictly encoded* Targum (not always still extant today, but we are fortunate to have here a written version), allows us to recite the following formula rhythmo-melodically:

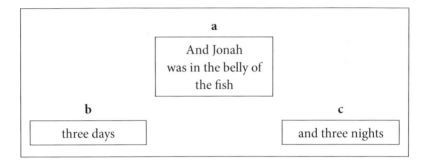

Thanks to the first element "As ..." or "Just as ..." of the comparative structure, we have an instant, ready-made recitative:

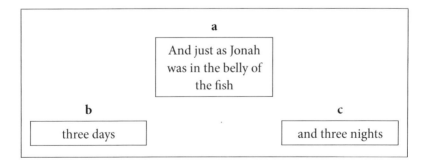

The Master of the house (or Master of the building = of construction = of instruction) will *build* his twin house, *construct* his symmetrical construction, *instruct* by ordering, according to the same architectural *style*, the old formulaic stones or bricks: "the *Bar'nâshâ*," and "in the heart of the earth." With the same rhythmo-melody, but using the second element, *thus* ..., of the comparative structure, he will rhythmo-catechize his lesson, at once new and old, in the following two parallel recitatives:

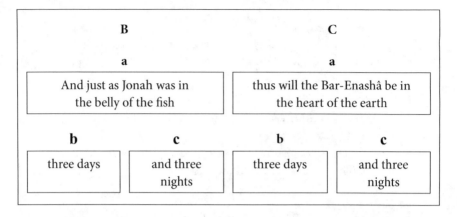

This first "twinned" construction thus gives us a double *didactic module* over which one or another targumic formula might cast the shadow of its structure and so allow a doubly formulaic "composite style." Thus, for example, this other targumic formula:

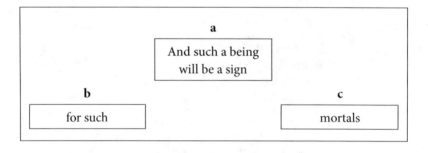

On the other hand, these other old formulaic stones or bricks, "the men of Nineveh," "the present generation," are there, solidly embedded in the old targumic constructions of the Orâyetâ (the Aramaic Tôrâh). With prodigious suppleness, these old stones or bricks remain marvellously docile and always ready to emerge when summonsed by the rhythm of the guiding, modelling melody, and to imbricate at the right and definite place in the new composite construction, whether it be doubly or triply formulaic:

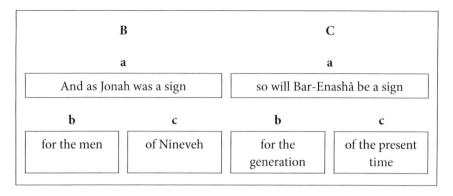

The Bilateralism of this comparative formulaic structure adapts itself at once to what we could call "the heavenly-earthly mechanism" of the Palestinian universe which is bilaterally constituted by the *invisible* world-from-on-high and by the *visible* world-from-below. The general wording of the law of universal gravitation, or better, of the law of universal theo-mimismologic gestualization, indeed borrows the bilateralism of this comparative structure:

However, whether symbolically, parabolically, metaphorically, comparatively or analogically, it is almost always through the gestes of the beings of the *visible* world-from-below that the gestes of the *invisible* world-from-on-high are expressed and announced as "signs" or "wonders" in the eyes of men. In addition, by a stroke of genius, the Palestinian formulaic rhythmocatechetization *pedagogically* inverted the original order of the bilateralism of things, reflected in the very order of the two balancings seen in the preceding binary. The demonstrative, convincing power of its concrete lessons rests entirely on the following new mimologic point:

How majestic the mimo-catechetization that with a flick of the wrist, commandeers for itself the whole indefinite number of interactional gestes of the visible world-from-below and pits itself pedagogically and *bilaterally* against the whole infinity of interactional gestes of the invisible world-from-on-high!

## Bilateralism and parable

The midrâshizing Targum developed the structure of the parable (or parabolized mâshâl) out of this formulaic structure of comparison (or mâshâl-proverb). Whence the double meaning that the word "mâshâl" gradually adopted in Palestine: proverb or parable. The comparison changes into parable simply by putting the structural formula of the parable before that of the comparison and so changing, or not, the latter from (*as* . . . ) to (*at* . . . ). So, for example, the following comparison:

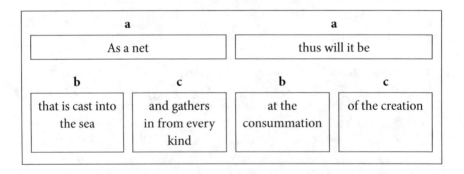

Before starting the recitation of these two parallel recitations, the rhythmocatechist would only have rhythmo-melodized his favoured, daily structural formula of the *Malkoûtâ of Shemaiah* in order to "compose" or, better, to "juxtapose" the most regular of mâshâls-parables as follow:

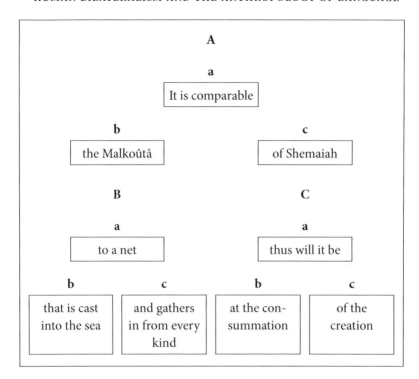

If he considered certain aspects of them too dense or not explicit enough, and in order to clarify matters for his rhythm-catechized, the rhythmo-catechist could "midrâshize" the mimodramatic tenor of the two basic parallel recitatives. He would then have each of the parallels followed recitationally by a variable number of complementary recitatives detailing the interactional gestes of the two mimodramas of the original comparison.

All the dramas, large or small, actually visible in the world-from-below or the present world, would thus be re-played formulaically in the supple global *meôd* (musculature) of the mimo-catechist and rhythmo-catechist, as well as in his *lêb* (heart-memory), and in his *néfesh* (reciting-throat). They would mimodramatize, and sound out parabolically, the hidden "mysteries," which are the dramas of the world-on-high and the world-to-come that are still invisible to us, but that were announced (besôraized) in the lessons of the *Malkoûtâ of Shemaiah*. These parabolically mimodramatized and concretely midrâshizing gestes awaken in the listeners all the "semantic harmonies" subsumed in the unique Aramaic term Malkoûtâ. Our own Greco-Latin ears cannot but very crudely distinguish these semantic harmonies by sounding them in succession, and harshly, in the various words lined for us in our dictionaries:

*Reg-ula Reg-num Reg-imen*

Rule Realm Reign

The inflexibility of our "semantic ear" is certainly aggravated by the endless polysemantism and pedagogical resonances of Palestinian nouns and verbs. Translated, they risk betrayal by our bookish languages, and lose all their delicate ethnological and pedagogical resonances: to give the Word-Lesson, to send or place it, to announce it, to sow it, to hide it, to take it, to receive it, to look for it, to reject it, to bear it, to hear or listen to it, to make, retain or keep it, etc. Such is the case, for example, with three pedagogical verbs, *to take, to sow, to hide*, in the two following parallel mâshâls:

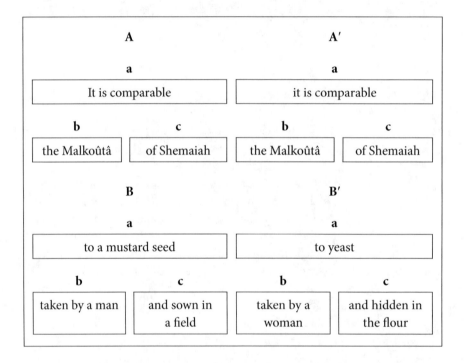

| **A** | | **A'** | |
|---|---|---|---|
| **a** | | **a** | |
| It is comparable | | it is comparable | |
| **b** | **c** | **b** | **c** |
| the Malkoûtâ | of Shemaiah | the Malkoûtâ | of Shemaiah |
| **B** | | **B'** | |
| **a** | | **a** | |
| to a mustard seed | | to yeast | |
| **b** | **c** | **b** | **c** |
| taken by a man | and sown in a field | taken by a woman | and hidden in the flour |

Another very characteristic example shows how difficult it is to translate such mâshâls *without extinguishing* the "pedagogical harmonics" of the original. Palestinian women indulge in putting a precious metal ring in the nose in which is inserted a *holy* pearl; hence its Aramaic name *qâdâshâ*—a term one could mistranslate by our word *holiness*. The Aramaic appellation *qâdâshâ* bestowed its piquancy of a double antithesis on the targumic mâshâl-proverb, felt so poignantly in this ethnic milieu where the pig (like the dog) was impure, *not holy*:

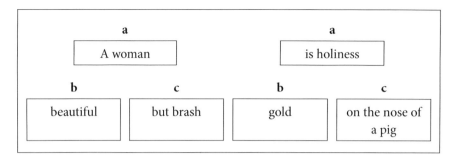

How can French speakers possibly grasp all the pedagogical, targu-mic, semantic, antithetical and vocal "harmonics" that are concealed in this gem of formulaic counsel that Rabbi Ieshua offered to the future rhythmo-catechists of his Malkoûtâ of Shemaiah?

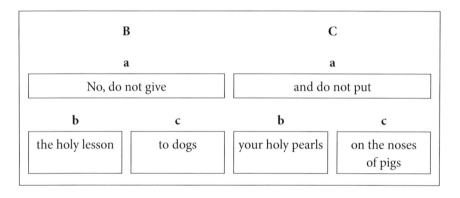

The more so as French speakers are ocular, silent readers, who do not recite this formulaic lesson aloud with the traditional rhythmo-melody that simultaneously balances and models another analogous formulaic lesson:

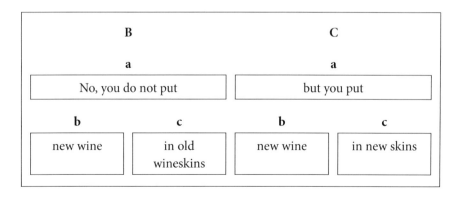

The Palestinians called such rhythmo-catechetical lessons "beautiful pearls." In the light of such mirrored sparkle of formulism and semantism, which reflect faithfully, continuously and holistically, we understand why and we can understand their need to "search" out such pearls as pedagogical "precious gems" in order to exploit their brevity of expression and their inexhaustible wealth of meaning. We are here, truly, at the heart of the mâshâl paradise, in that ethnic milieu where the "genre" of the parable synonymously parallels the "genre" of the enigma. Here the teacher teaches to enjoy the subtlety of midrâshing his own midrash; the apprehender or learner apprehends or learns to access his intelligence and understanding. We recognize too, pedagogically systematized or universalized, the aristocratic procedure of "the obscure clarity" of the style of our own Paul Valéry, well before his time, but almost with the same balancings of rhymes, if not of meaning:

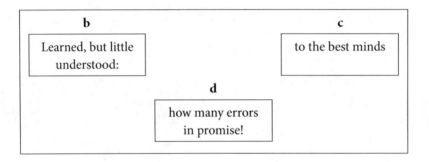

|   b   |   c   |
|-------|-------|
| Learned, but little understood: | to the best minds |

**d**

how many errors in promise!

King Solomon, in all his glory, orally rhythmed three-thousand mâshâls-proverbs. From the ends of the earth came the Queen of Sheba to test him with riddles. A few centuries later, the most prodigious of mâshâlists, Rabbi Ieshua of Nazareth, successfully undertook to transform the world with the rhythm of a few dozen parallel balancings of mâshâls-parables; moreover, he himself had to interpret and midrâshize them for his chosen apprehenders whom he would commission to carry his teaching to all the people of the earth.

## Bilateralism and opposition

The bilateralism inherent in the structure of the Palestinian rhythmocatechization was designed to juxtapose in order to *compare*, and to *oppose*—opposition being, as we saw, a kind of negative comparison. Thus we see rhythmo-catechists using one or the other with the same frequency. The formulaic structure of opposition is present schematically in the bilateralism of two elements, one negative (Not . . . ), the other adversative (But . . . ). This subtle semanticism is pedagogically profoundly Palestinian, and translates with great difficulty: a characteristic example is found in the following traditional lesson in which the geste of the manducation (or buccalization) of the bread plays on the curiously analogous geste of the manducation (either buccalization or oralization) of the word-lesson:

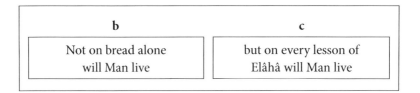

| b | c |
|---|---|
| Not on bread alone<br>will Man live | but on every lesson of<br>Elâhâ will Man live |

A mere glance tells us that the didactic modules are similarly structured and will be singularly appropriate material for *graphic abbreviations*. When putting the module in writing, one only needs to omit the last part of one of the recitatives. Here the original compositions are put in writing integrally, this is to say without graphic abreviations. The result feels intolerably pleonastic to anyone who lacks the rhythmo-catechistic urge for parallel recitatives and their imperious, guiding modelling rhythmo-melody embedded in his laryngo-buccal muscles from early childhood. No wonder then the literary repugnance of exclusively bookish philologists to add, even in obviously encoded Greek texts, a host of similar "pleonasms" as demanded by the formulism of parallel recitatives and by the rhythmo-catechetical melody. Only two kinds of people will accept, and even clamour for such integral rendering of the original: genuine people like our great Péguy, and anthropologists in daily contact with similar parallel recitatives in all the ethnic milieus where the balanced lessons of rhythmo-catechists are still "melodized" and transmitted.

Palestinian rhythm-catechistic "scriptions" were until recently jealously monopolised by Greco-Latinizing philologists and neglected with great abandon by the anthropologists. A most eminent and otherwise friendly master of bookish Palestinianism observed with a smile that only one researcher "saw at first glance what it had taken two thousand years for others not to see." That researcher was I. I had been more curious or less indifferent than the others were, perhaps. More important however, if I "saw," it was because I had remained alive and I had let myself "be informed" by the true milieux that have retained life and remained alive.

I discovered the Palestinian custom of graphic abbreviations by precise and meticulous verification of the living law of formulaic bilateralism. In each instance and without apparent reason, these graphic abbreviations give the impression of breaking the normal, anticipated development of the parallel rhythmic recitatives. At once then, the preformed and guiding rhythmo-melody does not guide anything anymore and runs idle. The following simple example shows how the first recitative obviously needs to be animated with a rhythmo-melody in order to "feel" that the recitation of the second recitative remains suspended in the air:

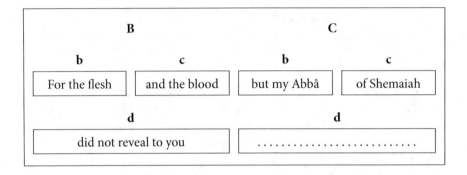

I repeat that the Palestinian compositions written-down as memory-aid should not be recited, nor even read aloud, slavishly, as they were written with customary graphic abbreviations known to all "users" of this aide-mémoire. Basic common sense demands that the recitation of these traditional graphic abbreviations be complemented orally by what the equally traditional formulaic bilateralism automatically brings on the lips. The old Sarthian women reciters from my childhood, so insistent on recitational fidelity, would have burst out laughing had they be made to listen to the recitation of their parallel recitatives as Albert Udry graphically abridged them in his book *Les vieilles Chansons patoises de tous les pays de France.*—"The old patois songs of the regions of France."

Even in our ethnic milieu of bookish people, would it not be the height of the ridiculous to hear an artist singing the Marseillaise during a gala concert and render the traditional refrain after the second and third couplets as "Aux armes! et cetera!"—"To arms! and so on!"? It would still be the case if the artist were to do so under the philological, scientific pretext that *all texts* that are printed in official songbooks must be sung as they are printed with the use of this *etc.* at the end of each of the two couplets in question. "That is how it is written, but that is not how one should recite it!" replies a pitiless ethnic milieu.

The Palestinian custom of graphic abbreviations has become just about as well known in the "ethnic milieu" of Palestinian specialists as our customary "etc." After me, Raymond Pautrel, among others, verified the use of graphic abbreviations as a Palestinian custom and published accordingly in important philological reviews. What is one to think, then, of those specialists who continue to tell us that the Our Father in Luke is "shorter" than it is in Matthew? There is yet another example: the parable of the two sons sent to the vineyard by their father. How much longer, as an improbable *Aux armes, etc.,* will we have to hear in the recto tono reading of this parable, the so very clearly parallel second recitative rendered in the following oral form.

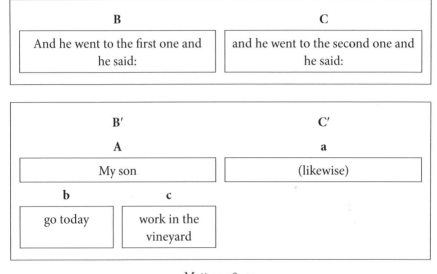

Matt 21:28–32

At the time I am writing these lines, the cost of paper has not quite reached the price of parchment for those Palestinians. Why not take advantage of this perhaps temporary situation and type out what is graphically abbreviated in these texts, or, at least, put a dotted line there to indicate the abbreviations? This would undoubtedly be the scientific procedure that would best respect, first, the very tenor of the text, in cases where we are fortunate to have the original (or its encoding); second, the integral parallel flow of the text, in cases where we have oral compositions put-in-writing. Such is the case, for example, with the two parallel recitatives of the Bread and the Word-Lesson that I presented a few pages earlier. While they might offend our literary taste in their perhaps "pleonastic" integrity, they conform, above all else and nonetheless, to the

Hebrew texts "put-in-writing" and to the Targum, and, above all, to the living laws of Palestinian oral style.

After what I said about the formulaic structure of opposition and how it facilitates the use of graphic abbreviations, it will come as no surprise that in some Greek encodings "put-in-writing," the scripter abbreviated graphically the second of the two recitatives, leaving out the last part, not essential to the meaning:

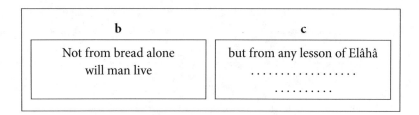

On the whole, graphic abbreviations were done so skilfully that, thus abridged, they altered neither the general meaning nor the grammatical correctness of the context. Which is why our philologists of purely bookish and Greco-Latin formation passed them over unperceived for so long and consider them, even today, to be negligible.

In the bilateral structure of opposition, the adversative element (But . . . ) is at times substituted by an equivalent (For . . . ). We find such substitution in the Aramaic targumization of the two above-mentioned recitatives and so we are able to trace the vicissitudes of their formulaic life throughout:

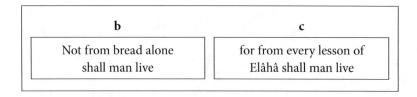

The bilateral structure of opposition appears with particular frequency in the fundamental formulaic Aramaic rhythmo-catechisms of Shâoûl of Giscala—he, too, a scholastic Rabbi who became a popular Rabbi. I will analyse the bilateralism of his different stylistic structures in an essay dedicated to him. I offer here today in graphic typescript the Greek encodings of his *Sunergoï*, who were his scripters and companions, as just an example among many to guide the methodical research of budding students in Palestinian oral style:

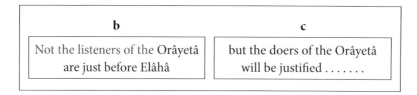

| b | c |
|---|---|
| Not the listeners of the Orâyetâ are just before Elâhâ | but the doers of the Orâyetâ will be justified . . . . . . . |

When classifying, structure by structure, all the formulae of these Palestinian rhythmo-catechisms of Rabbi Shâoûl of Giscala, former scholastic Berâ of Rabbân Gamaliel, the balancing d rhythmomelodizing of the famous pedagogical mâshâl-parable of Rabbi Ieshua cannot be glossed over. This mâshâl applies perfectly to this tireless memorizer and hoarder of formulae from the written Tôrâh, from the Aramaic oral Orâyetâ, and from the Malkoûtâ of Shemaiah:

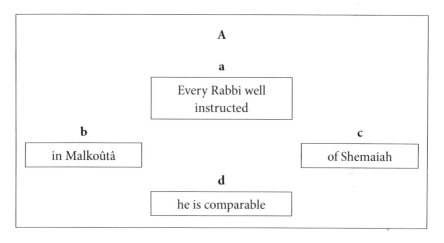

A

a
Every Rabbi well instructed

b
in Malkoûtâ

c
of Shemaiah

d
he is comparable

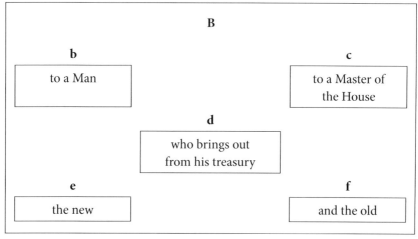

B

b
to a Man

c
to a Master of the House

d
who brings out from his treasury

e
the new

f
and the old

Matt 13:52

## Conclusion: French anthropology of language

We have witnessed the formulaic "flowing-out of the treasure house of the old and the new." We must now ask ourselves whether we, in our present bookish state, can fathom the full depth and extent of the subtle linguistic and rhythmic detail that plays out in the gestual and propositional bilateralism of rhythmo-formulaic composition. Experience has shown abundantly that no future observer should undertake research on this topic without thorough anthropological preparation, knowing full well that no matter how thorough, such preparation cannot ever equal the simple and almost instinctive, altogether infallible, "know-how" of the ethnic composer himself.

Is that not akin to how we, people of the pen, deal with that strange written-style genre called "verse"? "Verse," as I have shown, is no more than an artificial survivor and aesthetic mode of expression "in the manner of" our old French oral style, which was utilitarian and thus of necessity mnemonic and mnemotechnic. To better feel how adroitly, in the verse of one rhymer or another, old words jelled into new rhymes, a true expert makes repeated attempts at rhyming. Indeed, one knows well only what one has made oneself. *C'est en forgeant qu'on devient forgeron*—it is by forging that one becomes a blacksmith, or, practice makes perfect and one admires the master-blacksmith even more after having become one. One appreciates Virgil better after having written some bad Latin verse.

So much greater then the need, *mutatis mutandis*, to train oneself over many years in "formulaic" targumic sequencing in order to discover and appreciate its exceptional successes! Faced with a "composition" that presents an unusual "juxtaposition" of old formulae, in-depth knowledge of all the facts is needed before one can assent that indeed, "No, never has man composed as this man composes." Try, for example, to make a composition with targumic formulae "in the manner of" Rabbi Ieshua's *Our Father*. Yet, this *Pater noster*, which is so universally admired for its sublime beauty, is, as is Mâriâm's *Magnificat*, no more than a balanced juxtaposition of targumic formulae.

I secured the scientific and faithful backing of Father Frey, secretary to the Pontifical Biblical Commission by providing the anthropological proof of this for the first time, in Rome, in 1927. I did this with the evidence in hand, or rather, with the targumic formulae in my mouth. To his question: "Is the Paternoster a Jewish or a Christian prayer?" I answered: "Both: a *Jewish* prayer because of the traditional targumic *formulae*; a *Ieshuan* prayer because of the new and transfiguring juxtaposition of those same targumic formulae on the very lips of the young Rabbi Ieshua of Nazareth." The difference in length of the Greek Pater "put-in- writing" in Matthew and in Luke is solely due to the customary graphic abbreviations (analogous to our etc.

or our dotted lines) which the latter used at *the end* of the two recitatives that structure the *Pater* and which were orally known to all.

Such was the solution I printed as early as 1925 in my research outline on *The Oral Style*. This methodological and "graphically formulaic" essay by me, gestual anthropologist, was aimed at other gestual anthropologists and immediately understood and put to use by them (Drs. Pierre Janet, Georges Dumas, Joseph Morlaâs, André Ombredane, and Pierre Lher-mitte). Moreover, and most interesting to me as an observer of gestes in the ethnic laboratory, this anthropological essay proved to be a sort of *test-book*, setting off double quick "gestually graphic" reactions in quite a number of old French papyrovore specialists and monopolisers of purely book-oriented Palestinian studies. Their reactions—both gestual and ty-pographically registered—revealed some most curious and quite troubling lacunae in Palestinian anthropology, on the fundamental issue of the per-sistence of the oral style in Palestine at the beginning of our era, is just one example. No, indeed, *non omnia possumus omnes*: we can't all do every-thing—and we all have our limitations.

Times, however, have changed for philology. Palestinian oral-style for-mulism is publicly upheld now to prove the authenticity of the *Magnificat*, of the *Our Father* and of the parables. This in a flurry of grave philological com-mentaries, at times without even the slightest reference to the anthropologist-discoverer, and almost as if the discovery was common knowledge. This is the case in a recent, and contradictory, *Manual of biblical studies*, destined for the "formation" of our young French clerics. This manual, although published in Lyons, has an outlook that is decidedly "prelogical," as Lévy-Bruhl would have it. Indeed, having established, in its early chapters, philologically and thus definitely, that "oral style no longer existed in Palestine" at the beginning of our era, it finds occasion in subsequent chapters, to chide the negators of the authenticity of the *Magnificat* "for knowing nothing about oral style."

There we have it then: to understand the Palestinian compositions of the beginning of our era, no less an authority than bookish philology cau-tions us against the danger of "not know[ing] anything about the laws of oral style and its steadfast successes in highly gifted individuals." So, let us meet good fortune with goodwill, and let's be . . . anthropologists! I devoted my entire life to the experimental study of the anthropology of manual, oral and graphic geste and I cannot but rejoice today in the scientific success of these studies. Western civilization developed for two millennia thanks to the en-during lessons by which our French mothers rocked us, and it is our French anthropology of language that recovered these lessons as living structures and on the very lips of the prodigious Aramaic catechist, Ieshua.

# Index

abbreviation, graphic abbreviation, 267–91

abstract, abstracted, abstraction, abstractive, abstractively, x, 11, 17, 80, 103, 106, 113, 118–19, 121, 128, 149, 214, 218, 219, 229

action, cosmic action, 16, 18–19, 29. *See also* interaction

Adam, *adamâh*, 34, 38

adjust, adjustment, 18, 24, 78, 86, 186–87, 250

Africa, African, 10-11, 99, 172–73, 188–89, 212, 255

Alesia, 137, 139, 148–49

Alexander, 143

algebra, algebraic, algebreme, algebrism, algebrization, xiii, 12, 55, 57, 63–65, 75, 83, 88, 95–96, 98, 102–111, 129, 36, 176–77, 185, 187, 189, 198, 207, 218, 233, 240, 247

algebrose, algebroseme, algebrosis, 11–12, 45, 62-64, 76, 136, 138, 149

alliteration, 249, 256

alphabet, alphabetization, 64, 75, 91, 102, 105–6, 115, 165, 199, 207, 22, 264

Amerindian, 39, 52, 58, 84, 100, 103, 108, 112, 184, 189, 212, 231

an-acting-one, acting-on, an-acted-upon, 16–17, 20, 26, 33, 37

analogeme, analogical, analogically, analogy, phono-analogism, 23, 35, 37, 66-9, 78–79, 114, 142, 174, 220, 232–33, 279

animal, animalize, animalization, xvi, 4, 15, 21, 24, 26, 30, 37, 43, 46, 51, 56–7, 78, 80–105, 112, 130-131, 135, 158, 163, 165, 167, 170–71, 175, 189, 190, 210, 218–19, 225, 232, 236, 241, 257

animism, 19–20, 26, 76, 213

anthropoid, 6, 9, 30, 42, 55, 171, 223, 225–27, 229, 230, 232

anthropology, anthropology of geste, 6, 21, 47, 150, 186, 195, 264, 270, 274; anthropology of geste and rhythm, 85, 266; anthropology of language, 223–25, 235, 291; anthropology of life, 6; anthropology of mimism, 34–35, 51, 64, 75, 81, 191, 203, 212, 260, 263

anthropomorphism, 20, 229

anthropos, a human compound, 5–6, 15–17, 19, 21–22, 24, 27, 29–31, 37–38, 46, 55, 63, 65, 79, 104, 164, 209–10, 213, 215–17, 219–20, 222, 236, 245, 247, 262; a complexus of gestes, 8, 15,19, 21, 30–31, 46, 124,182, 243, 209, 236; a mimismic system, 15, 27, 31, 33, 226; anthropos and anthropoid, 6, 9, 24, 30, 223, 225–26, 229; anthropos and consciousness, v–vi, 11, 14–15, 21, 24–27; anthropos and cosmos, 4–17, 26, 28, 53, 60, 78; anthropos and memory 5, 24, 59, 210, 245